C000155299

Border Frictions offers an important, ⸝ practices and border control: the per agents and the organizational structure⸝ on impressive and unique ethnographi⸝ Côté-Boucher shows the messiness ⸝ therewith shines light on the challenges those who are tasked with this work are facing. It is at the border where sociopolitical, legal, organizational and individual goals, priorities and beliefs can clash hard. These clashes, and the ways in with individual agents deal with them are addressed in *Border Frictions*. In making sense of all this, the author looks at border control and bordering practices through, among others, a critical race and a critical feminist lens. The combination of unique fieldwork, a critical theoretical analysis and the focus on street-level border control agents and the various environments they are—often simultaneously—operating within makes *Border Frictions* a much needed and valuable addition to the ever-growing body of literature on borders and border criminologies.

Maartje van der Woude, *Professor of Law & Society,*
Van Vollenhoven Institute for Law, Governance & Society,
Leiden Law School, the Netherlands

This book by Karine Côté-Boucher is an essential read for anyone who considers that an investigation into human practices in context is the best antidote against exaggerations coming from those who adopt the radical hypothesis of a data revolution in security matters, be it to praise smart borders or to deplore the inexorability of data surveillance by algorithms. Her book is an absolute pleasure to read because of the attention she gives to the voices and practical work of border guards as well as her capacity to give a nuanced picture of this complex human tapestry. However, this empathy does not turn into an acceptance of actors' inner systems of justification. She explains how the transformation of borderwork is not driven by smart borders nor by integrated data management with the aim of simplifying life, but by a competition of positions inside a field among security professionals endowed with distinct professional socializations. What is crucial therefore is not technology as such, but these professionals' social use of the fraught integration of data in border management. The policing at a distance enabled by such deployment of data coincides with the reinforcement of dynamics of masculinization in bordering, as well as with the tensions created by unions and intergenerational conflicts within border agencies. All these elements lead to complex interactions between data management logics, officers' experience of data-led bordering and preoccupations for more rigid law enforcement practices. This "tour de force" presents a political anthropology of this professional milieu in Canada and will certainly inspire other researchers around the world to follow her rigorous path to a better analysis of the "investment" of sovereignty, technology and freedom into border mobilities.

Didier Bigo, *Professor of International Political*
Sociology at Sciences-Po Paris-CERI, France

Border Frictions

How did Canadian border officers come to think of themselves as a "police of the border"? This book tells the story of the shift to law enforcement in Canadian border control. From the 1990s onward, it traces the transformation of a customs organization into a border-policing agency.

Border Frictions investigates how considerable political efforts and state resources have made bordering a matter of security and trade facilitation best managed with surveillance technologies. Based on interviews with border officers, ethnographic work carried out in the vicinity of land border ports of entry and policy analysis, this book illuminates features seldom reviewed by critical border scholars. These include the fraught circulation of data, the role of unions in shaping the border policy agenda, the significance of professional socialization in the making of distinct generations of security workers and evidence of the masculinization of bordering. In a time when surveillance technologies track the mobilities of goods and people and push their control beyond and inside geopolitical borderlines, Côté-Boucher unpacks how we came to accept the idea that it is vital to deploy coercive bordering tactics at the land border.

Written in a clear and engaging style, this book will appeal to students and scholars in criminology, sociology, social theory, politics, and geography and appeal to those interested in learning about the everyday reality of policing the border.

Karine Côté-Boucher is Associate Professor at the Université de Montréal School of Criminology.

Routledge Studies in Criminal Justice, Borders and Citizenship

Edited by Mary Bosworth
University of Oxford

Katja Franko
University of Oslo

Sharon Pickering
Monash University

Globalizing forces have had a profound impact on the nature of contemporary criminal justice and law more generally. This is evident in the increasing salience of borders and mobility in the production of illegality and social exclusion. Routledge Studies in Criminal Justice, Borders and Citizenship showcases contemporary studies that connect criminological scholarship to migration studies and explore the intellectual resonances between the two. It provides an opportunity to reflect on the theoretical and methodological challenges posed by mass mobility and its control. By doing that, it charts an intellectual space and establishes a theoretical tradition within criminology to house scholars of immigration control, race, and citizenship including those who traditionally publish *either* in general criminological *or* in anthropological, sociological, refugee studies, human rights and other publications.

Criminal Justice Research in an Era of Mass Mobility
Edited by Andriani Fili, Synnøve Jahnsen and Rebecca Powell

Women, Mobility and Incarceration
Love and Recasting of Self across the Bangladesh-India Border
Rimple Mehta

Border Policing and Security Technologies
Mobility and Proliferation of Borders in the Western Balkans
Sanja Milivojevic

Re-thinking the Political Economy of Immigration Control
A Comparative Analysis
Lea Sitkin

Border Frictions
Gender, Generation and Technology on the Frontline
Karine Côté-Boucher

For more information about this series, please visit: www.routledge.com/criminology/series/CJBC

Border Frictions

Gender, Generation and Technology on the Frontline

Karine Côté-Boucher

Routledge
Taylor & Francis Group

LONDON AND NEW YORK

First published 2020 by Routledge

2 Park Square, Milton Park, Abingdon, Oxon OX14 4RN

605 Third Avenue, New York, NY 10017

Routledge is an imprint of the Taylor & Francis Group, an informa business

First issued in paperback 2022

Publisher's Note

The publisher has gone to great lengths to ensure the quality of this reprint but points out that some imperfections in the original copies may be apparent.

British Library Cataloguing-in-Publication Data
A catalogue record for this book is available from the British Library

Library of Congress Cataloging-in-Publication Data
Names: Côté-Boucher, Karine, author.
Title: Border frictions : gender, generation and technology on the frontline / Karine Côté-Boucher.
Description: Abingdon, Oxon ; New York, NY : Routledge, 2020. | Series: Routledge studies in criminal justice, borders and citizenship | Includes bibliographical references and index.
Identifiers: LCCN 2019055983 | ISBN 9780367136413 (hardback) | ISBN 9780429027680 (ebook)
Subjects: LCSH: Border patrol agents—Canada. | Border security—Canada. | Law enforcement—Canada. | Canada—Emigration and immigration—Government policy.
Classification: LCC JV7233 .C67 2020 | DDC 363.28/50971—dc23
LC record available at https://lccn.loc.gov/2019055983

ISBN: 978-0-367-13641-3 (hbk)
ISBN: 978-1-03-233653-4 (pbk)
DOI: 10.4324/9780429027680

Typeset in Garamond
by Apex CoVantage, LLC

MIX
Paper | Supporting responsible forestry
FSC
www.fsc.org FSC™ C013985

Printed in the United Kingdom
by Henry Ling Limited

Contents

Table

Series editor introduction

To better understand border control, as Karine Côté-Boucher points out, "we need to populate it." One of the many strengths of this book is that it manages to do precisely that. Through interviews with Canadian border officers and observation of their work, the author is able to bring rare empirical detail and nuance to our understanding of how borders work and those who make them work. The book is an analysis of the mechanisms and social forces that are transforming Canadian border officers from administrative officials to more aggressive law enforcers. And although this story may be by now familiar to many readers of this series, it is also often underpinned by numerous misconceptions. Karine Côté-Boucher debunks many of them—for example, that the adoption of firearms and various data technologies is a seamless process, unanimously embraced by politicians and officers alike. Côté-Boucher's grounded empirical analysis shows that this is far from the case. The securitization of borders is not a seamless process. A shift towards law enforcement does not come without friction. The book reveals that upon a closer look, borders are far from monolithic but rather are a space where competing narratives shape human actions. Guns and new IT solutions are embraced by many but also resisted by some. Where these lines are drawn often depends on gender, education and, importantly, age.

Border control is a deeply politicized scholarly field where passions run high—often for good reason. However, one of the dangers of working in the field is that nuance can be sacrificed for the sake of a greater good. Côté-Boucher never succumbs to this temptation. She successfully achieves a difficult balancing act that many border scholars, who are able to observe border control at close hand, face: how to do justice to the humaneness and diversity of those tasked with border work at the same time as they are swept over by the imperatives of harshness and security. Nevertheless, Côté-Boucher's meticulous analysis offers, precisely for this reason, all the more persuasive critique of the security ethos that is reshaping so many aspects of contemporary life and state practices.

Katja Franko, Oslo

Preface and acknowledgements

"Reader, I liked them." This is how Carol Cohn (1987) writes of her disbelief in realizing that she enjoyed the company of her unusual research participants: nuclear weapons specialists. These were men whose expertise threatened the future of humanity. While their work puzzled and alarmed Cohn, she liked them.

As I spent time with border officers, I experienced a related surprise. Coming from a background in refugee and migration studies, I entered fieldwork with stereotypical expectations: I would meet harsh border guards without much consideration for human dignity. They would confirm what I already "knew" about them: being fully empowered sovereign agents of the state, they would enjoy repression and a feeling of control. At times, this is exactly what I found. I admit that some officers effortlessly met my expectations and were quite skilled at performing the border enforcer role. After all, this book is about the mechanisms that are transforming street-level border officials into a harsher "police of the border." But my analysis comes as much from talking to those who somewhat fit the stereotype as it is indebted to their colleagues who were mordant in their scathing assessment of the "Rambo" border officer type.

I liked them. The officers I spoke with were often thoughtful and funny. They also took seriously the opportunity offered by my presence in their workplace to step back and reflect on their career and on the daily challenges of their job. For that, I am grateful to each and every one of them. As you will read about Richard, Sarah, Raymond, William, Elizabeth and others, you will meet flesh-and-blood border workers who share their aspirations but also their confusion and differences of opinions regarding how border control is changing. That is the point. I do not see what our radical critique of the severe impacts of bordering on global politics, social belonging and mobile individuals' rights gains from vilifying border workers. What I have learned throughout the years as I read about sovereignty, coercion, government and (state) violence is that ordinary people can manage to do both great and horrible things to each other given the right set of circumstances. Zygmunt Bauman taught us in his magisterial *Modernity and the Holocaust* that the material, legal and symbolic conditions in which bureaucrats work shape their (in)capacity to act ethically. Accordingly, I am more interested in tracing the trajectories that are turning border control into a tougher, more unforgiving endeavour than I am in being judgemental about individuals who, in an increasingly "flexible" North American economy, got a permanent government position as border officers that provides them with a rare stability, good wages and acceptable working conditions. After all, similar considerations influenced my decision to become a university professor.

I thus made the conscious choice to write about borders by using terms such as *job*, *work*, *workplace* and *unions*. Of course, I have long shared many scholars' outrage at the treatment of vulnerable migrants and racialized travellers and at the policies that have transformed borders into spaces of global exclusion. I am also occupied elsewhere at developing analyses on how border controls are now embedded in logistical regimes that sustain global capitalism and particularly at unpacking the consequences of this embedding upon highway transport workers. How labour and the economy become entangled in bordering and securitization is a particular interest of mine. For this reason, my book is about borderwork: the everyday labour that builds borders from the ground up, or, to use a militaristic language often repeated in bordering, from the "frontline" to headquarters. It may make bordering appear less threatening. It certainly makes it appear more mundane. That is a risk that I am willing to take. With all our talk about the purported exceptionality of borders, it is this simultaneously violent (even if sometimes only in potentiality) and techno-administrative character of border officers' practice that strikes me as a significant missing piece of the bordering puzzle. I hope this book will contribute to the collective endeavour of critical border scholars everywhere who try to untangle what makes bordering so quotidian yet so disturbing. Perhaps, together, we might clear the way for another kind of border transformation—one less concerned with facilitating global capital accumulation and excluding the world's poorest and most vulnerable and more concerned with building a more hospitable, safe and equitable world for everyone.

***

Many helped with this research and supported this book project. Without James Sheptycki's guidance as PhD supervisor, I would never have been able to expose myself to charges of sympathizing with the enemy. James introduced me to the sociology of policing and taught me much about how to do field research in one of the most puzzling domains of power in our contemporary world. This book owes him more than I can tell.

Years of conversation, reading, debate and laughter with Susan Braedley and Kate Pendakis run through these pages. I am lucky to have these brilliant women as friends and intellectual partners. Susan asked the good questions that got me started with the introduction. Kate reviewed the complete manuscript with her usual wit, mastery of sociology and beautiful command of the English language. Thanks also go to Mark Salter for his early support with this book project. A conversation with Matthew Light on a bright summer day in Toronto and another one with Luna Vives inspired the conclusion to this book. Ever the genius, Julien Jeandesboz took time to comment on my take on technologies and helped strengthen it in major ways. I thank them all for their time and generosity.

I would be remiss if I did not mention those students from the École de criminologie at Université de Montréal who work in policing, defence, intelligence and security and who took time to discuss with me the complex reality of their jobs. The ideas presented here have been polished during my years of teaching and exchanging with them.

Finally, I wish to thank the Criminal Justice, Borders and Citizenship Series editors, Mary Bosworth, Katja Franko and Sharon Pickering, for giving me the chance to publish my first book. It is a privilege to be included in a collection directed by these renowned scholars.

This book was too long in the making, as life, illness and learning how to tame this weird beast that is academia got in the way of writing it. But without Chris Braedley, who fills existence with love, optimism and delicious food, it would have never become reality. I dedicate this book to him.

***

Excerpts of my article (2016) The paradox of discretion, *British Journal of Criminology*, 56 (1): 49–57 may be found in Chapters 2 and 4. Reprinted by permission of Oxford University Press.

Excerpts of my article (2018) Of "old" and "new" ways: Generations, border control and the temporality of security, *Theoretical Criminology*, 22 (2): 149–168 may be found in Chapters 1 and 7.

First Published February 10, 2017 © 2017 by SAGE. Reprinted by permission of SAGE Publications, Ltd.

Chapter 1

Introduction

Changing customs: a cultural shift at the border

I first began to sense the cultural shift in Canadian border control during my interview with William in 2010. An experienced border officer, William had spent most of his career in a port of entry located on the Eastern Canada–US border.[1] Like many of his other senior colleagues, he came from the area. William loved his job; in his words, he was "tattooed with the organization" he worked for, namely the Canada Border Services Agency (CBSA). Throughout our conversation, he explained how things had changed since he started his career three decades earlier. Younger officers, he told me, now see themselves as "a police of the border." William was not certain how the change had come along, but he shared a few clues: new recruits are told to expect "people of real bad faith" at the border and that the job would entail fighting drug trafficking and crime and finding missing children. In fact, William tells me, recruits are selected and trained to become enforcers. They come to work licensed to carry a gun and expecting to catch bad guys. He adds that officers, and especially recruits, now expect to be respected (i.e. feared), just like American border guards.[2]

In contrast, William explains, experienced officers like him were hired as public servants to collect duties and taxes. They were satisfied with their role protecting the national economy from unwanted foreign competition. If someone crossed the border while driving drunk, border officers could not arrest him. They were not trained to use physical defence tactics, nor did they carry firearms, handcuffs or batons. Older officers like William liked to tell me that when they were young, their main tool was a passport stamp. They now carry more than 15 pounds of gear and wear a navy-blue police-like uniform, a bulletproof vest that makes them appear bigger than they are and leather black boots. Either shaking their head in disbelief or with a hint of nostalgia, these officers told me stories of the time when they came to work in light-blue shirts and regular shoes.

As I listened to William and his colleagues, I came to a realization: how they approach their work is different and disconnected from what I had learned from reading policy documents and the academic literature on borders, security and transnational policing. Border officers all participate in "border security," but they conceive of it differently. First, they disagree with each other on significant issues that run to the core of how borders are, and should be, policed—such as their mandate, the purpose of their work and their most important tasks and the best way to accomplish them. This variation is compounded by their diverse takes on what protecting the country means, what the risks are and how they categorize and act on such threats.

Second, when officers speak of *security* in policy parlance, they do so in law enforcement terms. Border officers working at the land border do not talk of algorithms or counterterrorism, nor do they speak of borders as if they were "smart" (that is reliant on technologies and capable of filtering risks) as North American and European policymakers would assume. Instead, they speak of the daily border processing and compliance work they do. In interview after interview, all of the officers described paperwork and boredom at the booth, telling tales of repetitive and uneventful days. But when officers spoke of guns, their expanded legal powers of arrest and the most recent time that they found drugs hidden in truck compartment, their eyes often lit up. These conversations often took a generational tone. While mid-career and older officers continued to speak about their public service role with pride, it was often the younger officers who discussed police-related themes with excitement.

Going along with fieldwork, I realized that I was doing research in a border control organization that was undergoing a transition. Perhaps this organization was moving towards "pre-emptive" bordering and the prevention of threats before they arrived at the border (or before they even occurred), as the literature on bordering would suggest. Above all, however, and when viewed from the frontline, this was an agency transitioning towards law enforcement. This transition remains controversial among officer ranks but also between officers, their union, management and government. The CBSA tells us that its job is about ensuring both *security* and *facilitation*. Accordingly, many of the officers I met are convinced that their work means letting travellers and trade in as swiftly as possible. Indeed, in overcrowded Canadian airports where waiting lines are the stuff of front-page news, officers who collect customs cards and whisk us through in a matter of seconds after we have answered a few questions at an automated border clearance (ABC) self-serve kiosk are called facilitators. Similarly, in the area of customs, the goal of enforcement enters into tension with other aims, such as removing impediments to smooth cargo traffic. But as far as most border officers are concerned, whether at the airport or at the land border, their job is not only to get stuff and people through but also to keep the line, to stay vigilant, to look for what seems out of the ordinary. When border officers told me that they were "a police of the border," they meant that they can now enforce the law at the state's limits and have the weapons to do so.

In this book, I argue that the shift towards enforcement is a major trend in border control, one that has become more and more significant over the years. We will see that bordering is a matter of technologized security and policing at a distance, but to the extent that it entails the ability to use force, to stop someone from moving and to search, question, arrest and detain, it is also more specifically concerned with law enforcement. Whether or not they use them, many officers take pride in these powers. This insistence on law enforcement by border officers indicates a perception of bordering as a tougher endeavour.

Focusing on the cultural shift towards enforcement, this book starts by asking a simple empirical question: what does the turn to border enforcement look like from the frontline? In investigating this turn, I also explore questions related to the recent history of contemporary changes in bordering and consider their effects for street-level border officials: How do border officers, and particularly those working customs, concretely handle the contradictory objectives of security and free trade? How do border officers deal with the adoption of new security technologies and border programmes that automatize and remove some part of their traditional tasks and discretion? What are the implications of these initiatives for the organization of work in ports of entry? Ultimately, these questions shed light on the forces that have been shaping the turn to enforcement as a strategy of mobility control not only for customs but for bordering in general.

I respond to these questions with interview material gathered in 2010 and 2011 with Canadian border officers working customs. Most of my interviewees are frontline border officers employed at the "commercial sections" of their port of entry; that is the way Canadian border authorities refer to those doing the work of customs and who are responsible for processing truck drivers, trucks and goods. In contrast to many countries where customs, border police and immigration officers are employees of different agencies, CBSA officers can be assigned to traffic, immigration, commercial or traveller processing. Commercial and immigration are generally seen as specializations because they require more-advanced legal and regulatory training. Further, Canada does not have an equivalent to the U.S. Border Patrol. The sections of the land border between ports of entry are patrolled by the federal Royal Canadian Mounted Police (RCMP).

The 33 interviews were conducted in French or in English onsite in five ports of entry on the Canada–US border located in the provinces of Quebec and Ontario.[3] They generally lasted about one and a half to two hours, but a few went over three hours. I met 21 men and 12 women. The great majority of my interviewees were border officers, but this number includes five port-of-entry supervisors, one chief of operations and one clerical worker. Some of my interviewees had low-grade data analysis experience, and I mention this when necessary. However, to respect anonymity and given the limited number of supervisors in ports of entry, in this book, I refer to all supervisors as border officers. All supervisors started their career as border officers. The tracing of the trajectory of borderwork towards enforcement became possible because the majority of my interviewees were officers with an accumulated experience of 15 to 35 years in customs. Further, as most of my interviewees had spent time in traveller processing and some in immigration control before being transferred to the commercial sections of their ports of entry, they led me to think about what we learn from the changes that they saw happening in customs and what these changes say about broader transformations in border control. As further explained in Chapter 2, since its creation in 2003, the CBSA is responsible for all taxation, customs, immigration and border enforcement at the country's ports of entry. Since the basic training of all frontline border officers is now related to the regulation of travellers and, with a slightly more specialized training, frontline immigration assessment, my conclusions can often be extended to the immigration and traveller control aspects of borderwork. I make the necessary distinctions between traveller migration control and cross-border trade regulation, when necessary.

In addition to these interviews, port-of-entry staff members offered me short tours of each site. I also spent between one and three weeks in the vicinity of each port that I visited. During this time, I discussed with locals and read regional newspapers. Archival research undertaken since that time provided legal jurisprudence, interpretations of border regulations and policy material. Recent civil rights and media reports, as well as continued informal conversations with border officers over the past nine years, suggest that the questions and issues that I explored during my research have kept their urgency and relevance.[4]

I locate this study in the global context of border control and do so by looking at the case of Canadian border services. Current scholarship is generally focused on the European and Mexico–US borders and pays particular attention to the control of aerial mobilities. It also speaks to the "mobile character of borders" (Pickering, Bosworth and Aas 2015: 382), so called because controls happen at a range of sites in a phenomenon that I elsewhere refer to as the "diffuse border" (Côté-Boucher 2008). So why focus on the uneventful Canada–US land border? First, the central-eastern Canada–US border is one of the busiest in the world for truck traffic: 10.9 million trucks transporting around Can$400 billion in value cross yearly and approximately 300,000 people cross daily.[5] Such high-volume trade is now in logistical tension with a sensitive post-9/11 security context. It has also come under scrutiny with tariffs imposed on Canadian aluminium and steel by the US and the renegotiation of the now-called Canada–US–Mexico Agreement (CUSMA) in 2018—which is expected to replace the previous accord (NAFTA) signed in 1994 between these countries. This case thus sheds light on the continuing importance of the land border as a site of border control.

Second, despite a large literature on the surveillance of human mobilities, customs remains understudied. To develop a more comprehensive appraisal of the kinds of privileges and vulnerabilities created by border control, we have to look at the second half of the equation: the securing of trade. It helps us to consider border control as a whole, since immigration, customs and traveller control often go hand in hand. By investigating how a recent political-economic agenda converted a taxation-focused customs into a global enterprise of security provision and trade facilitation, I make original contributions to the fields of criminology and of border, security and mobility studies.

Accordingly, the book investigates how the project of remaking customs and border control has created a group of frontline security professionals who think of themselves as law enforcers. It tells the story of how the considerable political effort and state resources deployed in this project have disrupted officers' work processes and of the extent to which these street-level officials have resisted, adopted and altered this project to their own ends. It uncovers some unique dimensions of what is often referred to as the hardening of borders, by revealing the inside dynamics that created a new generation of border officers more enthused by the oppressive side of their work.

Beyond denunciation: towards a grounded critique of border control

This book contributes to the significant scholarship produced since the beginning of this century, critically assessing how political authorities demonstrate a growing interest in shaping, channelling, tracing and interdicting how we move across spaces, territories and borders (Kotef 2015). This critical orientation denotes an acute and shared awareness that, in contrast to received wisdom, borders make people vulnerable; from migrants who take increasingly risky routes to avoid controls to those whose travel lives and work lives are subjected to unprecedented border surveillance. Through these scholars' collective efforts, we know that borders are increasingly mapped onto the social, economic and political divisions that make up our world. Indeed, we have learned that borders act as gendered, racialized and classed structures that enable the stratified classification of mobile people across the globe. We have also become more aware that borders contribute to the extension of state surveillance and that they sustain a transnational security governance detached from democratic oversight. Conceptually, this body of work is useful also because it sheds light on how contemporary borders interrogate traditional notions of sovereignty, citizenship and nation-building.

This book brings something else to the discussion. It adopts an alternative methodological sensibility, one that is anchored in an interpretive account of the shifting experiences of border control by frontline border actors. In doing so, I follow Mountz's (2010: xx) apt invitation to incorporate the "institutional memories" and "the voice of civil servants" in analyses of bordering. Her ethnography demonstrates that, in doing so, competing narratives emerge about bordering practices that shed light on a complex human tapestry. The literature on border control, and security more generally, often reads as if it were made of processes, power relations, technologies, categorizations and judgements but rarely of flesh-and-blood people with fears and hopes, conflicts and solidarities, convictions and doubts. In other words, to better understand border control, we need to populate it. Inspired by what Fosher (2009: 4) achieved in her study of the homeland security community in Boston, I examine border control not as a monolithic, cold technical object but as "an arena of socially and culturally constructed actions undertaken by real people."

In fact, when we hear officers' voices, we fall into the rabbit hole of bordering where things are not as they appear. Officers' narratives illuminate how they organize their activities and interactions around understandings of what constitutes border security and risk that differ from those mobilized by intelligence officers, technocrats and politicians. The latter are often the focus of border scholarship. Instead, border officers' narratives reveal the inconsistencies raised by the meeting of security policy, the oft-unfulfilled promises of high-tech bordering and the concrete delivery of border control by security professionals. Officers also provide crucial insights into the structuring effects of daily bordering activities on the control of mobilities. Through fieldwork research and thick description, the book expands on the research agenda approaching border control as practice (Côté-Boucher, Infantino and Salter 2014; see also Loftus 2015) and considers embodied border security workers and their changing labour processes. Many of us are studying border control, but we are neglecting the work that is done to sustain it and the people who do this work every day.

Taking officers' accounts of their day-to-day experiences seriously helps us with another critical task.[6] By retracing how Canadian frontline officers have been made—and make themselves—into border enforcers, I also consider why and how we got there. In this sense, I go beyond empirical research that privileges a "midrange problematizing" with the aim of improving security (Fosher 2009: 12). Certainly, there are elements in this book for those interested in such betterment. The following pages point to things that can be fixed with thoughtful budgeting, attention to detail and political will. For instance, it is not enough to buy technology and detection devices; one needs the staff to operate and repair them when broken. It is unfortunate that such basic problems in border security provision need media attention to be fixed. I found a port of entry where a VACIS truck—an oversized X-ray machine on wheels used to scan trucks and trailers for drugs—was sitting unused in a parking lot. Similar issues have since been made public. Known to be a major drug-trafficking hub for the Eastern part of Canada, the port of Montreal left unused its scanner for containers every one out of four days in 2015–2016, with officers reporting weekly breakage of these systems. Further, during research, officers did not have access in their booths to the federal police database, the Canadian Police Information Centre (CPIC), and could not therefore check for criminal records or whether there were warrants against a person wishing to enter Canada. This issue became known after a media investigation and, following public and union pressures, has since partly been fixed.[7]

Nonetheless, there are many issues raised in this book that do not easily lend themselves to administrative and technical fixes; they run deeper than repairing broken light bulbs in secondary inspection docks or figuring out a way for frontline officers to get data access. As I show in Chapter 2, these issues are the result of a series of political choices and reforms aimed at securing borders that began in the 1990s. These issues are multiple, ranging from border officers' perceptions of themselves as enforcers rather than public servants, the toughening of the border through expensive technologies and unnecessary weapons, the easing of the mobilities of goods and "trusted" travellers and the now-taken-for-granted idea that the Canada–US border is in need of more "security"—an idea that would have appeared ludicrous not that long ago. These issues are the outcome of political decisions made during a short historical period when we became increasingly concerned with policing mobilities in North America. This book looks critically at this trajectory, opening up a space to consider the possibility that bordering could have been (and could *still* be) done differently.

Disenchanting borderwork

As I talk to family and friends, to students and to the café owners where I often go to write this book, I realize that while border control is becoming more complex and capricious, our tools to understand what is happening in border spaces are limited. Borders are changing everywhere. In fact, we are living in a period when border control has become an international hot-button issue. We are concerned with ongoing drug trafficking and cross-border organized crime. Newspapers bring daily reports of hundreds of people crossing the Mediterranean and the Mexico–US border. We hear of European countries that have closed their borders to undocumented migrants or made agreements with neighbouring countries to "keep" migrants or prevent their passing across shared borders. Despite the optimism that followed the fall of the Berlin Wall, countries such as the US, India and Israel now erect border fences. In Canada, the crossing of thousands of migrants through the US land border since 2016 has also generated much public debate and even calls to further restrict access to that border for asylum seekers.

Meanwhile, our everyday experience of borders is also changing. When we pass security at the airport and are told, "you have been selected for a random check," we ask ourselves, "Why have I been selected? Is it because of skin colour? Behaviour? Is it *really* random?" In any case, the experience is not pleasant. At other times, we might stand in line for hours to pass through customs, or we may be whisked through in a matter of minutes by an automatized kiosk that scans our passport. These lines create impatience and confusion about how the decision has been made to allow or block our movement.

A kind of magic happens at the border, and we would like to better understand a few of the tricks that are played on us. This book argues that much of this magic can be understood if we look at border control as *work*. This is how Richard, a border officer I met on a cold and humid winter day, ended up disenchanting his job for me. You will read many times about Richard in the next chapters. Getting beyond artifices has been a challenge with Richard. Picture the interview: I sit in a meeting room in a port of entry somewhere in Eastern Canada along the US border. Across from me at the table gesticulates a funny, chatty and self-assured border officer. It has been almost two hours since we started our conversation when Richard unexpectedly wonders aloud what would make "the most entertaining interview." "How about a dull description of customs programmes or explanations on how to use databases?" he asks tongue in cheek. Amused, he immediately answers his own question and jokes that it would be like watching paint dry. I smile, thinking Richard must feel that I'm after quotable anecdotes (he was right, of course). Like other enforcement-oriented border officers I met during this research, my interlocutor is proud of captivating his audience with thrilling stories. But then, the show is over. Richard becomes serious and starts reflecting on what his days are really like: "You know, my work is business as usual. Most days, I do not arrest people like they do on TV shows. Most days, I just go to work."

When border officers like Richard go to work, they do what countless others have done before them, and most of these daily activities are not the stuff of police novels. Working at customs is generally a routine administrative job. Officers like Richard process trucks, truck drivers and goods and have done so for decades. They file paperwork; they accept and refuse documents. They spend hours asking the same questions to truck drivers who stop at their booth. They answer importers' queries about customs rules. They apply a mountain of regulations, verify the classification of goods and apply duties and taxes. They search trucks and open boxes. Once in a while, they find too much alcohol or the odd smuggled firearm, and more rarely, they arrest someone for drug trafficking.

In short, officers like Richard and William do *borderwork*. This term has been used previously to refer to the labour done by ordinary people in bounding space and making territories through a variety of strategies, including the use of nationalist narratives, making political demands and classifying the people and things that cross borders (Reeves 2014; Rumford 2008). With borderwork as frontline work, I mean something else. First, I assume a more labour-oriented definition of *borderwork*, which goes beyond bordering activities that are purely security based. When it comes to customs officers, despite their conviction that they make up "a police of the border," security is only a small part of what they actually do. My focus is therefore on the daily work of regulation, taxation, administration, policing and risk management performed by border officers and the context (political, economic and organizational) in which that work unfolds. Because it is a contested activity, a focus on borderwork allows me to examine the fraught relations between border actors through the prism of the multifaceted interactions between policies, regulations, organizational cultures, work routines and contexts of action that make up border control.

Second, despite the increased importance of policing at a distance in bordering (Bigo and Guild 2005), borderwork conveys the frontline and often-more-coercive aspect of bordering. In fact, border control is still often thought of in frontline terms by a range of oft-armed actors and in different countries and different sites—from private security guards involved in deportations (Gammeltoft-Hansen 2013) to vigilantes in borderlands (Shapira 2013) and police officers in cities (Provine et al. 2016). These actors often import military and policing imaginaries, along with related tools, weapons and tactics, into borderwork. By doing so, they assert what they see as the continuing importance of their physical presence and capacity to use force, especially at the state's geopolitical border, thus envisioning bordering as a labour of protection against intruders. As we shall see, the idea that it is vital to develop the capacity to deploy coercive bordering tactics at the land border and inside the country when needed has been central to the shift towards enforcement in border control in Canada.

For decades, borderwork has been its own métier—that is, a set of habits, tasks and assumptions that define an occupation and shape practice (Manning 2008; Sheptycki 2017). Border officers are what Lipsky (2010 [1980]) famously called street-level bureaucrats, or low-level state officials who work in hierarchical organizations. Like other bureaucrats, border officers hold permanent jobs. Thanks to this stability, they develop established routines sustained by ingrained dispositions that are not so easily disrupted—or, as the saying goes, old habits die hard in border control. By virtue of their position, street-level bureaucrats often exert direct authority on the public and are granted much discretion in doing so. Powers of this kind are an informal reward that compensates for the more routine and administrative aspects of the job (Gilboy 1991). However, as William, Richard and many others reminded me, border officers throughout the world enjoy a distinctively high level of statutory discretion. For instance (and as is the case in other countries), they can search and seize without a warrant, and they can do so in Canada on the basis of reasonable suspicion—a lower legal threshold than the one regulating the police (Pratt 2010; van der Woude and Brouwer 2017). This gives credence to moral assumptions and informal skills that come along with this métier—such as a putative sixth sense that officers believe makes them skilled at catching liars and criminals.

Given these long-standing trends, a critical analytical issue for much of the literature on border control has been how the symbolic significance of this métier resides in border officers' capacity to act as unaccountable "petty sovereigns" (Butler 2004: 56)—that is, as bureaucrats invested with the ultimate power to decide whether or not someone (or something) can enter a territory. Border guards have long performed these sovereign tasks at the states' limits, and as a result, my interviewees often felt invested with a protective mission. Nevertheless, borders are changing, and these changes shake the border officer métier to its core.

In this context, Butler's (2004: 65) oft-quoted jab at "petty sovereigns" appears of limited use. If border officers themselves relish the perceived image of having great powers and would like their decisions to be unencumbered, unilateral enactments of sovereignty, the reality of contemporary borderwork simply does not attest to this fantasy. This fact is well recognized by Huysmans (2011: 380), who tells us that "the process of securitizing does not work through these kinds of decisions." Indeed, in the next chapters, I show how borderwork is inserted in complex sociotechnical, organizational and infrastructural arrangements that shape, channel, sometimes reinforce but often limit officers' decision-making. Officers' effective legal powers are currently being rearticulated with the advent of risk-management measures, the automation of decision-making, new legal provisions and policy measures that expand borders beyond and inside territories. These trends have unsettled border officers' sense of being in charge of the border. Yet, paradoxically, this is also the context in which frontline officers have staked a series of political claims and made demands for more policing tools and powers in pursuit of *becoming* petty sovereigns.

Accordingly, if I pay attention to continuities in how bordering is done, the particular focus of this book remains on the altering labour processes that make up border control as well as the resistance, adaptation and realignments that officers collectively bring to these trends. This requires being attentive to five aspects of borderwork that have been neglected thus far.

Border frictions: five themes to renew the study of border control

Anna Tsing (2005), in her classic book *Friction*, unpacks the conflicting social interactions that make up the global; what these interactions produce across cultural differences and in our relations with nature; and how they are embedded in the capitalist forms that shape lives across the globe. By giving *Border Frictions* this very title, I instead explore a series of conflicts that emerged out of the current transformation of border control at the turn of the 21st century and that continue to impact borderwork as we know it in Canada. In the following pages, I look at how the border can be considered more broadly as a site of struggles. The struggles I refer to are not those of border crossers who might challenge the new bordered world order but *the tensions and disagreements that shape the relations between those actors who are tasked with bordering*. The book aims to illuminate these struggles and analyse what they teach us about the dynamics that shape border control from the inside.

Frontline borderwork is not a new occupation, but it is a transforming one, and this transformation creates its share of frictions, tensions and contradictions. Accordingly, this book examines these frictions by engaging with the multidisciplinary literature on border policing and mobilities through a series of arguments that either challenge some assumptions held dear by this literature or put forward propositions that have not yet been adequately discussed. The following interrelated themes offer the potential to investigate new questions relative to border control that expose some of these frictions: technologies, unions, gender, professional socialization and generations. These five key themes run throughout the book. I show that their interrelation has changed customs (and border control more generally)—contributing to making it into a market facilitation, a data-led endeavour and a hands-on law enforcement enterprise.

Technologies and devices: beyond the "smart" borders programme

In a 2015 short online video, the CBSA publicized its border modernization efforts, stating that "changing times demand it." Against a backdrop of exciting shots of its National Targeting Centre, its ABC machines for airports and X-ray trucks for containers, the agency raved about its trusted-traveller programme, NEXUS, and its associated biometric identity cards.[8] As we watch this promotional material, we are left wondering whether perhaps the agency embraces technologies too eagerly. In my dealings with customs, security and immigration technocrats since the beginning of my research on border control, I have come to agree with Feldman's assertion (2012: 23) that officials "idealize" technological systems. Technical tools such as databases, automated machines and detection devices are fantasized about as silver bullets that can tackle the wide-ranging policy problems faced by border agencies all over the world. These include reducing line-ups in airports, replacing border officers and their potentially faulty (or corrupt) decision-making and performing the difficult task of filtering trusted mobilities from risky mobilities at a distance.

If policymakers and technological providers exaggerate the capacity of borders to govern mobilities smoothly and predictively, some studies echo this idealization. Thanks to information technologies, border control is depicted as having gone beyond the model of "the Fordist production line, with its linear series of finite tasks and decisions," to now privilege "differentiated flows and modulated responses" in the governance of mobilities (Amoore 2013: 88). Borders, as the literature suggests, now showcase an uninterrupted capacity to fluctuate and vary their interventions depending on what and who crosses them. They are able to adapt to and pre-empt flows of dangerous people and things, to be fluid, "mobile and portable" (Popescu in Jones et al. 2017: 10). The smart border, Pötzsch (2015: 102) tells us, "acquires the capacity to see, think and act by itself." If we follow this line of thought, borders would be autonomous entities, free from human involvement.

Almost everybody likes sophisticated tech toys. As we study security technologies, we find that their undeniable coolness combines with an extraordinary surveillance potential. This both fascinates and alarms us. Yet there is an irony difficult to escape in the homology between current critiques of security technologies and the rhetoric of their promotors. They end up adopting a similar premise, which could be summarized in one short phrase: all of this works. The effects of technologies turn out to be those described in the promotional brochures. In a strange logical twist, critique ends up modelling, reinforcing and validating the common imaginary that it shares with that which it intends to challenge or resist. Perhaps we find in this homology an illustration of Bourdieu's critique of the scholastic point of view. As researchers, we are attracted to study those who abstract the social as we do since this is a habitus easy to recognize for us. Yet this fascination for the intellectualization at work in bordering policies and technologies pushes further the indifference shown by designers of smart borders towards the practical challenges experienced by street-level workers who deploy these tools every day.

In fact, technologies make security organizations particularly unstable because their ecological configuration is far from smooth. Technologies create frictions in the everyday provision of border control. By echoing technology providers' take on the capacities offered by technologies, we can exaggerate the coordination of security actors who use them. We can miss the glitches in the devices, the uneven quality of data, the lack of preparation of those in front of computers and the numerous other "organizational pathologies" that continue to plague intelligence systems—such as problems of interoperability and information silos (Sheptycki 2004).

Therefore, the dream of a perfect, fluctuating border remains aspirational and programmatic. To paraphrase Foucault (2001 [1980]: 847), it never happens as it was planned; how governing programmes play out in practice remains to be investigated.[9] Orlikowski (2000: 405–406) argues that technologies are enacted in specific social settings and contexts of action. She aptly reminds us that users "redefine and modify the meaning, properties and applications of technologies after development" and may "ignore certain properties of the technology, work around . . . or even contradict designers' expectations." For Cantens (2015), a specialist of customs, to assume otherwise is to fall prey to a "determinism of tools" that brings little to our understanding of borderwork as practised in diverse bordering settings. This open-endedness of technological practice is a goldmine for researchers, something researchers of policing have understood for quite some time. However, this insight is seldom taken up empirically in studies of security and borderwork through empirical investigations of "the way in which the devices promoted in programmatic security practices are embedded in the routines of security actors, understood as those who make security technologies *work*" (Davidshofer et al. 2016: 212).

Take, for instance, Nathan, an ageing officer whom we will meet again in the next chapters. As I sat listening to Nathan and others, the pre-emptive algorithmic border appeared more a myth than a reality—at least when seen from the frontline. Nathan had no previous training in information management when he became a low-level intelligence analyst. He benefited from union placement and was placed in front of a computer after he was injured on the job. Nathan works with a computer in dire need of replacement and on which some legacy databases, such as ACROSS (the main customs release database dating from 1997), still runs in DOS—yes, you read correctly, the computer language that predated Windows. This database remains in use at the time of writing. But most importantly, Nathan's case shows that the analyst in front of "modulating" databases might barely be able to make sense of the data on the screen. That is compounded by the fact that, as discussed in Chapter 3, Nathan's understanding of risk is neither flexible nor malleable; there are goods that present low risk and others that present high risk, and he classifies them accordingly.

Throughout this book, I draw from customs officers' narratives to investigate the role played by technologies in the shift to enforcement in border control. In Chapters 2, 3 and 4, I inquire into the more banal ways that technologies are mobilized by frontline border workers and their effects on the configuration of bordering. As we listen to officers describe their use, misuse and lack of use of databases, ion scans and X-rays, and as they reflect on the effects of automation on their work, street-level borderwork becomes a contested set of technologized activities. But the book also asks larger questions: To what degree do technologies reveal change, and as importantly, how are they used to account for change in border security organizations? How do technologies unsettle and reconfigure established power relations in border agencies? What passions, attachments, disaffections, dissentions and worries do they convey? In whose presence and when does an officer mobilize which technology? What are the consequences of this contextual and situated use for how borders govern the mobilities of transport workers and goods— and eventually of travellers and migrants? Finally, because technologies fast become obsolete, what is the technological politics of breaking and ageing in borderwork?

Technological determinism can be seductive to those who study borders. However, sociologists of organizations have taught us that, historically, machines have not driven change.[10] Instead, technologies have followed efforts to centralize the organization of work, redistribute labour and discipline workers (Thompson 1967; Zuboff 1988). This is also the case in border agencies. As reviewed in Chapter 2, the assumption of the neutrality, rapidity and efficacy of automated border control is especially pronounced in the case of customs, where information management is becoming more formalized and predicated on risk-management schemes. Advanced preclearance processing schemes and risk targeting were adopted because they were presumed to limit direct officer involvement in binary decision-making and have more predictable and neutral outcomes than traditional border-policing methods. However, we will see in Chapters 2, 3 and 4 that the reality of data-led bordering has revealed itself to be much more complicated. A series of difficulties impedes fluid data circulation in hierarchical border organizations, thus suggesting that the border is more often interrupted than "seamless."

Shall we then argue that despite all this talk of technologies and datafication, nothing has really changed in border control? I do not think so. I suggest that the practice of bordering has indeed been transformed, but in ways that do not exactly correspond to what was expected by smart border programme designers or those researchers who adopt their point of view. This book investigates the more complex effects of these transformations in the sociotechnical and labour arrangements that make up smart borders.

A final issue I consider in this book regarding technologies concerns the putative distinction that critical border scholars have drawn between conventional and non-conventional security tools. Entering the techno-material cultures of security by way of the gun, I take on Bonelli and Ragazzi's (2014) invitation to study the role played by "low-tech" tools in everyday security provision. Indeed, our warranted—if sometimes "epochal" (Amicelle et al. 2015: 295)—interest for biometrics, drones and algorithms should not prevent a close examination of the deployment of more-conventional policing tools in security work. Despite being understudied as security devices, guns are one of "the most significant, highly charged register[s] of material culture in the world today" (Springwood 2007: 2). In Chapters 5 and 7, I examine the role played by this low-tech device in promoting a culture of enforcement in border control.

That being said, I am also cautious about the distinction between "low-tech" and "high-tech" because it runs the risk of reinforcing (or at least replicating) the temporal hierarchies produced in the techno-material cultures we study.[11] In contrast, I suggest that it is more productive to look at the relational dynamics that characterize the adoption of information technologies and their use, together with more traditional policing and intelligence tools. More particularly, it is important to question the implicit chronology in studies of security technologies. We often assume that low-tech devices are more traditional tools that somehow belong to the past, while high-tech tools are associated with the present and future of policing. Yet in the case that I study, the firearm *followed* the introduction of computers and was an unintended consequence of trends like automation. I argue that the firearm is as transformative of bordering in the Canadian case, as the adoption of data-led technologies has been; it would be a mistake to study the one without paying attention to the other.

Following this insight, I investigate the ways different sociotechnical configurations are articulated with one another in border control. As they have been made professionally insecure by a combination of forces—including automation, informatization, the effective disappearance of aspects of their discretionary powers and the redistribution of labour between ports of entry—that come together to produce a *virtualization of borderwork*, officers have staked their protest on the gun as a powerful symbol of law enforcement. In the context of professional vulnerability, the firearm is one way that officers have been able to protest their partial marginalization by claiming that despite everything that conspires to take their grip on the border away, they are the tried and true "police of the border." Accordingly, firearms do not represent the essence of their métier but its transformation.

Unions matter

The arming of Canadian border officers has been the result of a long fight led by their union, which jumped onto guns as if its survival depended on it. In a way, it did. With its successful campaign for arming, the Customs and Immigration Union reinforced its ranks and obtained better working conditions for its members. It also accumulated political capital and established itself as a sought-after commentator on border security by national media. With a focus on the place of firearms in border politics, Chapter 5 sheds light on the complex relationship between union activism, security and border control policy, and it explores how their combination has been the driving force behind a turn towards enforcement-minded border control in Canada.

Power struggles often pit security agencies against one another. They influence how these agencies collaborate, shape agendas in matters of security and keep themselves relevant in the eyes of those who control the public purse (Bigo 2002, 2011; Nolan 2013). But what about turf wars *within* these organizations? What if we approached the "politicality of security practice" (Huysmans 2014: 11) and its influence on the security agenda from the point of view of organized security labour? We know little about how border officers act collectively and strategically in a rearranged security landscape. Yet if union struggles are central to understanding the division of labour in ports of entry, they are also crucial to comprehending why certain border policies and technologies are adopted while others are ignored. A greater number of public players and private players in border control are fighting for a piece of a shrinking budgetary pie. In this disputed security field, the design of security priorities is shaped not only by unions' concerted efforts to improve their members' working conditions but also by their defence of frontline workers' influence over security priorities (Dupont 2006: 92–93). My research pays attention to these neglected aspects of borderwork: the role that unions and security workers' associations have played in the making of security policy and their influence on budgetary, infrastructure and technological choices at the border. In doing so, this book uncovers officers' critical reading of the transforming landscape of border control while taking seriously their recourse to organized labour action in their bid to shape this control to their advantage and get their share of state security funding.

This research supports the claim that workers associations must be considered crucial actors in any effort to reform policing organizations. As Marks (2000: 559–560) argues,

> state change and changes in legislation, policy and constitutions alone, do not give rise automatically to police transformation . . . such transformation is dependent on police agents themselves. This involves a challenge from within police organizations, and such challenges are particularly effective when collectively organized.

Unions matter in border control. For instance, UK border officers disputed, through their 2011 strike, the requirement that they make systematic traveller verifications in databases, believing that they did not receive proper organizational support to carry out these tasks in a context of increased passenger flows in airports (Jeandesboz et al. 2013). The strike led to the dismantling of the UKBA.

As a "community of interest," unions can make or break security policy reform, obstruct progressive change and push for initiatives that favour their members even if they go against the public good (Fleming, Marks and Wood 2006; see also Berry et al. 2008). In the case of California's prison guards, Page (2011) tracks the part played by their union in shifting correctional policy away from rehabilitation and towards a "tough-on-crime" model—thus effectively resisting reforms to diminish prisoner and parolee numbers despite an overcrowded prison system. A conservative element in the larger—and more progressive—labour movement in North America, unions have been instrumental in the shift towards more aggressive, enforcement-oriented approaches to security and crime in policing.

The case of Canadian border officers' fight for the gun further illustrates this active involvement of unions in steering reforms related to border control. We will see that unions have an array of strategies at their disposal, such as administrative court battles over working conditions, media attention, lobbying with government and political parties and activist pressures in ports of entry and refusals to work, to push for security policies that they favour, garner political and public support and denounce unsafe working conditions. At the same time, unions are political bodies whose publicly united front hides more contentious internal politics. In light of recent organizational transformations and the political importance imputed to security questions by the public, policing and security agencies, union activism involves "internal conflicts over what policing [is] about, what principles it should follow, and how it should be practiced" (O'Malley and Hutchinson 2007: 163). When executives of border officer unions make political statements, they may do so with or without the support of their membership—as illustrated by the disputed endorsement of the candidacy of Donald Trump in the 2016 US presidential elections by the National Border Patrol Council.[12] In Chapter 7, I touch on this somewhat-sensitive relation between national executive and membership as I look at the fallout over arming in ports of entry for older officers.

Gendered and embodied borderwork

Decades of feminist research have made one thing clear: work is gendered. So is borderwork. To become a border officer today is to incorporate specific gendered practices; it is to tap into masculinist discourses and imaginations of state security that shape security officials' bodies and experiences in historically specific ways. While in the UK (Hadjimatheou and Lynch 2017) and Canada, borderwork is adopting a policing enforcement model, in other countries, such as the US, borderwork is said to be increasingly militarized (Jones 2012). These transitions rest on gendered assumptions that need to be fully investigated.

How did we get to the point of seeing border control as law enforcement, and what "particular modes of gender power" (Brown 1995: 167) are expressed through this vision? As they walked in ports of entry and showed around, as they entered the interview room with full uniform and gear, as they sat uncomfortably constrained by their bulletproof vests and as they spoke of enforcement and guns, border officers told a particular embodied gendered story. This story was about making borderwork masculine. Accordingly, this book presents a set of arguments concerned with gendered border control related to those offered by Prokkola and Ridanpää (2015) in their revealing archival study of "the gendered imaginations and rationalities" and "the politics of the body" deployed since the recent (yet limited) integration of women in Finnish border guarding.

But while these authors hold a legitimate wish to "feminize" border studies, I rather insist on how much labour it takes to masculinize borderwork. Theweleit (1989, 1987) and Connell (2005) have shown that becoming male, and making the social masculine, is an endeavour requiring repetitive re-enactment and is one that sifts the feminine out of the social and relegates it to the private sphere. As seen in Chapters 5 and 6, taking the feminine out of borderwork can be remarkably simple. For example, the challenging new physical fitness tests used by the CBSA to sift through new recruits sends the message that borderwork is a physical job for strong men. But generally speaking, making borderwork masculine has been a more subtle process. This book considers how the turn to enforcement has been made possible by a series of gendered political strategies, discourses and everyday interactions that work together to make borderwork a masculine affair.

How gendered are border frictions? How does one make borderwork "masculine"? This has been achieved, first, by changing the perception of borderwork as a tax and duties collection job and the cultural norms that sustain that perception. Both feminist scholarship and global employment statistics have taught us that work done by women, and work that is considered feminine, is less valued, paid less and benefits from fewer social protections. When it comes to borderwork, what does this insight mean? In Chapter 4, Nathan and some of his colleagues speak of the shift to enforcement as a step away from the more feminine, administrative aspects associated with customs and revenue work. In their bid to secure their position as chief border control actors and obtain pay increases and better working conditions, officers and their union have used arming as a strategy to take a distance from this clerical image, rather insisting on the dangers they putatively face at the border and boasting of their crime control credentials. They have done so through the firearm, a powerful symbol of hegemonic masculinity, and have succeeded in convincing elected politicians and border high officials that these weapons were necessary to their work. These strategies have made it easier for border authorities, as well as the general public, to imagine borderwork as a tougher and more physical endeavour. They demonstrate that shifting border masculinities are deployed to signify the protection of national borders by active and strong masculine subjects against imagined threats.

Second, the *masculinization of borderwork* rests on gendered constructions of authority and competence. On the one hand, we find continuity in the mechanisms that allow an officer to acquire the corporeal and affective dimensions associated with borderwork; from the 1980s to now, learning how to assert dominance at the border continues to be a gendered experience. Interviews with female officers speak to the importance of learning "masculinist behavioural codes and habits" (Prokkola and Ridanpää 2015: 1382) to affirm superiority. In Chapter 6, whether we listen to Marie (a career officer) or to Elizabeth (a younger officer) tell us about testing different strategies to project authority with border crossers, we become aware that learning to show who is in charge takes time and requires on the part of female officers[13] considerable emotional labour—the supplementary bodily, expressive and emotional regulation that usually women are expected to perform in the workplace.

On the other hand, this corporal and affective experience of authority has been transformed with the introduction of policing equipment. As we see in Chapters 6 and 7, these tools required that *all* officers incorporate new techniques of the body and to "know how to use their bodies" (Mauss 1934). Canadian border training allows recruits to acquire novel gendered embodied repertoires that have been developed by the police—a traditional institution of hegemonic masculinity. Sometimes, the training comes with the recruit: as has been done by the US for decades, Canadian border services has begun to hire former army trainees who already come equipped with the "durable somatic memory" of military drills (Higate 2012: 357). For new recruits, acquiring the "masculinized bodily capital" (Diphoorn 2015) that comes with enforcement entails becoming proficient in specific physical abilities, such as self-defence and control skills, use of weapons such as batons and cayenne pepper and the procedure for placing someone under arrest and in handcuffs. This insistence on the ability to physically control border crossers speaks to a new, more visible, embodied manifestation of authority at the border.

Third, this altered gendered embodiment affects both how border officers do their work and how travellers experience the border. Chapter 7 details how the training that comes with being licensed to carry a firearm has converted officers' bodily attitudes. Changing the corporeality of borderwork through the firearm meant adapting rules, equipment and buildings (for training and firearm storage). But it also meant reworking the relationship between these bodies and lethal tools, creating more suspicious, more careful officers in their interactions with border crossers. It inscribed suspicion not only as a cognitive dimension (Jubany 2017) but also as a corporeal manifestation of borderwork. By shifting officers' attention to what may be threatening in their surroundings, the firearm promises to reshape an entire workplace culture. It has been said that risk-management technologies and biometrics have reduced travellers' ability to offer complex and contextualized narratives about their mobility patterns (Aas 2006; Rygiel 2013). The gun further narrows the scope of relationships that can be established at the border, because armed officers are now compelled to keep their distance from travellers as a precaution against those who could potentially target them.

By virtue of being at the state's limits, border officers hold the legitimate means of violence and express sovereign power in one of its most unaccountable forms—at least as far as democratic countries are concerned. This is acknowledged by Salter (2007) and Pratt and Thompson (2008) following empirical studies in Canada. Additionally, I have found that the enactment of this power responds to a transformed gendered politics. Taken together, the recent masculinized portrayal of borderwork, the following of a gendered code of conduct to assert authority and the new enforcement training and incorporation of policing equipment have shifted the corporeal experience of frontline security actors in ways that allow them to now claim masculinist dominance over the border. This altered gendered politics has reshaped their bodies in a way that makes them more amenable to using violence—or, at least, to perform the capacity to do so in the eyes of the travelling public. If the masculinization of borderwork accompanies its transformation into an increasingly performative endeavour, it also makes that power even more visible.

The changing pedagogies of border control

To change borderwork is to change how border workers are made. No major project of conversion of a security organization can be successful without remodelling how its security professionals are selected and learn their jobs.[14] Despite this reality, we are quite uninformed about the professional socialization of security personnel—that is, about their selection and apprenticeship. Given the multiplication of security and "high policing" (Brodeur 2007)

bodies dedicated to combat transnational organized crime, irregular migration and terrorism (Andreas and Nadelmann 2006; Bowling and Sheptycki
2012), it comes as a surprise that we know so little about how security professionals learn their trade—especially in light of existing studies of street-cop
and military apprenticeships. If we are able to speak of the "securitization" of
a variety of areas of the social (e.g. migration), it means that those tasked with
this endeavour have had to acquire specific knowledges and competencies
that convert them into bona fide security actors.

A range of questions must be answered concerning the professional socialization of border control: How do border officers become acquainted with
the know-how (skills, practices, conduct) and the normative and subcultural
knowledge (values, assumptions, norms) that helps them integrate into border organizations (Chan 2003; van Maanen 1973)? Why do they choose that
profession in the first place? How did they acquire a disposition of suspicion
and distrust? As this book attempts to answer these questions by taking the
Canadian border as its case study, other comparative questions emerge that
would contribute to our understanding of the relations between professional
socialization and the securing of cross-border movement: How are border
officers chosen and instructed in different countries? Are there variations? If
so, what are the possible effects of these variations on the treatment of transport workers, travellers and migrants? This book offers a first exploration of
what novel aspects of bordering we discover by studying the pedagogies of
border control.

I begin this exploration with the premise that training in the security professions is a "transformative act"; Woodward and Jenkings (2011: 255) were thinking of soldiers when they made this observation, but it also applies, with nuances,
to the realm of border policing. In fact, pedagogies of border control focus particularly on selecting prospective officers with specific backgrounds but also
on altering border officers' subjectivities, attitudes and conduct. We will see in
Chapter 6 that officers' professional socialization has been completely revamped.
That process took years to implement, and it is still not complete. This required
significant spending and a substantive re-allocation of resources, developing new
hiring procedures and testing new training curriculums. It demanded a shift
from a local to a standardized model of selection and training and a new focus
in early officer training on a police academy model. New curriculums speak to a
conversion of formal training schemes with an emphasis on control and defence
tactics, gun training, data management and border regulations.

Despite these major changes, officers' narratives about their apprenticeship were not as much reminiscent of the skills they had learned via the
curriculum as they were filled with memories of more-informal aspects of
their training. I consider what we learn more broadly about modifications
in the formal aspects of officer training but also the more affective dimensions of the professional socialization of border staff. The latter is more difficult to grasp because it relates to the "soft," more relational side of officers'

occupation, whether this involves observing their more experienced peers' strategies of self-presentation, finding the right attitude in interactions with more combative border crossers or dealing with the stress of customs college.

Further, officers' practices can be traced back in great part to their learning trajectories. They train in the particular tools and techniques available to them at the beginning of their careers. As a result, it is more difficult (but not impossible) to have officers incorporate new habits as time passes for them. I have met experienced officers who began their career in the absence of enforcement tools now part of their arsenal and who looked at the arrival of the gun with disbelief. As Mario told me: he had never even used his baton, and now the CBSA wants him to carry a gun?! Others, as shown in Chapter 7, never really abandoned the objectives of economic protectionism. Years after the adoption of the North American Free Trade Agreement (NAFTA) in 1994, William and other experienced colleagues tried to convince me that "protecting the local economy" was still part of their job. Given these observations, Bigo's (2011, 2014) suggestion that we take heed of Bourdieu's work on the habitus and of Lahire's (2013, 2012) notion of the patrimony of dispositions—a shifting set of habits, capacities and schemes of thought that border officers tap into as they adapt to a new security context—becomes all the more relevant. For Lahire (2012: 49), these dispositions are how experience manifests itself in present interactions. The habits and experiences acquired during their professional socialization become resources for officers as they come to act, imagine, think and feel borderwork.

In short, if we are to understand the shift towards border enforcement, we also need to study how border workers are chosen and instructed. As William suggested to me, selection and training modify security outcomes and, ultimately, may alter how people on the move are treated. Border officers who think of themselves as enforcers do not appear out of thin air; they are made—and perhaps we should entertain the possibility that, eventually, they can be unmade.

The project to change customs and borderwork as an enforcement endeavour is full of tensions and contradictions. Despite the enforcement agenda, continuities remain in how borderwork is taught and practised. Officers still learn from their peers long-standing techniques that have characterized their occupation, such as how to listen and look for signs of deception, which forms to complete and how to search trucks. Further, former ways of selecting and training officers embraced before the creation of the CBSA continue to have an impact on everyday practice. It is this encounter between continuity and change in border control practice that bears the brunt of the responsibility for the intergenerational tensions that, I discovered, shape everyday interactions between officers in ports of entry.

Generational borderwork and security's logic of ageing

During our conversation, William suggested that my research would be useful if it could provide solutions to intergenerational tensions between senior officers and junior officers, whom he colourfully called "hush puppies and Dobermans." Talk of generational conflict and differences occurred frequently in interviews and proved to play a central role in shaping the "mundane forms of professional and personal self-understanding" in the ports of entry that I visited (Aas and Gundhus 2015: 2). It is an unexpected finding given the absence of concern for generations in the literature about borders, policing and security.

As shown in Chapter 7, officers refer to "generations" or to what they consider to be "old ways" and "new ways" when they describe their daily routines. "Old ways" refer to a variety of dispositions (i.e. ease with trade and national regulations on goods, traditional border enforcement skills such as interviewing and detection of behavioural "risk indicators") and a set of interests, affinities and preferences (i.e. public service, taxation, economic protectionism, good relations with local communities). Officers were seen to embrace "new ways" when they supported the adoption of the firearm and risk-management principles, showed an ease with databases and detection technologies and focused their attention on a type of law enforcement that adopted these tools and principles. Finding different generations of border officers taught me a simple but fundamental lesson: to become fully effective, the processes that we refer to as "militarization" or "securitization" require a change of guard in security organizations.

Accordingly, generational narratives indicate that the shift to enforcement and security in border control was neither immediately nor wholeheartedly embraced at the frontline. Taking these frictions into account, I present a take on borderwork that is inspired by the sociology of generations, which brings us momentarily beyond the world of security, policing and borders so that we can re-enter it with new eyes. Generations offer a unique entry point into dynamics of social change in border control, the conflicts created by the shift to enforcement and the reshaping of border officers' subjectivities in the process.

Social theorists have long drawn attention to how generation, as a cultural category, is less about birth cohorts than "social differentiation and conflict" (Aboim and Vasconcelos 2014: 168). Talk of "generations" relate to the ways that people draw boundaries between themselves and others in order to make sense of their historically specific experience; we label and differentiate ourselves as part of a collective anchored in a given social time (Foster 2013; Down and Reveley 2004). Therefore, generations of border workers are not "baby boomers" or "millennials" with distinct personality types that express changes in work attitudes and values created outside of the working world.[15] I am not interested in repeating this received wisdom, nor am I asking how imagined homogeneous social groups who share little more than being born at the same time fare in security organizations. Generations in border control are produced "in-house"; it is my contention that they can be traced back, in great part, to the remodelling of hiring procedures and training programmes.

Consequently, the book makes two points about generations and borderwork. First, it investigates the work done by generational discourses to classify and evaluate what is considered an appropriate security practice and what should be secured and by whom. Generational labels are intrinsically comparative, where a generation is positioned as lacking in something (skill, attitude, know-how) that another generation putatively excels in (Pritchard and Whiting 2014: 1620). Accordingly, borderwork is a manufacture of professional convictions. In interviews, officers had recourse to the popular cultural repertoire of "generations" and applied it to border policing—saying something like "there are young and old generations of border officers and let me explain to you the lesser value of what the other generation does."

By doing so, officers not only temporalize their work (those are "old ways"; this is "the future of the border") but also attribute positive or negative meaning to belonging to one or the other generation. The familiarity (or lack thereof) with technologies also gives shape to this idea, as does the notion that border policing has "entered another phase" or that border control should be about security and not taxation. In this sense, belonging to a "generation" of security professionals is revealed and signified in how these individuals engage with and mobilize technologies, devices, regulations, strategies of investigation and operating procedures. Officers classify their skills, training, regulatory knowledge, professional attitudes and work methods along a temporal scale of worth from which they determine what constitutes a job well done. It is this work of categorization and the practices it both reflects and sustains that I call *generational borderwork*.

My second related point concerns how these categorizations allocate prestige in border agencies, giving rise to classification struggles—where newcomers pit seniority against their higher educational achievements and their alignment with current border policy. Here, I follow Bourdieu's (1979) work on social fields where generations refer to how status, titles and resources are unequally distributed and where the related differences between young and old are not the product of general social trends. In the case of my research, these differences come from changes in border control that have renewed power struggles among security professionals endowed with distinct professional socializations. This is far from innocuous. Generational categorizations serve to establish leverage in security settings. Generational scales of distinction organize status through mechanisms that facilitate the obtainment of valued positions. They can also reduce access to and even prevent promotion. In fact, the educational, technological and law enforcement dispositions now favoured by the CBSA in their selection and training process are also those privileged when it comes to distributing rewards, ranks and promotions. This creates another source of generational conflict.

Taking generations seriously brings new insights to studies of border control. What generational borderwork tells us is that border guards' subjectivity not only is shaped by such concerns as the humanitarian–security dilemma (Pallister-Wilkins 2015), by a sense of powerlessness (Heyman 1995; Casella Colombeau 2015) or even by a confidence in their protective role (Pickering and Ham 2014) but is also predicated on temporal categories. To claim that a security practice is innovative or that another comes from a previous era is to pass judgement on its efficacy and relevance

(Fabian 1983; Hindess 2007). Such thought processes—whereby differences between practices are temporalized and read as separating contemporaries from those who are associated with the past—confirm the influence in security settings of classificatory modes that distribute individuals along scales of success and failure, of development and anachronism, and that judge people according to a present standard that is imagined as harnessing the best of security's future. The temporalization of categories of worth may have real-world consequences for border crossers. Imagine the implications for migrant rights advocates facing border workers who may deem issues of human rights to be a soft concern of the past, little aligned with the "way we do things now."

Further, if being in tune with the "future" of security can grant promotions and peer recognition, then inversely, it is also a way to disqualify, even render obsolete, those associated with an anachronistic past. Taking into account generational borderwork means shedding another light onto the struggles that make up the security field, including quarrels between the "ancients" and the "moderns" (Bigo 2005) over the legitimate framing of security objects (should borderwork be primarily about terrorism, refugees, legal amounts of alcohol, drug trafficking or counterfeit goods?) and the appropriation of budgets and resources to tackle them.

Border and security scholarship would be well served to investigate how ideas, but also technologies, methods, training and individuals, become older in security provision, by focusing on the internal history of security organizations and their "laws of ageing"—that is, on the dynamics that shape their transformation, ensure their stability or generate discontinuity (what Bourdieu [1984: 144] calls, the *mode de génération* of a social field). In fact, this scholarship often leaves us with a sense that security is the realm of potentiality and perpetual newness—with its pre-emptive approach and its adoption of technologies. This is not surprising, since it mirrors security agencies' official outlook, which supports approaches to security associated with youth and novelty—such as computing skills, physical strength, quick learning abilities and the capacity of adaptation. But it also means that a security professional, technology or enforcement practice can quickly appear outdated. By being a product of—and being produced by—generational dynamics, security reveals its own logic of ageing.

Conclusion

In many ways, this book has an exploratory character. Few incursions have been made into the daily practices of border security professionals in post-9/11 North America, and even fewer have approached the understudied area of customs. As it transitions towards enforcement, bordering has undergone profound transformations. As I show next, the magnitude of this change is impressive given the protectionist role that had defined customs for most of the 20th century. Accordingly, this book investigates the dynamics that are currently remodelling border control on the basis of an enforcement logic. It speaks to how this change not only is the result of a delocalized, technology-driven and intelligence-led surveillance over mobilities but also stems from the concrete labour performed by security professionals and from their efforts to remain relevant amid major policy, technological and regulatory changes. While it focuses on borderwork, I hope that this book will also offer food for thought to those concerned with cultural shifts in other types of policing and security-related workplaces.

To illuminate the specifics of this shift, I privilege the point of view of a particular group of border actors—namely the staff responsible for processing truck drivers, trucks and commodities at ports of entry along the Eastern Canada–US land border. Taken together, these frontline border officials reveal themselves to be a fascinating category of civil servants. As tax collectors and international trade regulators, they contribute to the classification, inspection and taxation of commodities entering Canada. But because they enjoy broad legal powers, they also increasingly consider themselves to be "a police of the border." Building an analytical bridge between the contemporary overhauls in security, the liberalization of trade in North America and the daily practices of customs officers, as well as the power struggles between these officers and other institutional actors who have a stake in border control, I revisit border control as a site of competing policing actors and strategies that are part and parcel of the reconfiguration of how we govern the circulation of people and things in border spaces. As a complement to studies that engage with the local experiences of those living in close proximity to North American securitized borderlands (Helleiner 2016: Rosas 2012), this book acquaints us with the more invisible labour that borders our lives.

Acknowledgements

Parts of this chapter are excerpts from the following article:

Côté-Boucher, K (2018). Of "old" and "new" ways: Generations, border control and the temporality of security, *Theoretical Criminology*, 22 (2): 149–168. First Published February 10, 2017 © 2017 by SAGE. Reprinted by Permission of SAGE Publications, Ltd.

With many thanks to SAGE Permissions, Ltd.

Notes

1 Given that the interviews have been carried out in French and in English, the fictitious names given to interviewees have been selected because they are used in both languages in Canada.

2 I experienced how seriously officers took the enforcement side of their work when I was scolded for calling them customs officers (a reminder of their time as tax collectors) rather than using border services officers, the new, more assertive designation.

3 I translated French interview quotes.
4 My current position in teaching security professionals, including border officers, also keeps me informed of developments at the border and in Canadian security organizations more generally. Further, I undertook another research project in the Canadian trucking industry about the impact of the border in truckers' working lives, and this also keeps me up to date on continuing policy and technological changes and the fate of border programmes in the customs area.
5 See CBC (2011), *The Canada-US Border: By the Numbers*, www.cbc.ca/news/canada/the-canada-u-s-border-by-the-numbers-1.999207 (last modified 7 Dec. 2011; last consulted 3 Mar. 2018); Transport Canada (2016), *Transportation in Canada 2016: Comprehensive Report*, www.tc.gc.ca/eng/policy/transportation-canada-2016.html (last modified 22 Aug. 2017; last consulted 4 Mar. 2018).
6 Following Boltanski's (2009: 29–30) categorization of the possible critical positions a scholar can take, I point to the contradictions between the official and the unofficial, to the lack of correspondence between that which is said about what is done and that which is actually realized in border control. It is perhaps a "less ambitious" type of critique than that proposed by many working on border control, yet it is "more likely to take advantage of the specific means offered by sociological description."
7 On port scanners, see Stéphane Baillargeon (2017), La surveillance des conteneurs est défaillante au port de Montréal, *Le Devoir*, www.ledevoir.com/societe/actualites-en-societe/497114/la-surveillance-des-conteneurs-est-defaillante-au-port-de-montreal (last consulted 2 Jan. 2019). On the availability of CPIC, see J. Lancaster and S. Bridge (2015), Canada's border agents armed with new information to screen visitors, *CBC News*, 3 Dec., www.cbc.ca/news/canada/toronto/canada-s-border-agents-armed-with-new-information-to-screen-visitors-1.3349779 (last consulted 2 Jan. 2019).
8 See CBSA (2015), *Border Modernization: Transforming for Tomorrow*, www.cbsa-asfc.gc.ca/multimedia/bomo-prio/menu-eng.html (last modified 15 June 2015; last consulted 2 Jan. 2019).
9 For Foucault, programmes propose a set of "reasoned and calculated prescriptions" that can be followed to "organize institutions, design spaces [such as borders] and regulate behaviours." Programmes can be left "in suspension," yet they remain significant because they point to a way of thinking about an object or an institution (here the border, the control of mobilities, security, etc.).
10 Coleman (2010: 489) reminds us that anthropologists of technologies have since the 1990s cast "doubt on the autonomous power of technologies to engender change," showing that "digital technologies in many instances facilitated social reproduction." A similar conclusion is proposed by the sociology of organization. "Analytically and historically," organizational change happens before the need is felt to incorporate technological innovations (Clawson 1980: 57, cited in Thompson and McHugh 2009: 20).
11 I thank Julien Jeandesboz for helping me make this point clearer.
12 Richard Marosi (2016), Union for Border Patrol agents under fire for endorsement of Trump, *Los Angeles Times*, 12 May, www.latimes.com/nation/politics/la-na-border-patrol-trump-20160511-snap-story.html (last consulted 2 Jan. 2019).
13 This emotional labour is probably equally demanding for racialized officers, although because the great majority of my interviewees were white, my data is limited on this aspect and would therefore require more research.
14 This has been demonstrated by Nolan's (2013) study of the CIA, where the unchanged selection and training of officers—traditionally intended to protect secrets, generate pride in being part of an elite secret group and detach themselves from the outside world—undermined the agency's post-9/11 efforts in collaborating with the National Counterterrorism Center (NCTC).
15 See Lyons and Kuron (2014) for a management studies take on generations.

References

Aas, K. F. 2006. "The body does not lie": Identity, risk and trust in technoculture. *Crime, Media, Culture* 2 (2):143–158.

Aas, K. F., and H. Gundhus. 2015. Policing humanitarian borderlands: Frontex, human rights and the precariousness of life. *British Journal of Criminology* 55 (1):1–18.

Aboim, S., and P. Vasconcelos. 2014. From political to social generations: A critical reappraisal of Mannheim's classical approach. *European Journal of Social Theory* 17 (2):165–183.

Amicelle, A., C. Aradau, and J. Jeandesboz. 2015. Questioning security devices: Performativity, resistance, politics. *Security Dialogue* 46 (4):293–306.

Amoore, L. 2013. *The Politics of Possibility: Risk and Security beyond Probability*. Durham, London: Duke University Press.

Andreas, P., and E. Nadelmann. 2006. *Policing the Globe: Criminalization and Crime Control in International Relations*. Oxford, New York: Oxford University Press.

Berry, J., G. O'Connor, M. Punch, and P. Wilson. 2008. Strange union: Changing patterns of reform, representation, and unionization in policing. *Police Practice and Research* 9 (2):113–130.

Bigo, D. 2002. Security and immigration: Toward a critique of the governmentality of unease. *Alternatives: Global, Local, Political* 27:63–92.

———. 2005. La mondialisation de l'insécurité? *Cultures & Conflicts* 58:53–101.

———. 2011. Pierre Bourdieu and international relations: Power of practices, practices of power. *International Political Sociology* 5 (3):225–258.

———. 2014. The (in)securitization practices of the three universes of EU border control: Military/Navy-border guards/police-database analysts. *Security Dialogue* 45 (3):209–225.

Bigo, D., and E. Guild. 2005. Policing at a distance: Schengen visa policies. In *Controlling Frontiers: Free Movement into and within Europe*, edited by D. Bigo and E. Guild. London: Routledge.

Boltanski, L. 2009. *De la critique. Précis de sociologie de l'émancipation*. Paris: Gallimard.

Bonelli, L., and F. Ragazzi. 2014. Low-tech security: Files, notes, and memos as technologies of anticipation. *Security Dialogue* 45 (5):476–493.

Bourdieu, P. 1979. *La distinction. Critique sociale du jugement*. Paris: Les éditions de minuit.

———. 1984. *Questions de sociologie*. Paris: Les Éditions de minuit.

Bowling, B., and J. Sheptycki. 2012. *Global Policing*. London: Sage.

Brodeur, J. P. 2007. High and low policing in post 9/11 times. *Policing: A Journal of Policy and Practice* 1 (1):25–37.

Brown, W. 1995. *States of Injury: Power and Freedom in Late Modernity*. Princeton: Princeton University Press.

Butler, J. 2004. *Precarious Life: The Powers of Mourning and Violence*. London: Verso.

Cantens, T. 2015. Un scanner de conteneurs en « Terre Promise » camerounaise: adopter et s'approprier une technologie de contrôle. *L'Espace politique* 25:2–18.

Casella Colombeau, S. 2015. Policing the internal Schengen borders: Managing the double bind between free movement and migration control. *Policing and Society* 27 (5):480–493.

Chan, J. 2003. *Fair Cop: Learning the Art of Policing*. Toronto: University of Toronto Press.

Clawson, D. 1980. *Bureaucracy and the Labor Process: The Transformation of US Industry, 1860–1920*. New York: Monthly Review Press.

Cohn, C. 1987. Sex and death in the rational world of defense intellectuals. *Signs*. 12 (4): 687–718.

Coleman, G. 2010. Ethnographic approaches to digital media. *Annual Review of Anthropology* 39 (1):487–505.

Connell, R. W. 2005. *Masculinities (Second edition)*. Cambridge: Polity Press.

Côté-Boucher, K., F. Infantino, and M. B. Salter. 2014. Border security as practice: An agenda for research. *Security Dialogue* 45 (3):195–208.

Côté-Boucher, K. 2008. The diffuse border: Intelligence-sharing, control and confinement along Canada's Smart Border. *Surveillance and Society* 5 (2):142–165.

Davidshofer, S., J. Jeandesboz, and F. Ragazzi. 2016. Technology and security practices. In *International Political Sociology: Transversal Lines*, edited by T. Basaran, D. Bigo and E.-P. Guittet. London: Routledge.

Diphoorn, T. 2015. "It's all about the body": The bodily capital of armed response officers in South Africa. *Medical Anthropology* 34 (4):336–352.

Down, S., and Reveley, J. 2004. Generational encounters and the social formation of entrepreneurial identity: 'young guns' and 'old farts'. *Organization* 511 (2):233–250.

Dupont, B. 2006. Power struggles in the field of security: Implications for democratic transformation. In *Democracy, Society and the Governance of Security*, edited by J. Wood and B. Dupont. Cambridge: Cambridge University Press, 86–110.

Fabian, J. 1983. *Time and the Other: How Anthropology Makes Its Object*. New York: Columbia University Press.

Feldman, G. 2012. *The Migration Apparatus: Security, Labor, and Policymaking in the European Union*. Stanford: Stanford University Press.

Fleming, J., M. Marks, and J. Wood. 2006. "Standing on the inside looking out": The significance of police unions in networks of police governance. *Australian & New Zealand Journal of Criminology* 39 (1):7–89.

Fosher, K. B. 2009. *Under Construction: Making Homeland Security at the Local Level*. Chicago: University of Chicago Press.

Foster, K. 2013. Generation and discourse in working life stories. *British Journal of Sociology* 64 (2):195–215.

Foucault, M. 2001 [1980]. Table ronde du 20 mai 1978. In *Dits et écrits volume II 1976–1988*, edited by D. Defert and F. Ewald. Paris: Quarto Gallimard.

Gammeltoft-Hansen, T. 2013. The rise of the private border guard: Governance and accountability in the involvement of non-state actors in migration management. In *The Migration Industry and the Commercialization of International Migration*, edited by T. Gammeltoft-Hansen and N. Nyberg Sorenson. Abingdon, UK: Routledge.

Gilboy, J. 1991. Deciding who gets in: Decisionmaking by immigration inspectors. *Law & Society Review* 25 (3):571–600.

Hadjimatheou, K., and J. K. Lynch. 2017. "Once they pass you, they may be gone forever": Humanitarian duties and professional tensions in safeguarding and anti-trafficking at the border. *British Journal of Criminology* 57 (4): 945–963.

Helleiner, J. 2016. *Borderline Canadianness: Border Crossings and Everyday Nationalism in Niagara*. Toronto: University of Toronto Press.

Heyman, J. McC. 1995. Putting power in the anthropology of bureaucracy: The immigration and naturalization service at the Mexico-United States border. *Current Anthropology* 36 (2):261–287.

Higate, P. 2012. The private militarized and security contractor as geocorporeal actor. *International Political Sociology* 6 (4):355–372.

Hindess, B. 2007. The past is another culture. *International Political Sociology* 1 (4):325–338.

Huysmans, J. 2011. What's in an act? On security speech acts and little security nothings. *Security Dialogue* 42 (4–5):371–383.

Huysmans, J. 2014. *Security Unbound: Enacting Democratic Limits*. London: Routledge.

Jeandesboz, J., D. Bigo, B. Hayes, and S. Simon. 2013. *The Commission's Legislative Proposals on Smart Borders: Their Feasibility and Costs*. Brussels: European Parliament. https://doi.org/10.2861/39726

Jones, R. 2012. *Border Walls: Security and the War on Terror in the United States, India, and Israel*. London, New York: Zed Books.

Jones, R., C. Johnson, W. Brown, G. Popescu, P. Pallister-Wilkins, A. Mountz, and E. Gilbert. 2017. Interventions on the state of sovereignty at the border. *Political Geography* 59:1–10.

Jubany, O. 2017. *Screening Asylum in a Culture of Disbelief: Truth, Denials and Skeptical Borders*. Cham: Palgrave Macmillan.

Kotef, H. 2015. *Movement and the Ordering of Freedom*. Durham: Duke University Press.

Lahire, B. 2012. *Monde pluriel. Penser l'unité des sciences sociales*. Paris: Seuil.

———. 2013. *Dans les plis singuliers du social. Individus, institutions, socialisations*. Paris: La Découverte.

Lipsky, M. 2010 [1980]. *Street-Level Bureaucracy: Dilemmas of the Individual in Public Services (30th anniversary expanded edition)*. New York: Russell Sage Foundation.

Loftus, B. 2015. Border regimes and the sociology of policing. *Policing and Society* 25 (1): 115–125.

Lyons, S., and L. Kuron. 2014. Generational differences in the workplace: A review of the evidence and directions for future research. *Journal of Organizational Behavior* 35:S139–S157.

Manning, P. 2008. *The Technology of Policing: Crime Mapping, Information Technology, and the Rationality of Crime Control*. New York: New York University Press.

Marks, M. 2000. Transforming police organizations from within: Police dissident groupings in South Africa. *British Journal of Criminology* 40 (4):557–573.

Mauss, M. 1934. Les techniques du corps. *Journal de Psychologie* 32 (3–4).

Mountz, A. 2010. *Seeking Asylum: Human Smuggling and Bureaucracy at the Border*. Minneapolis: University of Minnesota Press.

Nolan, B. R. 2013. *Information Sharing and Collaboration in the United States Intelligence Community: An Ethnographic Study of the National Counterterrorism Centre*. PhD Dissertation in Sociology. Philadelphia: University of Pennsylvania.

O'Malley, P., and S. Hutchinson. 2007. Converging corporatization? Police management, police unionism, and the transfer of business principles. *Police Practice and Research* 8 (2): 159–174.

Orlikowski, W. J. 2000. Using technology and constituting structures: A practice lens for studying technology in organizations. *Organization Science* 11 (4):404–428.

Page, J. 2011. *The Toughest Beat: Politics, Punishment, and the Prison Officers Union in California*. Oxford: Oxford University Press.

Pallister-Wilkins, P. 2015. The humanitarian politics of European border policing: Frontex and border police in Evros. *International Political Sociology* 9 (1):53–69.

Pickering, S., M. Bosworth, and K. Franko Aas. 2015. The criminology of mobility. In *The Routledge Handbook on Crime and International Migration*, edited by S. Pickering and J. Ham. London: Routledge, 382–395.

Pickering, S., and J. Ham. 2014. Hot pants at the border: Sorting sex work from trafficking. *The British Journal of Criminology* 54 (1):2–19.

Pötzsch, H. 2015. The emergence of iBorder: Bordering bodies, networks and machines. *Environment and Planning D: Society and Space* 33 (1):101–118.

Pratt, A. 2010. Between a hunch and a hard place: Making suspicion reasonable at the Canadian border. *Social & Legal Studies* 19 (4):461–480.

Pratt, A., and S. Thompson. 2008. Chivalry, "race" and discretion at the Canadian border. *The British Journal of Criminology* 48 (5):620–640.

Pritchard, K., and R. Whiting. 2014. Baby Boomers and the lost generation: On the discursive construction of generations at work. *Organization Studies* 35 (11):1605–1636.

Prokkola, E.-V., and J. Ridanpää. 2015. Border guarding and the politics of the body: An examination of the Finnish Border Guard service. *Gender, Place & Culture* 22 (10):1374–1390.

Provine, D. M., M. W. Varsanyi, P. G. Lewis, and S. H. Decker. 2016. *Policing Immigrants: Local Law Enforcement on the Front Lines*. Chicago: University of Chicago Press.

Reeves, M. 2014. *Border Work: Spatial Lives of the State in Rural Central Asia*. Ithaca: Cornell University Press.

Rosas, G. 2012. *Barrio Libre: Criminalizing States and Delinquant Refusals of the New Frontier*. Durham: Duke University Press.

Rumford, C. 2008. Citizens and borderwork in Europe. *Space and Polity* 12 (1):1–12.

Rygiel, K. 2013. Mobile citizens, risky subjects: Security knowledge at the border. In *Mobilities, Knowledge, and Social Justice*, edited by S. Ilcan. Montreal, Kingston: McGill-Queen's University Press, 152–177.

Salter, M. 2007. Governmentalities of an airport: Heterotopia and confession. *International Political Sociology* 1 (1):49–66.

Shapira, H. 2013. *Waiting for José. The Minutemen's Pursuit of America*. Princeton: Princeton University Press.

Sheptycki, J. 2004. Organizational pathologies in police intelligence-systems: Some contributions to the lexicon of intelligence-led policing. *European Journal of Criminology* 1 (3):307–332.

———. 2017. Liquid modernity and the police métier: Thinking about information flows in police organisation. *Global Crime* 18 (3):286–302.

Springwood, C. F. 2007. The social life of guns: Introduction. In *Open Fire: Understanding Global Gun Cultures*, edited by C. F. Springwood. Oxford, NY: Bert.

Theweleit, K. 1987 [1977]. *Male Fantasies Vol. 1 Women Floods Bodies History*. Minneapolis: University of Minnesota Press.

———. 1989 [1978]. *Male Fantasies Vol. 2 Male Bodies: Psychoanalyzing the White Terror*. Minneapolis: University of Minnesota Press.

Thompson, E. P. 1967. Time, work-discipline, and industrial capitalism. *Past & Present* 38:56–97.

Thompson, P., and D. McHugh. 2009. *Work Organisations. A Critical Approach (Fourth edition)*. London: Palgrave Macmillan.

Tsing, A. 2005. *Friction: An Ethnography of Global Connection*. Princeton: Princeton University Press.

van der Woude, M., and J. Brouwer. 2017. Searching for "illegal" junk in the trunk: Underlying intentions of (cr)immigration controls in Schengen's internal border areas. *New Criminal Law Review* 20 (1):157–179.

van Maanen, J. 1973. Observations on the making of policemen. *Human Organization* 32 (4):407–418.

Woodward, R., and K. N. Jenkings. 2011. Military identities in the situated accounts of British military personnel. *Sociology* 45 (2):252–268.

Zuboff, S. 1988. *In the Age of the Smart Machine: The Future of Work and Power*. New York: Basic Books

Interlude

The slipper section

It is a sunny spring day at the land border. I am touring a port of entry, spending some time in the traffic section, where car drivers and bus passengers are processed. Some officers have their heads buried in paperwork; others sit at their computers. As I observe these daily activities, a middle-aged officer engages me in a conversation, wondering who I am and what I am doing there. After hearing my explanations about my research, she gives me a perplexed look, asking aloud, "why would you be interested in 'commercial' work?" "What on earth are you doing 'back there' when traffic and immigration is where the action happens?"

This reaction is typical of the view taken by border officers when it comes to customs work, a type of border control perceived to be more administrative and rather monotonous. As mentioned in introduction, all border officers in Canada, whether they work customs, immigration or traffic and traveller control, are employed by the Canada Border Services Agency (CBSA). Yet there is a clear division of labour between these responsibilities, which are also differently valued by officers. As a distinct kind of border personnel, commercial officers have long understood themselves to be more oriented towards compliance with customs, trade, and agricultural and environmental regulations as well as with the collection of duties and taxes rather than with strict law enforcement activities. To understand the shift to enforcement in border control, including for customs workers, let's first shed light on what makes customs a specific type of street-level bureaucratic labour.

Working commercial

The spatial arrangements that make up land ports of entry are indicative of the division of labour between customs, traveller processing and immigration, and they do much to sustain the view that customs is a special kind of borderwork. With the exception of small and remote ports, most land ports of entry comprise at least two buildings—which is also the case in the US and in many other countries (Heyman 2004; Chalfin 2010).

In Canada, the first building is referred to as the traffic section, where traffic and immigration officers are posted. Traffic officers process car drivers and bus passengers. After the creation of the CBSA in 2003, immigration officers have been incorporated into the border agency and have since been required to take on traffic work as part of their duties. In this main building, immigration officers also decide on admissibility into the country (e.g. verifying permanent residency, handling work visas, etc.). Trucks, truck drivers and goods are processed elsewhere, in the commercial building, where the great majority of my interviewees were located.

These two sections—traffic and commercial—practically operate as two different ports of entry. Often, officers are not acquainted with their colleagues attached to the other building. The spatial metaphors they use when speaking of this micro-geography of the port illustrate this separation and their perception that commercial officers operate behind the scenes. Officers frequently refer to commercial services as "the back" of the port and traffic operations as "the front" or "up there." This backstage position of the commercial section reflects the more monotonous and clerical character of customs work, which includes many computer-related and paper-based tasks and involves less contact with border crossers. The organization of the work week also differs in the two buildings. The week at the commercial section starts slowly and picks up as trucks start coming back from the US. Weekend and night shifts are less busy, requiring more week-based work schedules than at the traffic section where cross-border shoppers, vacationers and sports fans cross south of the border for the weekend.

Further, working commercial requires more training in complex regulations, including trade, the environment and food safety. Accordingly, while some ports decide to have officers begin their work in commercial, it is generally admitted that traffic is where rookie officers should first learn the ropes of their new job. Transfers occur later in their career, and it is common to see in the commercial section those officers who decided to finish their careers there. As a result, the customs buildings are usually staffed with more-experienced officers.

Most of the officers I met emphasized the more routine character of the commercial section, and many explained that this atmosphere played a great part in their choice to work there. Elizabeth, an officer with previous traffic experience, nicknames her current work building the "slipper section" of her port of entry. An experienced officer, Suzanne, told me she "loved" commercial, calling it her "home." In contrast, working in a "relaxed" environment is given a more negative connotation by those who were forced to transfer to the commercial section for health reasons. In the latter case, these officers feel restless in commercial. Nathan, whom we met in the previous chapter, confided that he "would have given his right arm to get back in traffic." Arthur, another officer with a similar set of circumstances, said he appreciated traffic because he was not scared of "getting into a little scuffle." Interestingly, this representation clashes with actual seizure records at the CBSA. As monotonous as the commercial section may be, it is customs officers who are responsible for the most significant drug seizures when assessed by weight—given the room afforded by containers and commercial vehicles for smuggling operations. But since these large seizures are rare events, they are not as typical of the daily experience of commercial work as are smaller seizures and finding irregularities in documentation, traveller stories and status in traffic and immigration work.

The repetitive and bureaucratic feel of the job makes commercial work more comfortable, or dull, depending on whom you talk to. Raymond, an experienced officer, calls the commercial section "a lot happier work environment" and contrasts it with traffic work: "Some people can't stand it back here. They come back here for a little bit and they hate it. They find it boring. They want to be up front. They consider that action, they enjoy the confrontation I suppose." Raymond pauses, thinks of his first years when he himself worked traffic, and goes on:

> I always found that part of the job [traffic], unless you were helping somebody on the phone, it was almost 90% negative. Because unless you were just questioning somebody believing them and letting them go up the road, as soon as you were sending somebody down, you were sending them down for two reasons: Either to pay, which pissed them off, or because you didn't believe what they told you.

Raymond then gives me an example:

> You're essentially looking at somebody saying, "I think you're lying to me." And who likes to be called a liar? And then so you're getting dirty looks and then, if you're the person searching the car, (he imitates an irritated voice): "I don't look like a smuggler." It was always confrontational where you never. . . . I don't want to use the word never . . . but you almost never have that back here.

Commercial officers' narratives are replete with evidence of discomfort regarding the parts of their responsibilities that require them to display oppressive and invasive authority—secured by their extensive search-and-seizure powers[1]—especially when this involves direct conflict with travellers over small quantities of merchandise. This was particularly true of older officers, whereas the younger ones tended to display more enthusiasm for any type of enforcement activity. In the following chapters, I explore the reasons for this change in mentality. But the fact remains that many interviewees, especially experienced officers having spent a large part of their careers at the commercial section, expressed a dislike for traffic work. They were forthcoming in their portrayal of traffic duties as stressful and riddled with daily conflicts with travellers. To quote Raymond again, working traffic is a "cat and mouse game" played with those travellers who are inclined to lie, and searching private luggage, purses and wallets is a "petty" and unnecessary kind of work. Another experienced officer, Catherine, remembers with irony how she did not like hassling people: "Oh my God! You have an extra shirt you didn't declare! Big deal!" Seeking less "action," those officers sometimes attempt to get transferred, seeing the regulatory compliance work involved in customs as a respite from the pressures experienced in the traffic section.

Underplaying one's formal authority

Perhaps overly influenced by Butler's remarks about "petty sovereigns" and by works that, in the wake of Agamben and Schmitt, theorized bordering as an instance of the normalization of the state of exception, I entered ports of entry assuming that security professionals would be eager, coercive agents of the sovereign state. Yet I found much-more-contradictory social actors. Officers are not always at peace with their extended search-and-seizure powers and the strictness that their profession requires them to display publicly. Since the conclusion of my research, scholarship on humanitarian biopolitics at borders (Aas and Gundhus 2015; Pallister-Wilkins 2015) has demonstrated that borderwork presents border personnel with ethical dilemmas, daily frustrations and even malaise regarding some of their duties. A similar observation has been made in criminology, by Waddington (1999), for whom policing represents an "inherently problematic occupational experience," and more recently by Ugelvik (2016), who underscores the various ways Norwegian immigration detention officers legitimize their morally challenging occupation. In the Canadian case, I have found a similar uneasiness displayed by many customs officers with the more oppresive aspects of their work. In fact, similarly to what Bosworth (2014: 100) found in the case of UK immigration detention staff—that their "views of detainees also shaped their sense of self"—commercial officers' stance towards what they call their "clients" (truck drivers) influences how they rationalize their role at the border.

Customs officers tend to rely on a particular legitimation strategy when speaking of their work, which consists in undervaluing their formal authority over truck drivers. An experienced officer's description of commercial work touched on how officers downplay their power differential with truck drivers, singling them out as model border crossers. Catherine explains that "In commercial, the brokers, the truck drivers and customs, we all know we are here to do a job. We know it's something that has to be done, we put up with it and we try and make it as easy for each other as possible." Officers insist that they appreciate "working commercial" because truck drivers, they argue, are "just like them": workers who try to make a living, "pay their mortgage" and "feed their families." For these reasons, there is "mutual respect" between officers and truck drivers.

This refusal to acknowledge the salience of the power dynamics that characterizes interactions between border officers and truck drivers was a repeated theme in those conversations. At times, this denial relied on familiar generalizations about working-class men, such as truck drivers being jolly, accommodating and hard-working people. As Lipsky (2010 [1980]: 54) reminds us, "clients in street-level bureaucracies are nonvoluntary." A coercive element can always be found in this relationship, which varies depending on the particulars of the power differential between clients and bureaucrats and on the level of dependence of the former on the services provided by the latter. High reliance on a particular bureaucracy diminishes the ability to complain or seek accountability. In the case of truck drivers, this dependence is significant. Paid by the kilometre, their compliance with border officials' authority provides them with access to the country and impacts the swiftness of border crossing. It limits to a minimum the time spent at ports of entry. It even bears on the possibility of keeping one's job, since noncompliant truck drivers at customs may be disciplined by their employer with job termination. Drivers' dependency on swift border processing and a spotless customs file is productive of a high level of compliance with customs regulations and officers' instructions.

By insisting on their putatively equal relationship with truck drivers, my interviewees tended to undervalue the ways they perform their authority, which make up what Salter (2007) aptly refers to as the "confessionary complex" in border spaces. These ways involve legal, material and symbolic elements, such as extended legislated powers, navy-blue policing uniforms and oppressive tools (e.g. batons, guns and pepper spray). Compounding matters, such authority is expressed through the spatial arrangements that make up ports of entry. These are designed to ensure a high level of compliance from truck drivers—including making them wait in line at the booth, answer questions in order to gain entry and submit to searches of their personal belongings and trucks without judicial warrants. In addition to this infrastructural shaping of truck drivers into tamed subjects, the technological remodelling of customs requires them to provide an ever-expanding amount of information before they present themselves at the border. It is now an integral part of cross-border truck drivers' everyday experience of labour discipline to be exposed to an increasingly intrusive routine of revelation about themselves engineered by preclearance and automated border programmes, along with more traditional questioning by officers when crossing the border.

The making of confession at the border relies on the meeting of unequal actors and is inevitably subject to a hierarchical dynamic between these sovereign state representatives and those they question. In the "unequal configuration" inherent in the "general economy of the interrogation" (Proteau 2009) in the policing world, those who interrogate are authorized to exert symbolic violence (not to speak of occasional emotional and even physical violence) over the interrogated. They in turn may experience anxiety, coercion, intimidation and even, as shown by Villegas (2015) in the case of immigration checks at the border, feelings of humiliation.

When it comes to Canadian customs, this confessionary infrastructure appears quite efficient at creating a behaviour of compliance in truck drivers, but with nuances. Customs officers agree: truck drivers seldom create trouble. As I was often reminded, they are also much more familiar with customs regulations than the average traveller is. As a result, some officers give more weight to instances when truck drivers smuggle the odd bottle of alcohol or carton of cigarettes. A rookie officer, Sarah wondered why some truck drivers did not conform to her expectations of truthful speech and compliant behaviour: "They could be lying about the length of time they were gone, about their declaration, about alcohol or tobacco. Uh . . . they just, I don't know. It's frustrating! Because if they just told the truth in the first place, it wouldn't be as big of a deal."

The downplaying of the power differential between officers and truck drivers is based on a variety of legal, organizational, material and symbolic displays of state authority. Whether working commercial, traffic or immigration, customs officials have long been representatives of the sovereign state at its borders. Yet through a narrative emphasizing the business-as-usual nature of a job that legally grants them the most important powers held by law enforcement officers interacting with the public in Canada (and in many other countries), commercial officers are able to obscure their power relationship with truck drivers.

The land border as a space of familiarity

The land border I visited was far from the cold, anonymous, technologized space we often imagine borders to be. Rather, land border control has long shaped, and been shaped by, local kinship, friendship, neighbourly and intimate relations but also personal dislikes and memories of slights. It is a milieu of long-standing contact where land border officers have a deep knowledge of local family histories, of smuggling enterprises gone wrong and of those drivers and trucking companies that they should keep a close watch over. Some try to find solutions when the local forestry industry goes through yet another Canada–US lumber trade dispute, putting many out of work. This milieu of long-standing contact also creates expectations on the part of local residents and drivers who frequently cross there, as is the case when truck drivers and locals affirm that a particular supervisor oversteps their powers at the same time as they confide that they bring back goods (such as tires) bought in the US on separate trips in order to avoid duties.

While airports see flows of people come and go, familiarity develops over the years at the land border between local residents, transport workers and border officers. In particular, long-distance truck drivers may cross twice a week at the same port, whereas short-distance drivers who come from nearby villages and towns may cross up to five times a day. In rural areas and border towns with border crossings—and because officers used to be hired locally—it is not uncommon for local drivers and experienced officers to know each other well, sometimes from childhood. Commercial sections are social milieus that have sustained the development of limited but nevertheless tangible acquaintance between border crossers and those who control their passage. Such familiarity built over decades has long informed officers' decisions and sometimes even moderated their scrutiny. How many times, an officer asked me, can you search a local who crosses the border regularly?

Therefore, the land border is a special policing space. In contrast to the police, border officers at the Canada–US land border do not interact with "those most marginal and least powerful in our society" who are considered "police property" (Reiner 2010: 9). In contrast, the land border is a space of whitened familiarity.[2] As far as class, gender and race are concerned, land border officers often search and question people who are not used to those oppressive tools of policing that shape many interactions of poorer and racialized people with state authorities. Further, unlike racialized people, who have learned early to respect or fear the police, privileged white border crossers are known to boldly speak back to border officers (a not-so-uncommon occurrence at the traffic section, I was told), complain to their superiors or take to national and social media when they consider they have been treated unfairly. Helleiner (2016) further illuminates this phenomenon when she describes the surprise of her white Canadian border crossers interviewees at their being submitted to random checks by US authorities after 9/11 while, in the same breath, justifying that those racialized may experience the same fate for "security reasons." As shown in the next chapters, it is this particular social arrangement at the border as a space of familiarity and privilege that is challenged by automation and targeting and by the arming and the novel professional socialization of officers. These trends announce a new, more securitized form of bordering that takes a turn towards more stringent law enforcement.

Notes

1 Canadian border officers' search and seizure powers were extended in 1998 to allow for the enforcement of the Criminal Code in ports of entry. See Chapter 2.
2 This space of whitened familiarity is in part a product of policy. Since 2003, crossings of the land border by refugees diminished as a result of the Safe Third Country Agreement. In this accord, Canada and the US problematically consider each other as safe countries to claim asylum, thus justifying the refoulement of asylum claimants to the country of first arrival—generally the US. The capacity to effectively push back refugees to the US as a result of this accord has been challenged since 2017. With the Trump administration's erratic migration and border policy, migrants with vulnerable status in the US started irregularly crossing the

border into Canada. When they do so, they are first processed by the federal police, then by the CBSA. These crossings have increased the pressures on these ports that were not staffed to process such numbers of asylum claims. From February 2017 to June 2019, 45,000 people crossed the land border irregularly into Canada and made a refugee claim.

References

Aas, K. F., and H. Gundhus. 2015. Policing humanitarian borderlands: Frontex, human rights and the precariousness of life. *British Journal of Criminology* 55 (1):1–18.

Bosworth, M. 2014. *Inside Immigration Detention*. London: Oxford University Press.

Chalfin, B. 2010. *Neoliberal Frontiers: An Ethnography of Sovereignty in West Africa*. Chicago: University of Chicago Press.

Helleiner, J. 2016. *Borderline Canadianness: Border Crossings and Everyday Nationalism in Niagara*. Toronto: University of Toronto Press.

Heyman, J. McC. 2004. Ports of entry as nodes in the world system. *Identities: Global Studies in Culture and Power* 11:303–327.

Lipsky, M. 2010. *Street-Level Bureaucracy: Dilemmas of the Individual in Public Services (30th anniversary expanded edition)*. New York: Russell Sage Foundation.

Pallister-Wilkins, P. 2015. The humanitarian politics of European border policing: Frontex and border police in Evros. *International Political Sociology* 9 (1):53–69.

Proteau, L. 2009. Interrogatoire. Forme élémentaire de classification. *Actes de la recherche en sciences sociales* 3 (178):4–11.

Reiner, R. 2010. *The Politics of the Police (Fourth edition)*. Oxford: Oxford University Press.

Salter, M. 2007. Governmentalities of an airport: Heterotopia and confession. *International Political Sociology* 1 (1):49–66.

Ugelvik, T. 2016. Techniques of legitimation: The narrative construction of legitimacy among immigration detention officers. *Crime, Media, Culture* 12 (2):215–232.

Villegas, P. E. 2015. Moments of humiliation, intimidation and implied "illegality": Encounters with immigration officials at the border and the performance of sovereignty. *Journal of Ethnic and Migration Studies* 41 (14):2357–2375.

Waddington, P. A. J. 1999. Police (canteen) subculture: An appreciation. *British Journal of Criminology* 39 (2):287–309.

Chapter 2

Changing customs

From taxation to secure trade

Experienced officers who spent their careers at the commercial sections of major border crossings remember the 1990s with a hint of nostalgia. Back then, their workplace had its own outdoor hotdog stand. A social committee organized Christmas parties funded by onsite pop machines, where truck drivers emptied their pockets while waiting in lines to submit their paperwork for approval. The parking lot was full of trucks waiting to be processed. Two decades later, parking lots are empty save for the odd confiscated trailer, and the pop machine is mainly used by thirsty border officers. Drivers are swiftly cleared and rarely step out of their trucks. What happened to bring about such a change in the social life of these ports?

Ronald has a theory. Armed with a social science degree obtained after he left his old job to join border services, Ronald gives me a crash course in the recent history of the border's political economy. At times, our conversation reminds me of Andreas and Biersteker's (2003) oft-quoted argument about the successive debordering and rebordering of the Canada–US border. Europe eliminated its internal borders in the 1990s and, as North American "free trade" grew, Ronald recalls that some thought the same fate awaited the Canada–US border. But then came 9/11, he says, and the border tightened up again, making it more difficult for people and freight to pass through. During the next 10 years, this rebordering was accompanied by renewed efforts at expediting trade—through programmes that preclear imports before they reach the border and other ones that promise swifter border crossing by granting some transportation companies a "trusted trader" label after a lengthy risk-assessment process.

Ronald tells me that he would not want to be a new employee today. He believes that it has become too labour-intensive to have officers asking questions to travellers and truck drivers at the border. He then offers a prediction: ultimately, we'll see the border dissolve and officer jobs vanish, especially for commercial trade. Considering Ronald's explanation, I wondered how significant was 9/11 in this scenario? Is 9/11 responsible for the deserted parking lots and abandoned pop machines in ports of entry? Some officers agree with this interpretation. Others, like Ronald, go back to the 1990s, stressing the importance of global trade to changes in border governance.

Event-based thinking has its limits when it comes to understanding the forces that have shaped border control, customs in particular. For nearly two decades, 9/11 has come to dominate how we view security, with a sense of the before and after of this event. However, there are both discontinuities and parallels between these periods in regard to the policing of goods through borders. On the one hand, this chapter shows that the 1990s were a decisive decade in North America for changing customs—as is the case too for the border interdiction of asylum seekers, which was well underway in the decade before 9/11 (Dauvergne 2016: 48). We will see that after centuries of treating customs as a taxation body and after more than a century of economic protectionism, much of what is now accepted as normal customs procedure was first tested in the 1990s—including a tentative but growing role for automation in risk assessment, the presence of new security players at the border and the legal granting of extended enforcement powers to border officers. This is also the decade when border authorities clumsily experimented with traveller preclearance and trade facilitation programmes and introduced electronic data exchange. These trends picked up steam after 9/11 as the Canada–US border became a full-fledged security concern for security and political professionals in both countries. On the other hand, other trends only appear during the 2000s—such as the creation of a new border agency, the partial devolution of border risk management to the transportation industry through preclearance and trusted trader programmes, leaps in data collection capacity and the subsequent centralization of intelligence-led policing in border spaces. By discussing how and to what extent these developments contributed to the enforcement shift in Canadian border control, this chapter challenges the popular claim that the event of 9/11 singularly "changed everything."

Through the case of the Canada–US border, the chapter also presents evidence of changes in bordering that go beyond the common concern for the control of peoples' mobilities and the production of migrant irregularity. As Mezzadra and Neilson (2013: 7) remind us, "isolating a single function of the border does not allow us to grasp the flexibility of this institution" since borders are also "devices of inclusion that select and filter people and different forms of circulation in ways no less violent than those deployed in exclusionary measures." If it is undeniable that borders make an increasing number of people vulnerable, then border authorities are also pressured to enable the mobilities of ever-increasing numbers of people and commodities. Despite the fact that customs regimes are essential to the workings of global capitalism, they remain understudied by those interested in borders. This oversight engenders a lopsided analysis that is oblivious to the extraordinary human and financial investments made to enable the mobilities of privileged people, freight and capital.

While refugees, undocumented migrants and many racialized travellers have seen their movements increasingly encumbered by borders since the 1990s, significant political efforts, public resources and technological advancements have nevertheless contributed to opening up border trade during the same period. A politico-economic agenda has emerged that conceives of borders as mechanisms essential to both enhancing the speed of circulation in line with liberalized "market logics" (Chalfin 2010) and establishing points of control for securitizing global economic integration. This agenda has required major transformations on many fronts, including new regulations, redesigning border infrastructures, reorganizing state institutions and incorporating new public and private actors in border control, all in the name of enhancing the speed of circulation for goods. In North America, this agenda has meant the development of a regional "free-trade" zone. Following this upheaval, customs has become less a state institution with the ultimate sovereign power to decide whether something, or someone, may enter the country and more a component inside an apparatus that has been assembled for extending supply chain security. This chapter traces this evolution.

Some historical signposts

Until recently, Canadian border officers would not have described themselves as law enforcers and security actors. After all, customs fulfilled three major purposes at different moments of its history: revenue collection, economic protectionism and the regulation of smuggling—not as a criminal but as a tax evasion matter. Recalling this history helps us measure the depth and extent of the recent changes in border control. For centuries, wars were funded, revolutions started and postal services provided because of duties collected at borders. Events such as the Boston Tea Party particularly remind us of the significance of import duties in North American history. Tongue in cheek, McIntosh (1984: 34) alludes to this history: "It has been suggested that the only reason Canada and the Maritime colonies did not join the [1776 US] revolution was that they were expert smugglers and consequently were not as enraged by customs duties as were the Americans." Aptly called a "key pillar of modern state sovereignty" by Chalfin (2010: 26), customs controls shaped colonial and mercantile flows of commerce—especially in the Americas. The European colonial powers' plundering of the continent's resources soon made necessary the creation of customs infrastructures or "a type of capability we think of as modern: the apparatus to implement, organize, manage, and service cross-border economic transactions" (Sassen 2008: 88).

A major source of revenue for the French and then British colonial authorities during the 17th and 18th centuries, customs enforced import regulations and high tariffs (McIntosh 1984). In a bid to protect the domestic industry against unwarranted foreign (US) competition, a nationalist policy of economic protectionism imposing prohibitive tariffs on US imports was adopted in the 1870s and remained in place for most of the 20th century (Blake 1956; Norrie and Owram 2002). From the Canadian Conservatives'

1911 election slogan "no truck nor trade with the Yankees," to the battle that won the same party a second mandate after reversing its historical rhetoric and signing a free-trade deal with the US in 1988, Canadian elections were won and lost over the question of trade with its southern neighbour for more than a hundred years.[1]

During this entire period, customs officers focused on revenue generation and trade regulation while remaining dedicated to combatting tax and duties evasion. But as a regulatory body, they also held a historical role in the creation of smuggling. When products—such as drugs or, during the 1920s US prohibition, alcohol—were made illegal and their entry into national territories was banned, customs regulations somewhat unintentionally contributed to the making of underground smuggling routes. Some of these routes are still in use today (Farfan 2009).

Since the official protectionist mandate for Canadian customs lasted for more than a century, it is important to challenge the assumption that protectionism represents a past trade regulation mechanism now irrelevant to contemporary border control. The 2018 trade spat that led to the imposition of tariffs on Canadian and Chinese aluminium and steel by the US testifies to this fact. In this book, I stress the contemporaneity of protectionism by pointing at its continuing manifestation in everyday borderwork. As presented in Chapter 7, a good number of the officers I met entered customs when the protection of the Canadian economy was considered one of their fundamental responsibilities. We will also see how this economic sensibility is being successfully challenged by promoters of border enforcement in a context of (mostly) liberalized trade.

What spurred the shift towards liberalized trade? What are its consequences on customs authorities worldwide? Chalfin (2007) suggests that international trade organizations have been actively promoting a facilitation paradigm for customs since the end of WWII. Economic protectionism has been gradually replaced by a market-based, neoliberal mode of economic regulation that fosters global capital accumulation through intricate cross-border production and distribution networks (Harvey 2007). This evolution builds on decades of regulatory changes carried out at different institutional levels—through free-trade agreements, transport deregulation, the elimination of fiscal barriers, the implementation of integrated cargo management and restructuring customs authorities' mandates and practices. These global trade governance trends have modified what is expected of customs organizations. Showing the importance of this regulatory convergence over trade is the creation in 1995 of the World Customs Organization (WCO) alongside the World Trade Organization in order to become the WTO's "enforcement arm" (Bowling and Sheptycki 2012: 58). Responsible for issues of compliance and taxation and for coming up with a comprehensive nomenclature of traded products (called the harmonized system), the WCO also championed the adoption by member states of standardized customs enforcement practices—including a reliance on customs automation, the centralization of data analysis and a more limited recourse to discretionary inspections by frontline officers. As we shall see later in this chapter and again in the next, these practices have been implemented by Canadian border authorities.

In North America, these changes impacted transport labour mobility and removed a wide range of duties, with consequences on how fast goods may cross borders. For instance, the deregulation of the US and Canadian trucking industries, in 1982 and 1992 respectively, made it possible for truck drivers of each country to drive loads across the border—instead of transferring them onto another truck as is sometimes still the case at the Mexico–US border. In turn, this regulatory change paved the way for the signature of NAFTA in 1994 (Madar 2000). North–South trade corridors were put in place on the East Coast and West Coast, which rely on new forms of organization of transport and border labour. We will see in the next section of this chapter that while these macroeconomic changes had, at first, little impact on border officers' handling of travellers and migrants, they spurred significant transformations for those officers who worked "commercial."

Customs as enforcers: extended legal powers and smart borders

The Canada–US land border has long held the status of the "longest undefended border in the world." Of course, "dominant constructions of a benign and even 'friendly' Canadian border" (Helleiner 2016: 8) are challenged by alternative histories that highlight the arbitrary colonial drawing of that border over Indigenous peoples' territories (LaDow 2002) and the heightened control still experienced by Indigenous, migrant and racialized people who live close to—or cross—this border (Finn, Hennebry and Momani 2018; Kalman 2016). Meanwhile, for much truck traffic and (predominantly white) border crossers, enforcement remains minimal. Before 2001, criminal records were seldom used by both of these national authorities to prevent entry, as is done now, and the US made passports mandatory to cross the border with Canada only after 2006. But the rhetoric stressing an "undefended" status for the border really started to unravel at the end of the 1990s. Since then, bordering policies and programmes have proliferated, initiating a process of securitizing the border that is still in full swing.

The first indication of the shift to law enforcement in Canadian border control can be found in the law that regulates bordering. Before the 1998 modifications to the Customs Act, officers held search, seizure and arrest powers without warrants but only in compliance with this Act.[2] These powers continue to be used to this day, including for searches of cell phones and computers. Border officers have long been granted more legal discretion; that is, their enforcement actions are subject to a lower legal test—that of reasonable suspicion (Pratt 2010). In Canada, searches and seizures were performed only by the police with a warrant in hand and who has to conform to the test of reasonable doubt enshrined in Canadian law. But in 1998, officers' powers were extended to matters relative to the Criminal Code. Since then, Canadian border officers can arrest and detain drunk drivers and people with outstanding warrants. Experienced officers recall that their inability to search in those cases was a significant source of frustration. In our conversations, officers often referred to this period of transition as the moment when they first started thinking of themselves as "a police of the border." These new-found powers are the first in a series of changes reviewed throughout this book that ushered an enforcement mentality into ports of entry.

Meanwhile, following the transformation of customs' mandate away from economic protectionism, a series of agreements began to articulate free trade alongside calls for increased border enforcement. Canada and the US set the ball rolling with a little-known bilateral accord that closely followed NAFTA—the 1995 Canada–United States Accord on Our Shared Border. The first of its kind in the region, the document experimented with a new language that explicitly connected the elimination of trade hindrances to the tightening of controls for irregular flows of people and goods. These efforts began to build a cross-border network of North American law enforcement agencies claiming a stake in border control. Among other measures, the accord established the Canada–U.S. Border Crime Forum in 1997, a still-active regional coordinating body including law enforcement and justice ministerial officials.

After the border was shut down by US authorities for a week, after 9/11, these trends were further entrenched. Both countries soon adopted a "smart border" approach, the central features of which remain in place today. Signed three months after 9/11, the 2001 Canada–US Smart Border Declaration laid out a 32-point action plan aiming to "identify security threats before they arrive in North America," facilitate low-risk mobilities of people and commodities, improve cross-jurisdictional and interagency cooperation and intelligence exchange, invest in land border infrastructure and, finally, minimize the impacts of security measures on trade. In the subsequent decade, the policy language adopted to speak of border security and trade was little altered despite changes in government in both countries. It was similarly repeated in the 2006 Security and Prosperity Partnership between the United States, Mexico and Canada—now abandoned. The last instance of these agreements, the 2011 U.S.–Canada Beyond the Border, is no exception and continued to promote border security by pushing the border away from the "North American security perimeter" in order to facilitate trade.

The Smart Border Accord not only aimed to tackle cross-border criminality but also construed refugees and terrorism as dual security concerns to be hindered through bordering. Involving technological, legal and administrative measures, the smart border programme intends to extend border controls outside and inside the geopolitical border between the two countries while promoting a differential filtration logic for mobilities seen to present a "low"

and a "high" risk (Côté-Boucher 2008). Ever since, the Canadian government has been deploying significant diplomatic efforts to retain its access
to the American market; much of its border control policies are organized
around that objective.

An upheaval in federal public safety also followed 9/11. Immediately after
the events, the minister of citizenship and immigration was put in charge of
federal interventions in border matters. Soon afterwards, the US overhauled
its security agencies—creating, among others, the Department of Homeland
Security and a novel border agency, the US Customs and Border Protection. Mirroring these changes north of the border, Public Safety Canada was
launched in 2003. This department took responsibility for an array of intelligence and law enforcement agencies, including the Canadian Security
Intelligence Service (CSIS), the RCMP and Corrections Canada, and for a
new border agency, the CBSA. The CBSA is itself created out of three "legacy"
agencies: the customs segment of the Canada Customs and Revenue Agency
(CCRA) and the enforcement sections of Citizenship and Immigration Canada (CIC) and of the Canadian Food and Inspection Agency (CFIA).

The significance of this institutional conversion should not be lost on us;
it inaugurates a revolution for border control in Canada. Since the colonial
period, much of border regulation and customs had been placed under the
jurisdiction of the Ministry of Revenue—a fact that was clear to most of my
interviewees who started their careers as revenue employees. Taken together,
these legal and institutional changes suggest a major transformation in how
border control and its purpose are conceived and governed at the highest level.
By 2004, bordering had become a "secure trade" enterprise in the minds of
security professionals, policymakers and politicians, with important consequences on borderwork. Although 9/11 has been viewed as a turning point in
bordering, we can see that contemporary changes in border control date much
further back and respond to market, security and law enforcement logics.

The multiplication of border control players

In contrast to the US, Canada never had an independent border patrol.[3] Nevertheless, frontline border officers have long acted as enforcement and taxation agents for areas surrounding ports of entry—policing tobacco, alcohol
and drug smuggling. After the 1998 modifications to the Customs Act, border officers gained greater control over the border for a few years. However, in
a parallel development, new public policing and private industry actors began
investing in the border. These investments take different forms, from outsourcing and assistance agreements to more or less formalized cooperation.

Some authors have examined this proliferation of private and public policing actors in border settings. In the case of ports, Brewer (2014) argued that
these arrangements make possible a better, more networked form of security
governance by fostering collaboration between these actors. Critiques of these

arrangements recognize the multilayered character of contemporary border control but insist on paying attention to the rivalries that continue to epitomize security provision. These antagonisms are still very much alive, because divergent historical trajectories have fashioned security agencies into distinct organizational cultures. In the current era, when discourses about interagency collaboration are legion, competition over budgets and resources remains fierce. But struggles also ensue over the symbolic authority to designate what threats ought to make us feel uneasy or scared—whether it is specific forms of crime, terrorism or irregular migration (Bigo 2002, 2011, 2014).

In the case of the Canada–US border, a sense of competition is very much alive as more-complex border issues are now treated as matters warranting the attention of other policing and industry actors. Frontline staff and their union are particularly weary of the federal police influence over the territory spreading along the Canada–US borderland, including via interagency task forces. At the same time, border residents unaccustomed to such police presence in their villages and towns must now experience the increased surveillance of their daily activities. Meanwhile, the transportation sector is enrolled in border control through strategies intending to bring customs risk assessment "upstream"—that is, in highway transportation and maritime yards. Taken together, these trends favour as mode of control the traceability of goods in transit from point of departure to that of arrival, thus flagging the shift to a "securitization of globalized and revolutionized logistics" (Cowen 2014: 55). In the process, border officers saw their newfound legal grip on the border challenged, leaving them feeling out of the loop.

Enter competition: integrated task forces and the intensification of surveillance at the land border

Everyone competes for a piece of the resources spent on securitizing the land border: federal, provincial and state police on both sides of the border; US border patrol officers; integrated law enforcement teams; and Canadian border authorities. But it is the increasing hold of the RCMP over sections of the border between ports of entry—as well as the task forces and multiagency border-policing teams that it leads on Canadian soil—that was most debated among the border officers I met and by their union.

On the Canadian side, the RCMP oversees a range of bilateral task forces. In a similar but more limited way than in Europe and other regions across the globe (Hufnagel 2013), these policing cooperation strategies rework traditional divisions of labour in policing. Spearheaded in Canada by the RCMP and in the US by Customs and Border Protection (CBP), integrated border enforcement teams (IBETs) were created in 1996 to tackle cross-border crime. IBETs now include elements of the CBSA, the US Immigration and Customs Enforcement (ICE) and the U.S. Coast Guard, and at times, they work with provincial and municipal police. Since 2004, IBETs post agents along the land border with the mandate to prevent terrorism and the smuggling of people and contraband. As the Canada–US border becomes a matter of transnational policing through cross-border cooperation and information-sharing on a range of issues, from cross-border crime to refugee claims, these task forces pit border officers against other policing actors over the responsibility to oversee cross-border mobilities.

Evidence of this competition brought by binational border initiatives is found in how they target border communities through an "unprecedented reconfiguration of jurisdictional practices" (Pratt 2016: 250). Indeed, there are social consequences to the current intensification of policing activities, and these are experienced throughout borderland communities. This brings harmful effects on Indigenous communities whose ancestral territories criss-cross the border and are narrowly conceived by law enforcement as ridden with crime. It adds a more coercive colonial state presence over these oft-unceded territories on which many people, such as the Haudenosaunee Confederacy, assert their sovereignty (Simpson 2014). As a result of this expanded border enforcement, other local residents are faced with increased impediments to what used to be mundane activities. Robicheau illustrates in her web documentary how the quality of life at Stanstead-Derby Line, a Quebec—Vermont cross-border community, has been seriously altered since American authorities imposed higher border enforcement on a border formerly quite porous to neighbourhood and kinship ties.[4] Helleiner (2016) dissects similar processes for the Niagara region in Ontario. Others, such as Núñez and Heyman (2007), have shown how a more militarized form of border enforcement at the southern US borderland is making migrants and racialized citizens living in the area more vulnerable to over-policing.

The effects of increased everyday surveillance in the lives of borderland residents inspires caution, especially when presented with the Canadian border officers' union requests that authority be granted to their members to police border areas now under RCMP mandate. The discussion was fierce in Quebec during my fieldwork when a pilot project for a task force dedicated to policing the land between ports of entry was tested close to Lacolle (a major port of entry located in the vicinity of Montreal). Since there had been discussions to give the CBSA the responsibility for that project, I was told that some border officers interested in joining had undergone complementary enforcement training. In the end, however, the RCMP was put in charge and today remains responsible for all land border policing between ports of entry. The discussion was still going strong in 2017 and 2018, when the RCMP was tasked with picking up irregular border crossers at the land border following fears of deportation among undocumented migrants under the Trump administration.

The Canadian officers' union demand to extend powers to search, seize and apprehend to areas between ports of entry has thankfully been ignored by the legislator. If enshrined in law, it would likely further increase policing encounters in the lives of borderland residents. In addition, if we take the U.S. Border Patrol case as our compass, because such powers are less restricted by constitutional rights, such measure would usher in conditions ripe for abuse and violation of fundamental rights.[5] Current research indicates that it also presents a recipe for amplified racial profiling at the border (Pratt and Thompson 2008; Mountz 2011). This proposal to extend the reach of border officers' increased enforcement powers outside of ports of entry in Canadian borderlands ought to remain unfulfilled.

Enter the logistics world: precleared and trusted "partners" do security

Another trend that has unsettled officers' monopoly over the border is the market-based liberalization of commerce that has pressed customs to adopt a trade facilitation logic. This happens as "free trade" intensifies bilateral commerce and, as a result, wait times at the border. Experienced officers recall the kilometres-long truck line-ups at major border crossings in the mid 1990s after NAFTA's implementation. At the time, these delays caused headaches for importers dependent on just-in-time manufacturing.[6] To tackle bottlenecks, border authorities began testing preclearance cards for car and truck drivers in 1998. The project was shelved but then resuscitated after 9/11; it is now known as the NEXUS (car drivers and air travellers) and FAST (truck drivers) bilateral preclearance programmes. The expansion of preclearance has indeed "intensified since 9/11, as it is seen as a way to promote cross-border mobility while enhancing security" (Gilbert 2018: 10). Customs preclearance emerged to improve the swiftness with which commodities cross borders in a context where global capital accumulation strategies are designed with the assumption of the speedy and reliable delivery of commodities and where the exploitation of transport workers has intensified (Bonacich and Wilson 2008). Accordingly, preclearance cards are viewed by customs authorities as a means to increase the mobility rights of freight in exchange for heightened surveillance through the personal data provided by truck drivers (Côté-Boucher 2010).

Wishing to secure the transportation corridors newly opened by NAFTA in 1994, Canada created that same year the first trusted trader programme of its kind: Partners in Protection (PIP). PIP was followed in 2003 by its US counterpart, the Customs and Trade Partnership Against Terrorism (CTPAT), now the main customs-based security programme in the world. Involving transportation and logistics companies in the business of risk assessment, preclearance, customs self-assessment and trusted trader programmes gained pre-eminence first in North America and then worldwide.[7] In short, these programmes have tested the devolution of border functions to the North American transportation sector: the transfer to this industry of surveillance responsibilities over transport workers and goods. As mentioned in countless official documents by the World Customs Organization, such programmes are meant to bring "supply chain security upstream" and promote industry self-regulation in fostering "secure trade."

However, not everyone is convinced that trade and security can be so easily married. For some of the officers I spoke to, supply chain security involves creating an intimate relationship between trade facilitation and self-regulation that leaves out security. This was Marie's opinion. Marie is an officer with more than 30 years' experience working at her port of entry:

> The Agency [CBSA] tells us that "we need to trust our clientele." For instance, people who go "in bound" to another office. They give us a little paper that says "we go to x" with this cargo and this quantity. That is all we have as information. Before, we would require a seal to lock the trailer's doors and we put it there and checked whether it was there. No one could break that seal. Now the guy gives us his little paper, we give him a seal and he is supposed to go and put it himself. We don't even check if the seal is on!

Continuing with a short laugh, she ends in sarcasm: "All these programmes, they are meant 'to help the clientele, to speed up the economy.' (. . .) Clients are satisfied." Security for Marie requires being able to intercept contraband, but for trusted trader and preclearance schemes, it means allowing the unimpeded circulation of goods. Throughout the book, we will see how these different understandings of what border control is about creates conflicts in how it is policed from the frontlines and from the offices at headquarters in Ottawa.

Trusted trader programmes arguably apply the policing-at-a-distance logics tested in immigration control to customs (Menjívar 2014). While the border officers whom I met are critical of this transfer of surveillance responsibilities to an industry whose main objective remains profit, border agencies in many countries wish to expand such "partnerships" with the transportation industry. Yet if this industry is not paid for its involvement in security programmes, it is increasingly harnessed to compile and transfer massive numbers of data for compliance purposes. Invited to take on some security responsibilities, these companies also carry out onsite reviews of their security and customs compliance practices and the surveillance of workers, yards and transport fleets. They are made responsible for reducing criminal opportunities by physically securing access to their trucks while on the road. In an enlightening intervention that speaks volumes about the global spreading of this partnership rhetoric, a senior manager of the UK Revenue and Customs declared,

> We need to return to basics and re-assess why we are in business. In the United Kingdom (UK) we have re-confirmed that we collect revenue, facilitate trade, protect society and collect trade statistics. But we are throwing away the old Customs textbooks on how we do that and

looking to see if we can make best use of electronic data which is part of businesses' everyday operations to assess revenue, compliance, admissibility and security risks. This means working in partnership to drive up compliance and bear down on noncompliance using IT systems and intelligence-led risk management. *But even more radical is the idea of shifting our emphasis from the point of importation to as far upstream in the supply chain as possible and considering the role of the consignor in feeding accurate information into an electronic data pipeline.*

(Heskett 2009: 27, emphasis added)

Chalfin (2007) argued that this type of border control involves a customs-at-a-distance focus: it operates through automated processes and a displacement of border controls inside transportation yards. As a result, such controls duplicate border authorities' capacity to inquire into many more economic, trade and labour processes that previously remained beyond their reach. Nevertheless, these programmes have also changed the rules of the game for cross-border policing along supply chains because they rest on a largely uninvestigated assumption. By virtue of being located "on the frontline," workers in all kinds of industries—from transportation and banking to hospitality—are now considered to be those who are best placed to detect and report suspicious activities (Ritchie 2015). Customs at a distance thus displaces much of the securing of commodity flows inland and abroad along supply chains. It does so away from the hands of customs officers by expanding the notion of what constitutes "the frontline" into multiple social spaces that are becoming securitized through the involvement of a range of private for-profit and public policing actors in bordering.

So far, we have seen that a series of macroeconomic processes, global political changes and border security policies have unsettled customs officers' traditional monopoly over the control of border mobilities and that this is the case despite having been granted extended enforcement powers. Having reviewed the general facets that have shaped border control since the 1990s, I now consider the erosion of this monopoly after the introduction of information technologies in borderwork.

Automating borderwork

Towards the end of the 1990s, border authorities in Canada and elsewhere began introducing detection devices and data analysis into risk and customs compliance assessment. Meant to speed up the flow of goods, this improved technological capacity helps border authorities to experiment with what has since become a staple of bordering: policing at a distance—that is, moving the border temporally and spatially beyond ports of entry and before people, trucks, ships and aircrafts reach them. Until now, this recourse to technologies has been more fully studied in the cases of immigration and traveller control in publications on topics such as biometrics and data-led border policing. While tracking mobilities and stopping people conceived by border agencies to be "illegal" or "risky" from reaching wealthier and more-stable countries is a troubling part of what border control has become, we often forget that confronted with the hyper-circulation of people and cargo sustained by contemporary global capitalist arrangements, border authorities have also been hard-pressed to find solutions to avoid bottlenecks and waiting lines, whether in airports or at land borders. This has been particularly true when it comes to customs. Because it is considered a lower-risk domain by border agencies—that is, one where the trade of goods should be favoured over other security considerations—customs is an area of border control where automation has been pushed the furthest. It is thus a textbook case for investigating information technologies' impact on borderwork. In this section, I examine the transformation of border policing through its informatization; in the next two chapters, I analyse the consequences of this process on officers' work routines and self-understanding.

While many technologies studied thus far by border scholars have counterterrorism or the prevention of migrant smuggling as their rationale, the introduction of digital technologies into customs responds to another policy concern: it offers a response to a global economic context characterized by the turn towards logistics in the management of supply chains. As aptly argued by Danyluk (2018), enabling the global intensification of the circulation of commodities has required a range of infrastructural and technological interventions on the part of the corporate world. I build on Danyluk's (2018: 632) emphasis on the "materiality of global economic restructuring" and argue that to become truly effective, this logistics revolution has also required considerable public investments in expediting the risk assessment and evaluation of exporter–importer compliance with national regulations. Together with the recourse to standardized containers, port infrastructure, just-in-time production and other market-friendly business and regulation models that revolutionized distribution at the turn of the 21st century, customs ushered in new bordering strategies to ease the intensified circulation of cargo and further enable capital accumulation on a global scale. This happened at the same time that borders became increasingly difficult to cross for refugees and impoverished migrants because of more-restrictive border controls. We see then the entrenchment of a mobility regime that grants differential rights to people and market and that articulates a form of global inequality that is still very much alive today.

Such novel mobility-governing strategies aiming to ease the circulation of goods became effective at European, West African, US and Asian maritime ports but also at the land borders that Canada and Mexico share with the US, where truck traffic increased steadily right after NAFTA. The results have been staggering from a border control point of view, enabling and expanding state authorities' security claims along supply chains. In fact, the extraordinary accumulation of data about cross-border economic exchanges made possible by customs automation has brought intelligence-led policing practices into customs. Drawing from officers' narratives, this section details the successive automation of customs and the centralization of risk evaluation in Canadian bordering in the context of the promotion of "secure trade" in North America. The partial automation of decisions to allow or refuse entry into the country and of the routine administrative activities that used to fill border officers' workdays has reorganized the division of labour in border agencies, ultimately exerting new pressures on frontline officers to legitimate their presence at the border. This section consolidates the evidence of technologized borders but in a particular context: trade facilitation, where the flexibility of data circulation is seen as both a security and an economic priority.

Electronic declarations

Until recently, Canadian commercial officers heavily relied on their discretion and covered the whole release process at the border, that is, they were solely responsible for evaluating and clearing shipments. This included assessing truck drivers for smuggling (sometimes for concealed drugs but most often for tobacco and alcohol), sending trucks for secondary inspection and determining how to inspect them. It also involved the classification of documents such as cargo manifests[8] and administering quantities of forms while ensuring compliance with a number of national regulations (environmental, sanitary, dangerous goods, etc.). They were also responsible for collecting duties and taxes.

This means that before electronic declarations, the transportation industry and importers experienced the land border differently. Before the progressive introduction of e-declarations during the 1990s, truck drivers, customs brokers (intermediaries between importers and customs), carriers and importers relied on officers' knowledge of revenue and customs regulations. During the time they spent at the port of entry, drivers had to step down from their trucks and wait in line to submit their paperwork; this is when they spent their small change in the pop machine mentioned in the introduction to this chapter. At that time, drivers brought copies of cargo manifests and other forms to their customs broker[9] working in the same building or in a small office nearby. Back again to the main customs office with the full declaration, truck drivers had the document signed by a border officer, and they or their brokers paid duties and taxes owed on the shipment. The whole process lasted at least 45 minutes, often longer at major ports on busy days. Afterwards, the paperwork was treated by clerks, and duties collected that day were deposited in a neighbouring bank by a supervisor on their way home.

After political pressures by major economic actors who were losing money in the kilometres-long truck line-ups that were the result of the post-NAFTA trade increase, Canadian border services introduced, in 1997, a major change to this established routine. Developed to speed up customs processing, electronic declarations—or electronic declaration interchange (EDI) in customs parlance—eliminated much of the paperwork required to release a shipment at the border. With the introduction of EDI, exporters began submitting information about shipment and means of transportation electronically.[10] As a great part of shipment evaluations could now be completed before crossing, this drastically reduced decision-making times at the border.

What changed for logistics at the border after EDI? Interestingly, electronic declarations spurred a major upheaval in an associated industry understudied by those interested in borders: customs brokerage. Since the advent of electronic declarations in Canada and the United States, and the remodelling of customs to follow the World Customs Organizations recommendations in trade facilitation, the North American customs brokerage industry has been overhauled by mergers.[11] In fact, EDI reduced the number of operations necessary to process a shipment, thus making superfluous brokers' physical presence at the border. When driving towards the land border, this shift can be observed in the microeconomy surrounding ports of entry as most customs brokerage offices are now closed. In case of missing paperwork or incomplete data, truck drivers now call representatives working remotely in major cities or meet with a local staff member hired by a cluster of brokerage companies to serve that port.

EDI not only reshaped customs brokerage but also transformed borderwork. Steeve, who started working as an officer at the beginning of the 2000s, illustrates this well. When I first visited the port of entry where Steeve works, I was surprised to see numerous empty desks on the main floor. Steeve told me that before EDI, an officer used to sit at each of these desks for a number of hours, each looking at a big stack of paper in front of them. In contrast, officers can now spend several hours of their daily shifts in front of computer screens reviewing customs declarations—even when the shipment is not bound for their port of entry, as we shall see later on. Simply put, electronic declarations make possible shipment evaluation without visual assessment. EDI introduced border officers to the more abstract "modes of visualization" (Amoore 2009) that have since become a staple of border control: ways of seeing cargo mobilities that are less reliant on physical assessments and more dependent on remotely analysing shipments through data capture.

Therefore, at about the same time as "remote control" border mechanisms were tested in Europe and North America for monitoring irregular migration (Zaiotti 2016), a variety of tools were introduced to do the same for customs and supply chains (Cantens 2015). Whether in maritime ports (Chalfin 2007; Eski 2011) or on land borders, these tools have meant the decoupling of decision-making from physical assessments of shipments and transportation and from the face-to-face questioning of transport workers. In this novel border control paradigm, the port of entry is no longer a place where truck drivers linger to receive paperwork approval and spend their hard-earned money on pop; instead, it becomes the last site in a chain of decision-making concerned with permitting entry into the country. In Table 2.1, I present how electronic declarations and automation changed border officers' daily work.

Machine release or the automation of customs

Growing data capture and retention for future analysis also made possible the automation of decision-making at the border. The automation of customs has been essential to speeding up border crossing and has greatly contributed to facilitating logistics operations worldwide. Gone are the days when officers went through every single customs declaration. Depending on the month and the port, officers I spoke to estimated that between 40% and 60% of declarations are recommended through an automated system. That system releases shipments from importers deemed to present a lower risk, namely those with a history of compliance with customs regulations. Importantly, the release recommendation is performed automatically and without the intervention of a customs officer—who nevertheless keeps the final authority to decide to clear shipments and truck drivers at the primary inspection line. For companies deemed to represent a low risk, the automated system also

Table 2.1 Customs officers' main everyday tasks after automation

Office	• Electronic entries
	  1) Review manifests
	  2) Review import permits
	  3) Recommend release (online)
	• Process paperwork
	• Answer questions (in person, phone)
	• Interrogate drivers suspected of noncompliance

Booth (in about 30 seconds)	• Collect documentation
	• Collect driver ID
	• Admissibility questionnaire
	• Evaluate drivers for "risk indicators"
	• Review screen for
	  1. Targets
	  2. Precleared release recommendation
	  3. Aleatory inspection recommendation
	• Decision
	  1. Entry in country
	  2. Send to main office for paperwork problems
	  3. Send for inspection

Inspection Docks	• Physical inspections of cabs, trailers and freight • X-ray trucks (some ports) • Check customs and enforcement databases • Recordkeeping on inspection process/results • Seizures and arrests

generates random requests for inspection on which officers must then act. In fact, automated machine release includes random checks of compliant exporters at the level of about 2% of all shipments entering the country—a percentage quoted in interviews and consistent with standard international levels of inspection of shipments and travellers (Chalfin 2007). As an indication of the lowering rate of inspected shipments and the privileging of cargo mobilities in a neoliberal logic of trade facilitation in border spaces, the CBSA now intends to inspect less than 1% of shipments carried by members of trusted trader programmes.[12]

Customs automation is related to the creation of a new position in busier ports: the officer responsible for the automated machine-release system. This is a minor data analysis position coveted among officers I interviewed because it granted considerable operational discretion. This officer may consult reports about local seizures and national strategic risk evaluations to assess the risk presented by local companies and review their inclusion in the system. They could also adjust the percentages of random secondary inspection, thus influencing the work load at inspection docks. At the same time, however, while the release of goods previously represented a time-consuming and paper-based responsibility at the centre of their work, automation has restricted the part taken by other frontline customs officers in this activity.

In short, EDI was the first step in a series of technological and policy changes that increased reliance on the automated verification of compliance with customs regulations in a bid to speed up customs processes at the border. As I shall further discuss in the next chapter, electronic declarations and databases now integrate the primary inspection line into a network of data collection processes going from cross-border trade statistics to information about mobility trends that are used for subsequent risk analyses.

Targeting and risk-analysis centres

Port-based analysts were short-lived. Automation and EDI made it possible to push even further the limits of the policy rationale driving customs-at-a-distance programmes by centralizing the analysis of data transmitted by logistics actors to border authorities and thus opening the way for risk-analysis centres. The most recent step in the securitization of logistics chains through customs involves intelligence-based use customs and border data through targeting. What exactly is a "target"? The notion is an abstraction relied on by policing and intelligence actors for its plasticity and the ease with which it can be deployed onto a range of objects and behaviours. Targets can be applied to criminal, immigration, taxation, customs and environmental compliance issues under the banner of risk. Based on information provided by different internal intelligence reports, targeters may put "targets" on specific products, truck drivers, trucking companies and exporters that they recommend for further inspection. For instance, a local trucking company has a history of past enforcement (e.g. drug trafficking) inscribed in its file; it could therefore be targeted, requiring officers to perform more-frequent secondary inspections on its trucks. A tree species has been regulated by environmental authorities because it contains an insect damaging to forests; it can also be targeted nationwide. An importer with overdue duty payments or customs penalties may also be targeted for noncompliance. From a strictly law enforcement perspective, it is unclear whether targeting fulfills its promises. In a 2016 document, the CBSA estimates to be able to substantially improve the quantities of illegal product seized at the border through intelligence-led targeting. Compared to seizures achieved through officers' "cold hits"—seizures done by border officers without prior intelligence—the ratio intelligence seizures to cold hits would be nine to one. However, the results of targeting change according to whether people or goods are targeted. While 25% of searches and examination of air passengers result in enforcement action, it is the case for only 1.5% of containers in maritime mode.[13]

If growing data capture and retention through electronic declarations made it possible to automatize part of the decision-making process in customs, it also led to the creation of another pivotal position to which border officers may be appointed, that of targeter. At first, targeters were responsible for local, low-level risk management in the commercial sections of major ports of entry. After 9/11 and during the following decade, the preferred border control strategy has been to multiply local intelligence-gathering possibilities. Targeters were then located in major and mid-size ports of entry. However, these local positions have since been mostly eliminated by the centralization of targeting in Ottawa, an ongoing process that is much discussed internally. Centralized targeting happened at the conjunction of technological advancements, policy projects stemming from a difficult meeting of market-based orientation and securitization in border control and the fiscal crisis of the state. While studies of the "informationalization" of border policing do not pay much attention to states' budgetary limits, the fact remains that making borders "smart" is expensive. After the 2008 economic downturn and subsequent years of fiscal restraint at the federal level, the CBSA saw it as more cost-effective to regroup these activities than to maintain local intelligence personnel across the country.

The centralization of targeting has been ongoing. It brings together multiple databases (enforcement, immigration and customs), aiming for the automation of risk analyses and the generation of recommendations for inspection by a more limited number of intelligence personnel. More-detailed risk analyses are now made possible through the integration of customs release and risk management facilitated by a platform called e-Manifest. The Canadian version of ACE—Automated Commercial Environment, the US-based equivalent implemented in the early 2000s—e-Manifest was developed as a response to the World Customs Organization's 2005 SAFE requirements for the transmission of advanced commercial information by the private sector to border authorities. Implemented at a cost of more than Can$400 million, its use has been compulsory for carriers, freight forwarders and importers since 2017. E-Manifest is a disciplinary mechanism for both truck drivers and trucking companies. Data includes EDI-transmitted information but also additional information such as routes and port of crossing taken by drivers. Following e-Manifest, less leeway is left to drivers to modify their driving plans, and since implementation, fines have started being applied to transporters who have failed to transmit documentation before a truck shows up at the border.

In a lack of public transparency typical of the CBSA, its plans regarding this new step in the securitization of commercial flows are not clearly laid out in public documents. At the time of research, the CBSA was experimenting with a commercial risk-assessment hub concerned with assessing highway transportation flows by means of advanced information provided by importers and carriers about cargo, means of transportation and drivers. Based in Windsor between 2009 and 2011, the pilot project tested undisclosed "risk indicators" that are now processed through algorithms that automate targeting.[14] According to interviewees, the CBSA was at the time contemplating opening a risk-assessment centre in Windsor and then hubs in different regions in Canada. However, these plans have since been modified towards an even greater centralization by which regions become less and less involved in the production of intelligence knowledge. Since 2017, the agency is working towards the centralization of rail and highway targeting, which will ultimately be placed under the responsibility of the National Targeting Centre (NTC) located in Ottawa. The NTC is already responsible for air passenger, marine and air cargo targeting.[15]

Automated and centralized targeting brings about the erosion of decisions made at the border that used to rely on officers' detailed localized knowledge about border crossers, regional criminal trends and types of commodities. Increasingly asked to enact decisions made elsewhere, customs officers (and presumably all border guards) are made to feel delegitimized as decision makers. Over the next two chapters, I investigate the consequences of this growing sense of virtualization in the daily work of border officers.

Conclusion

Returning to the image of the abandoned pop machine in a port of entry that used to be bustling with activity, it is now easier to understand its desertion. If the case presented here is a product of North American bordering history, this chapter also traced a series of shifts that transformed the port of entry as we knew it. Hitherto located at the centre of customs activities, it was downgraded to one of the many control points spread along securitized supply chains. By studying customs transformations, we begin to appreciate how both securitization *and* neoliberal considerations have shaped the governing of contemporary border control. As early as the

1990s, customs authorities set off on the road of monitoring the mobility of goods while leaving taxation to slowly fade away in the rear-view mirror. They did so not only to remove impediments to circulation but to foster cross-border capital accumulation. Undeniably, 9/11 has ushered in political shifts that must be taken into account when considering border control. Yet, as shown in this chapter, the overhaul of customs was shaped by a range of policy priorities that both include and go beyond security. Changing customs practices are anchored in pilot programmes, legislative changes, technological tests, trade agreements and policing initiatives that emerged in the 1990s only to find more financial resources, political willingness, organizational restructuring and the technological advancements necessary to enact a major shift towards automation, electronic assessment and targeting, after 2001. In this sense, border control is shaped by both security and market rationalities. Of course, attitudes towards trade are historical and may change. Signalling a trend towards limited economic protectionism, the US renegotiated its regional trade agreement with Mexico and Canada in 2018 while imposing new tariffs on Chinese products. But for now, the general border mechanisms detailed in this chapter do not seem to be affected much by these global economic convulsions. This could change, and we should keep our eyes open for the transformations that could follow in customs regulations and practices.

The last pages of this chapter began to explore how automation and targeting have progressively been dovetailed by customs authorities in their project to smooth the control of cross-border commodity flows. Accordingly, the chapter prepared the ground for considering how technologies impact border guards' work routine. As decision-making in bordering is spreading along a chain increasingly difficult to untangle, I turn now to officers' declining grasp over the border that results from the novel division of labour induced by digital technologies.

Acknowledgements

Parts of this chapter are excerpts from the following article:

> Côté-Boucher, K (2016). The paradox of discretion, *British Journal of Criminology*, 56 (1): 49–57, reprinted by permission of Oxford University Press.

With many thanks to Oxford University Press.

Notes

1 The same has been true for the US in its relations with Canada and Mexico. Donald Trump won the 2016 US presidential election partly on promises that he would reopen the 1994 North American Free Trade Agreement (NAFTA). He launched negotiations in the summer of 2017.

2 How these decisions must nevertheless be anchored in quasi-scientific risk knowledges has been particularly well analysed by Anna Pratt (2010) in her review of Canadian jurisprudence on the topic. For a summary of the changes in enforcement powers, see Parliament of Canada (1998), *Bill C-18: An Act to Amend the Customs Act and the Criminal Code*, https://lop.parl.ca/About/Parliament/LegislativeSummaries/bills_ls.asp?lang=F&ls=C18& Parl=36&Ses=1 (last consulted 14 Aug. 2018).

3 *Just-in-time manufacturing* (a term now more often replaced, mutatis mutandis, with that of *lean manufacturing*) refers to a management method that, among other things, better aligns production and distribution while limiting warehouse inventories and improving delivery times to customers.

4 N. Robicheau (2012), *The Border between Us*, www.theborderbetweenus.org/ (last consulted 11 Jan. 2019).

5 American Civil Liberties Union, *The Constitution in the 100-Mile Border Zone*, www.aclu.org/other/constitution-100-mile-border-zone (last consulted 22 July 2019). See also note 6.

6 Since 1924, US authorities have counted on the Border Patrol, which evolved into a formidable tool for the policing of Mexican and Central American migration at the Rio Grande and an instrument of state building and identity making (Lytle Hernández 2010). Traditionally associated with the Mexico–US border, the Border Patrol saw its resources significantly increased at the Canada–US border in the aftermath of 9/11. Now a subsection of the U.S. Customs and Border Protection (CBP), Border Patrol officers are granted extended powers not unlike those conceded to Canada and US border officers. However, they can legally use them in a much larger geographical area—that is, while patrolling areas between ports of entry within 100 miles of the border. These powers allow for normalized immigration status checks in public places such as train or bus stations, which adversely affect people of colour, citizens or not, in higher numbers (Mountz 2011).

7 See the WCO SAFE framework of standards adopted in 2005 by the World Customs Organization and since then implemented by various customs and border agencies throughout the world.

8 Cargo manifests list information such as the type of merchandise being imported, where it comes from and where it is headed, shipper and consignee, weight, etc.

9 A custom broker is a private intermediary that helps businesses to ensure compliance with national regulations, pay tariffs and provide customs officers with the information they need about a shipment to clear its importation into the country.

10 This information includes data about the merchandises and quantities transported, the exporter's name and address and the port of entry where the crossing will occur. Permits for regulated commodities can also be obtained and transmitted electronically by other governmental agencies (e.g. Health Canada for pharmaceutical products).

11 One of the most important strings of takeovers in North American customs brokerage to date includes the buying of established companies such as Norman G. Jensen, Inc., and M.G. Maher & Company, Inc., by Livingston International in 2012.

12 See CBSA (2016), *Part III: Departmental Expenditure Plans: Reports on Plans and Priorities*, www.cbsa-asfc.gc.ca/agency-agence/reports-rapports/rpp/2016-2017/report-rapport-eng.html (last modified 5 May 2016; last consulted 22 July 2019).

13 Ibid., pp. 21–22. Numbers for targeting trade on the land border (commercial highway mode) are not available in these documents. In addition, these statistics have not been confirmed by an independent third-party. With the exception of this cost-efficiency evaluation, there is no publicly available data that would allow us to compare the effectiveness of targeting before and after centralization—in terms of the number of seizures and arrests made or even in more general cross-border crime prevention.

14 CBSA (2012), *E-Manifest Initiative: Evaluation Study Final Report August 03, 2012*, www.cbsa-asfc.gc.ca/agency-agence/reports-rapports/ae-ve/2012/emi-ime-eng.html (last modified 31 Oct. 2012; last consulted 9 Jan. 2019).

15 CBSA (2016), *Part III: Departmental Expenditure Plans: Report on Plans and Priorities*, www.cbsa-asfc.gc.ca/agency-agence/reports-rapports/rpp/2016-2017/report-rapport-eng. html (last modified 5 May 2016; last consulted 22 July 2019).

References

Amoore, L. 2009. Lines of sight: On the visualization of unknown futures. *Citizenship Studies* 13 (1):17–30.

Andreas, P., and T. J. Biersteker. 2003. *The Rebordering of North America*. Edited by P. Andreas and T. J. Biersteker. New York: Routledge.

Bigo, D. 2002. Security and immigration: Toward a critique of the governmentality of unease. *Alternatives: Global, Local, Political* 27:63–92.

———. 2011. Pierre Bourdieu and international relations: Power of practices, practices of power. *International Political Sociology* 5 (3):225–258.

———. 2014. The (in)securitization practices of the three universes of EU border control: Military/Navy-border guards/police-database analysts. *Security Dialogue* 45 (3):209–225.

Blake, G. 1956. The customs administration in Canadian historical development. *The Canadian Journal of Economics and Political Science/Revue canadienne d'économique et de science politique* 22 (4):497–508.

Bonacich, E., and J. B. Wilson. 2008. *Getting the Goods: Ports, Labor and the Logistics Revolution*. Ithaca: Cornell University Press.

Bowling, B., and J. Sheptycki. 2012. *Global Policing*. London: Sage.

Brewer, R. 2014. *Policing the Waterfront: Networks, Partnerships and the Governance of Security*. Oxford: Oxford University Press.

Cantens, T. 2015. Un scanner de conteneurs en « Terre Promise » camerounaise: adopter et s'approprier une technologie de contrôle. *L'Espace politique* 25:2–18.

Chalfin, B. 2007. Customs regimes and the materiality of global mobility: Governing the port of Rotterdam. *American Behavioural Scientist* 50 (12):1610–1630.

———. 2010. *Neoliberal Frontiers: An Ethnography of Sovereignty in West Africa*. Chicago: University of Chicago Press.

Côté-Boucher, K. 2008. The diffuse border: Intelligence-sharing, control and confinement along Canada's Smart Border. *Surveillance and Society* 5 (2):142–165.

———. 2010. Risky business? Border preclearance and the securing of economic life in North America. In *Neoliberalism and Everyday Life*, edited by S. Braedley and M. Luxton. Montreal, Kingston: McGill-Queen's University Press, 37–67.

Cowen, D. 2014. *The Deadly Life of Logistics: Mapping Violence in Global Trade*. Minneapolis: University of Minnesota Press.

Danyluk, M. 2018. Capital's logistical fix: Accumulation, globalization, and the survival of capitalism. *Environment and Planning D: Society and Space* 36 (4):630–647.

Dauvergne, C. 2016. *The New Politics of Immigration and the End of Settler Societies*. Cambridge: Cambridge University Press.

Eski, Y. 2011. "Port of call": Towards a criminology of port security. *Criminology & Criminal Justice* 11 (5):415–431.

Farfan, M. 2009. *The Vermont-Quebec Border: Life on the Line*. Charleston: Arcadia Publishing.

Finn, M., J. Hennebry, and B. Momani. 2018. Canadian-Arab youth at the border: Cultural dissociation, fear management, and disciplining practices in securitized spaces. *Journal of International Migration and Integration* 19 (3):667–682.

Gilbert, E. 2019. Elasticity at the Canada-US border: Jurisdiction, rights, accountability. *Environment and Planning C: Politics and Space*, 37 (3): 424–441.

Harvey, D. 2007. *A Brief History of Neoliberalism*. Oxford: Oxford University Press.

Helleiner, J. 2016. *Borderline Canadianness: Border Crossings and Everyday Nationalism in Niagara*. Toronto: University of Toronto Press.

Heskett, D. 2009. Seamless electronic data and logistics pipelines shift focus from import declarations to start of commercial transactions. *World Customs Journal* 3 (1):27–32.

Hufnagel, S. 2013. *Policing Cooperation across Borders: Comparative Perspective on Law Enforcement within the EU and Australia*. Farnham: Ashgate.

Kalman, I. 2016. Framing Borders: Indigenous Difference at the Canada/US Border, PhD. dissertation in Anthropology, McGill University, Montreal.

LaDow, B. 2002. *The Medicine Line: Life and Death on a North American Borderland*. New York, London: Routledge.

Lytle Hernández, K. 2010. *Migra! A History of the U.S. Border Patrol*. Berkeley: University of California Press.

Madar, D. 2000. *Heavy Traffic: Deregulation, Trade, and Transformation in North American Trucking*. Vancouver: UBC Press.

McIntosh, D. 1984. *The Collectors: A History of Canadian Customs and Excise*. Toronto: NC Press, Revenue Canada, Customs and Excise, Canadian Government Publishing Centre, Supply and Services Canada.

Menjívar, C. 2014. Immigration law beyond borders: Externalizing and internalizing border controls in an era of securitization. *Annual Review of Law and Social Science* 10 (1):353–369.

Mezzadra, S., and B. Neilson. 2013. *Border as Method, or the Multiplication of Labour*. Durham, London: Duke University Press.

Mountz, A. 2011. Specters at the port of entry: Understanding state mobilities through an ontology of exclusion. *Mobilities* 6 (3):317–334.

Norrie, K., and D. Owram. 2002. NAFTA and Canada: Economic policy and national symbolism. In *NAFTA in the New Millenium*, edited by E. J. Chambers and P. H. Smith. La Jolla, Edmonton: Centre for U.S.-Mexican Studies University of California San Diego, The University of Alberta Press.

Núñez, G. G., and J. Heyman. 2007. Entrapment processes and immigrant communities in a time of heightened border vigilance. *Human Organization* 66 (4):354–365.

Pratt, A. 2010. Between a hunch and a hard place: Making suspicion reasonable at the Canadian border. *Social & Legal Studies* 19 (4):461–480.

———. 2016. The Canada-US Shiprider program, jurisdiction and the crime-security nexus. In *National Security, Surveillance and Terror*, edited by R. K. Lippert, K. Walby, I. Warren and D. Palmer. London: Palgrave Macmillan, 249–272.

Pratt, A., and S. Thompson. 2008. Chivalry, "race" and discretion at the Canadian border. *The British Journal of Criminology* 48 (5):620–640.

Ritchie, M. 2015. Feeling for the state: Affective labor and anti-terrorism training in US hotels. *Communication and Critical/Cultural Studies* 12 (2):179–197.

Sassen, S. 2008. *Territory, Authority, Rights: From Medieval to Global Assemblages*. Princeton: Princeton University Press.

Simpson, A. 2014. *Mohawk Interruptus: Political Life across the Borders of Settler States*. Durham: Duke University Press.

Zaiotti, R., ed. 2016. *Externalizing Migration Management: Europe, North America and the Spread of "Remote Control" Practices*. London: Routledge.

Chapter 3

Border interrupted

Technologies and the fraught circulation of data in bordering

Accompanied by a supervisor, I tour the commercial section of a major port of entry known for its historically high levels of truck traffic. The Windsor–Detroit border crossing represents a vital logistics link, the busiest for truck traffic between Canada and the US.[1] While truck queues are not as long as they used to be in the 1990s, they still occur—for example, 2.5 million trucks crossed the bridge in 2017.[2] Part of that traffic comes from what is called in the region the Big Three—automakers Chrysler, Ford and GM. Before arriving in Canada, trucks cross the Ambassador Bridge, which is owned by a controversial family of American billionaires. The Morouns have earned their reputation by letting this major corridor for the North American economy reach such a state of disrepair that construction on a new toll bridge funded by Canada has begun and is scheduled to be completed in 2024— despite years of legal opposition by the Morouns to the project.

In addition to this bit of local politics over cross-border infrastructures, it is the peculiar way that truck inspections are done that stands out at the Windsor port. Given inadequate customs installations at the Ambassador Bridge exit, trucks cannot be searched at the main port-of-entry site. In fact, customs installations are located seven kilometres away from the border. This is quite unusual. When it was built, this inspection site was meant to be temporary. Yet it had already been operating for about 20 years at the time of my visit and is likely to remain so until the replacement bridge and attached customs sections are finalized in 2024. Until then, when a truck is referred to secondary inspection, it must cross the city to reach inspection docks. The local CBSA authorities have proven themselves creative by putting in place a procedure that involves tagging trucks designated for inspection and escorting drivers to the site. Before these measures were put in place, trucks have been known to sometimes get "lost" on the way, failing to appear for inspection.

There are additional issues with this arrangement. Temporary infrastructures are rarely built to withstand the test of time or to accommodate different types of needs and situations. This is the case in Windsor. At the time of my visit, only some of the doors where trucks back up for inspection are fully functional, while dock openings do not fit all trailer sizes—thus making searching certain types of trailers for contraband more difficult. Windsor is a special case, but not an insignificant one. For years, its inadequate border infrastructures have impacted border enforcement and facilitation at the most important land border for cargo crossing into Canada.

Throughout fieldwork, I found more ports with similar infrastructure issues, some minor, others major. I have observed a few of these issues during supervised visits and learned about others as officers explained how they used inspection devices and often commented about broken tools or old and underused equipment. For instance, on inspection docks in another port, I saw broken mirrors and burned light bulbs that could easily be fixed to offer simple but effective means for looking inside and under a trailer. In a third port, an officer sarcastically mentioned that he could use the ion scan "when it worked."[3] As stated in Chapter 1, officers also told me about a VACIS scan (a massive mobile X-ray inspection vehicle for trailers and containers operated by a team of officers) sitting in a parking lot due to a lack of budget to staff it properly—an issue also faced by the port of Montreal.[4]

Why should I insist on these infrastructural matters in an introduction to a chapter concerned with the circulation of data in border control? As illustrated by the Windsor–Detroit border-crossing example, sometimes simplicity is key: all the preclearance, border automation and commercial targeting in the world do not make up for the fact that without the proper infrastructures and basic work tools, searches and seizures of illegal cargo will not happen. Despite promises that the arrival of automation and targeting would translate into an increased rate of inspections and more time to dedicate to law enforcement and complex decision-making, officers have since become disenchanted. In the end, however, officers told me that inspection rates have not gone up. This is confirmed by public documents that show that inspection rates for international trade tend to go down, an understandable trend when we factor in the emphasis placed by border agencies on trade facilitation, as explored in the previous chapter.[5] Part of the problem has been a disparity between existing port-of-entry infrastructures and computer risk analyses. This gap further restricts the implementation of decisions made remotely. Similar disparities between technological improvements and lack of corresponding infrastructural investments have been observed by Heyman (2009) in the case of US ports of entry.

But the Windsor case is an illustration of a larger issue with significant consequences on how we study the role of technologies and data in bordering. According to a policy assumption often echoed in scholarship, borders would be rendered "seamless" by reducing human input and safeguarding a smooth circulation of data between actors loosely connected across the policing networks that make up borders. By virtue of this smooth circulation, this data would enable intelligence-led decision-making.

This chapter aims to unpack this assumption by looking into how data circulation unfolds in bordering. In the following pages, I ask, how does data circulate in border spaces, and how actionable is this data? It is often said that intelligence and risk knowledge are geared towards action, or as Amoore (2013: 162) argues, "risk-based security technologies . . . appeal to an expansion of forms of knowledge that can always be rendered as actionable intelligence." Accordingly, and in light of the widespread adoption of predictive technologies for the purpose of acting on border mobilities, Amoore (2013: 87) asks, "Where does the border materialize and how is it decided?" Inquiring into the development of fluid borders through data derivatives and pixelated modes of visualization, her response is anchored in how these abstractions are produced from the particular vantage point of high border officials and technological designers.

In view of my findings, I make two propositions, which contrast with Amoore's vision, to investigate anew the putative seamlessness of technologized borders. First, I suggest, as did Davidshofer, Jeandesboz and Ragazzi (2016) and Bigo (2011, 2014), that we contextualize how bordering actors think about technologies and what they do with them, particularly as it comes to their socio-professional dispositions and their social positioning in the bordering world. Accordingly, rather than assuming fluctuating, mobile and unencumbered borders, the chapter delves into the concrete intricacies that shape, channel and interrupt data circulation in everyday bordering. Doing so allows us to give back to algorithmic borders their sociological texture through a contextualized rendering of the situated practices involved in the deployment of bordering technologies.

However, we need to go a little further by inquiring into the moments where everyday bordering practices and imaginaries of data fluidity collide. In this chapter, I am intrigued by the points of frictions between these imaginaries, how they shape frontline border guards experience of bordering and, in turn, how this experience feeds back into data collection, circulation and analysis. In fact, a range of issues make data production and circulation as well as the enactment of bordering decisions on the basis of data less certain and more fraught. This includes border infrastructures, of course, but also, as we shall see, an immanent variability in understandings of risk. This further involves spotty data access at the frontline and officer distrust in the validity of available data. As a result, these issues affect not only decision-making at the border but also the desired feedback loop between frontline officer data gathering and centralized targeting. In short, rather than a top-down or bottom-up analysis, I propose to look at the variegated effects of data circulation on bordering, paying attention to how and when data moves and to how it both transforms borderwork and is altered by it in the process.

Neither are these points of frictions temporary, nor are they side effects or externalities that can be ignored; rather, they are intrinsically constitutive of the materialities that make up data-led bordering. After years of studies concerned with single border technologies (e.g. body scanners, biometrics, etc.), it is fruitful to shift our focus in order to investigate these points of friction. Examining the complexities of data circulation as experienced from ports of entry should expand our understanding of the register of variables conceivably at work in technologized border control. While much ink has been spilled on surveillance technologies and bordering, generally with a focus on a programmatic vision where mobilities are meant to be controlled upstream, I explore what is produced by those moments when this vision and the practical contingencies involved in the "datafication" of borders collide. Accordingly, opening up to scrutiny those fantasies of automatized borders where "actionable" data seemingly circulates unimpeded, I make room for contextualized inquiries that recast our critical engagements with datafied bordering.

The "seamless border" programme: a limited analytical framework

My interactions with upper echelons in security and border agencies over the years have taught me an important lesson: their border has little to do with that of street-level officers. Imagining a high-tech space built through automation, risk algorithms and unimpeded data circulation, those who work in border agencies' headquarters fetishize technologies for their "smartness" and efficiency while pitting their purported neutrality against what they see as the problematic messiness of officer discretion.

These flexible, intelligent, quasi-ubiquitous borders that "can be invoked anywhere, anytime, for anyone" (Amoore 2013: 83) are assumed to have many qualities. They are seen to promote a better use of officers' time by first automating and then eliminating binary decision-making in ports of entry—that is, decisions to let in or to intercept for further screening. This would, in theory, focus officers on more-complex decisions that require human input and on inspections of border crossers and freight. Further, data-led bordering would formalize, without human input, the criteria through which new threats are identified and low-risk individuals and cargo assessed, with the promise of reduced and better-targeted inspections. Automated border decisions would also be less likely to be contested in court or denounced on social media by disgruntled citizens unhappy about their treatment at the hands of overzealous border officers.

In short, the silver bullet of information technologies is seen to solve it all. It promises more-efficient and more-secure borders while speeding up cargo assessment. It pledges to do so by reducing discretionary decisions, decreasing rates of faulty decision-making and promoting more-consistent and more-accurate judgements on who and what should be allowed entry.

This "dreaming of the seamless border" (Broeders and Hampshire 2013) by policymakers and upper-level management is a common but not very realistic occurrence.[6] In a study about predictive policing, Manning (2008: 72) calls such fictions "technology as a caricature," where "the situational, adaptive, and creative aspects of using technologies are ignored, while the managerial profiles are highlighted and dramatized." Zuboff (1988: 268) argues in her classic study on the effects of automation in a range of industries that this enthusiasm for technologies "reveals an underlying but potent fantasy, one in which perfect control through total automaticity allows [managers] to avoid the messiness and potential conflict of real human interactions."

Unfortunately, this fantasy is taken too literally by some critical border scholars quick to give credit to border authorities' vision of technologized border control, and such scholars at the same time eschew questions related to whether and how this vision is deployed and enacted on the ground.[7] Amoore's (2013) work illustrates this problem. Relying on UK border high officials' and EU policy documents, Amoore develops an approach to border automation as a smooth, fluctuating and iterative process, conjecturing that border decisions emerge in a continuous back and forth between a variety of border actors—from software designers to targeters and frontline officials. This would create a border in "real time" in which targeting depends on risk scores that are, Amoore (88) assumes, "conveyed to frontline border guards" through modalities that remain unexplored. At the centre of her research, Amoore looks at how in those conditions, the border "simultaneously discriminates among and within bodies, dissecting into degrees of risk and visualizing as a series of fragments"; new forms of intelligence would thus allow border analysts to go beyond the search for real information and expand intelligence production "into a world of possibilities [that] lends greater weight to the fragments, making them actionable" (103). In this sense, targeting would rely on risk derivatives, adopting a longer view of risk. Predictive security would then bypass traditional concerns for data validity but also permit the future enactment of risk predictions on the basis of "inferences to make links between partial elements of information" (89).

Amoore's work has been influential, not the least because of its careful dissection of the anticipatory logics that populate security imaginaries—that is, the desire of high-level decision makers in security agencies to harness information technologies in order to create new connections between disparate data to predict future threats. Amoore takes these imaginaries seriously, and so should we. They signal the constitution of a truth regime that views drawing data correlations and automated decision-making as superior security strategies worth spending billions in public money on a global scale. Assuredly, we are witnessing a "datafication" of bordering that dovetails with these imaginaries; a massive human, technological and budgetary effort is now made to "measure, record and analyse" border mobilities globally and put them "in a quantified format so [that they] can be tabulated and analysed" (Mayer-Schöneberger and Cukier 2013: 78). These fictions about technologized bordering are symbolically powerful; they shape bordering for border workers, and as exposed by authors such as Feldman (2012), they mediate their experience while making the effects of bordering invisible to the eyes of bordering agents—including fostering moral indifference towards migrants' plights and challenges. Conveying the idealizations of elite policymakers and technological providers as they imagine an orderly, standardized and efficient bordering, they tell us about aims to standardize and simplify the control of complex cross-border flows.

Whether they are called "smart" or "seamless," technologized border programmatics constitute an inescapable horizon of action for border workers. The accepted wisdom that bordering should now be done through data creates the contemporary conditions of possibility of borderwork. Nowadays, much of what happens in frontline bordering is enabled by the circulation of data—including data access, whether or not one should take data into account when making a decision, the requirement to participate in data collection or the fact that this data is now analysed beyond ports of entry. For these reasons, the imaginary of the "seamless border" constitutes a useful framework for understanding the role played by data circulation in bordering.

Yet it is also a limited framework. When things do not work as they were planned to (as they rarely do), these fictions enter in tension with the disorderly everydayness of bordering. As argued by Bourne, Johnson and Lisle (2015: 313),

> at the heart of the bordering process (. . .) is an important structuring tension between the belief that technology can provide total security on the one hand, and the everyday practices of human/technological assemblages that are riven with competing agendas, unexpected failures, tangents, and miscommunications, on the other.

Following this important insight, I open up to scrutiny some moments of friction when technologized border imaginaries and bordering practices do not dovetail into a "seamless" circulation of data but produce something else. To explore these moments, the question of whether and under which conditions data is really actionable seems like a good place to start.

Friction moments in data-led bordering

As established by ethnographic research on policing and technologies, there are "structural disconnections between technological solutions and actual policing" and, by extension, borderwork (Sheptycki 2017: 294). If border decisions conceal a "complex of calculation, consulting, analysis, algorithmic modelling and risk management" (Amoore 2013: 2), then these decisions are also made amid a context of subcultural conflicts in security agencies over the purpose of bordering, the distribution of enforcement and risk-management responsibilities, distrust over the qualifications associated with distinct positions within the border, hierarchical access to fragmentary and unverified data, gaps between decisions and the infrastructures to enact them and disjunctures between frontline data collection and centralized data analysis compounded by the varied risk imaginaries that underpin these processes. As a result, security agencies' aim of "integrating human and machine reasoning at each step of processing relevance and learning how to distinguish significant and non-significant information from each other" (Aradau and Blanke 2015: 5) encounters important roadblocks when the time comes to make this goal a reality.

Variability in risk taxonomies

On the basis of material provided by a deputy director of the UK e-border programme, Amoore (2013: 66) argues that border risk derivatives work

> with a mobile norm, a norm that is itself modulated and aleatory. (. . .) The e-borders official describes a customs officer who can visually scan pages of data on multitransit point sea routes, identifying an apparently suspicious set of travel association (. . .) as normal in specific circumstances.

Rather than presenting them as rigid categorizations, this interpretation of the flexible character of risk imaginaries deployed in security settings aptly underscores the immanent nature of risk taxonomies. However, it neglects one of the most trenchant features of risk imaginaries, technological or otherwise: they come in multiple forms (Douglas and Wildavsky 1984). Some phenomena are selected and designated as risk and others ignored, and all are attached to historically situated cultural norms and moral politics, themselves now powered by technological infrastructures. Further, and as shown by works in critical security studies influenced by Bourdieu and Lahire, this selection also depends on specific actors endowed with a repertoire of dispositions anchored in their socio-professional position. Amoore generalizes to all bordering sites a disposition towards risk, one that actually reflects that of specific border actors. In contrast, I have found a variability in risk taxonomies and in the organizational factors that shape them.

First of all, where some adopted the circumstantial vision of risk not unlike that espoused by the UK official interviewed by Amoore, others embraced a much more essentialist risk classification. Samuel and Nathan exemplify well this distinction. Before the centralization of targeting, both held risk-analysis responsibilities at some point in their careers. Yet risk carried different meanings for each officer. Samuel's version is closer to the trope of a modulating and adaptable border. As he explains how he comes up with a drug traffic target, Samuel sheds light on how targeting introduces a temporal variability in risk classifications. His description of a targeter's main task concentrates on the conduct of random checks on carriers, drivers and importers informed by known trends in cross-border criminality. In that risk-assessment scenario, past enforcement histories and recent developments in smuggling are reinterpreted and probed for out-of-the-ordinary routings or for types of shipments worthy of further inspection. To illustrate this point, Samuel comes up with the following example: if cocaine has been found hidden amid ceramic tiles, then ceramic tiles would become a high-risk commodity and be targeted accordingly. This would especially be the case if these tiles originate from a region known to be a drug-trafficking hub (e.g. California for Columbian cocaine smuggled through the US–Mexico border, then transferred on Canada-bound trucks). But if smugglers then adapt their practices to avoid detection—such as by changing their routing to have another point of origin appear on a truck driver's manifest—and intelligence analysts at the CBSA become aware of these changes, then targeting is adjusted accordingly, and the ceramic would then be dropped from the high-risk list. In this explanation, levels of risk are modulated according to context, events and what is currently known about organized crime strategies.

Then comes Nathan, the officer we met in Chapter 1 who became a low-level data analyst following an injury. I asked Nathan, "what constitutes a risk for you?" Offering a fixed classification, Nathan's answer implies that he holds risk as self-evident. For him, low risk is alcohol and tobacco. Medium risk is child pornography, drugs and guns. Lastly, animal or human-born contagious illnesses such as mad cow disease represent high risks. Nathan thus mobilizes risk definitions that represent embedded, immediate and essential attributes of an object. In many ways, his risk taxonomy is reminiscent of the static biopolitical categorizations and enduring sanitary practices that have long been part of border control and continue being so—such as 19th-century quarantines of Irish and Chinese migrants to Canada (Mawani 2003); more recently, airport screenings during the global SARS epidemic outbreak; or even colour-coded situational risk assessments (green, yellow, red).

Hall (2017: 491) found in her study that European targeters held "an ambivalent view of their decision-making," influenced simultaneously by the "apparent objectivity of data" and by these targeters' "judgemental calls." I was made aware of a parallel ambivalence in Samuel's and Nathan's explanations. Risk readings can dynamically fluctuate according to context, or they can be quite rigid, but in both cases, these readings are likely to influence targeting decisions. It would be a mistake to think that more-static classifications are now a thing of the past for borderwork and that Nathan's risk associations remain an anomaly. In fact, border control is now made of "dynamic sociomaterial configurations" that "affect the kind of organizational realities that are produced" by technologies in workplaces (Orlikowski and Scott 2008: 434, 436). This is illustrated by the fact that risk analysis at the CBSA is considered a viable alternative placement for incapacitated officers; their union even lists the Targeting Centre in Ottawa as a potential accommodation position for officers having failed their firearm certification or having been injured, as was the case for Nathan. These are often older officers with much field experience but not necessarily chosen because of their advanced IT skills.

Different forces and tensions on the frontline collide with the seamless border vision when it comes to developing the intellective and technical skills associated with risk targeting schemes. These forces include unionized staff placement, the level of border workers' education, professional socialization[8] and the need for IT training in the wake of constant upgrades and technological change, and they point to the diverse risk taxonomies that are deployed in producing data and enacting border decisions.

The frontline, data access and the trickling-down hypothesis

As I spoke with officers about the steps that they took while processing truck drivers, a discovery surprised me: officers do not have much access to databases when officers do not have much access to databases when in their booths. If they wish to inquire further into a driver, they must send this person to the main office, where a colleague would then be able to look into different databases—for instance, the Integrated Border Query (IBQ) or, until recently, the CPIC, the main federal criminal database. Officers can also then check ICES (integrated customs enforcement system), which contains a history of past customs enforcement actions with drivers and carriers and which includes motives for secondary inspection, notes from past questioning and receipts and invoices previously found on drivers.[9]

For years, this limited data access has been at the centre of an ongoing debate between frontline officers, their union and upper CBSA management, the latter being reluctant to make the necessary investments (from the officers' point of view) to facilitate such access.[10] In 2015, the issue was made prominent in national media after a foreign Catholic priest with an outstanding arrest warrant for sexual assault was allowed re-entry at an airport. In reaction to the media attention garnered in the aftermath, access to criminal records was granted to frontline officers.

My disbelief at learning about this limited data access arose from the portrayal of data circulation in border scholarship, which often speculates about the flowing of intelligence and data analyses down to ports of entry where decisions to allow or prohibit entry would then be enforced. I term this assumption the *trickling-down hypothesis*. It is based on a mechanistic top-down reading of the dynamics of information flow in security and policing organizations that is not corroborated by research. Data is often difficult to access in security organizations, for a range of reasons, including hoarding, information silos, lack of interoperability and budgetary limitations that impede acquiring costly equipment to make use of such data (Sheptycki 2004; Sanders et al. 2015).

Some of these problems can be found in Canadian bordering but must be given their proper context. As I argued in the previous chapter, border authorities operate customs and much of traveller surveillance under a facilitation paradigm. The objective is clear: border agencies must process billions of dollars of cargo and millions of air passengers each year. Following agency standards, the time spent at the booth by drivers and travellers can seldom go beyond 30 seconds. Accordingly, having officers search databases would represent an impediment to an expeditious management of global flows, particularly if we take into account that the past two decades have seen the explosion of border-related databases—dozens are now listed in CBSA public documents—which often have compatibility problems.[11]

Further, this difficulty of access is compounded by the fact that, in contrast to the current political push to foster collaboration and data-sharing in intelligence and security, the datafication of borders has not eliminated the hierarchical and secretive organizational culture of security agencies (Nolan 2013). The effects of such a culture are amplified by the formal norms and procedures that frame data circulation. This includes content limitations embedded in databases that constrain recording qualitative risk data and includes privacy and data protection rules,[12] which circumscribe who has access to and can exchange distinct categories of sensitive information. Difficulty of access is also compounded by the need-to-know principle, which continues to be associated with distinct secret clearance levels. As a result, the CBSA indicates in an evaluation of its targeting programmes that "though the targeting officer can include a narrative in the system, they are limited in the number of characters that they can use. Targeting officers are also limited, by legislation as well as regulation and policy, in the type of information that they can share with the frontline."[13]

What does this tell us about the actionable character of border data? Together, these obstacles feed long-standing debates in security organizations over differential access to information and the leverage that such access may grant, including the capacity to speak legitimately about security in these organizations and beyond (Dewerpe 1994; Linhardt 2005). Under these circumstances, border officers' insistence on gaining access to data must be understood not only as a desire to be more efficient in their enforcement work but also as a bid to receive more recognition and establish themselves as still-relevant security actors. Whereas data circulation does sustain bordering, it actually follows specific political, budgetary and organizational modalities that channel such data to particular actors while eluding others. As a result, whereas the seamless border thesis assumes data circulation to the frontline, strategic access to data as a way to maintain influence in border decision-making remains a major point of contention in border agencies and security institutions more generally.

Distrusting data

Amoore (2013: 67) argues that risk derivatives call into question "scientific notions of evidence and accuracy. . . . What matters is not the accuracy gleaned from large volumes of data, analyzed and statistically assessed but the intelligibility of the derivative as an instrument, its precision as a basis for deci-sion." From a targeting point of view, this may be a correct statement. Jeandes-boz (2017) proposes that targeting centres can be best understood via a detour with Latour's notion of "centres of calculation," where knowledge production requires the mobilization of a variety of technical and social resources, the stabilization of knowledge claims and the extension of the networks created by these centres in order to validate and disseminate that knowledge. How-ever, my research suggests that this stabilization is never completely achieved, because legitimation problems recurrently affect how data circulates and is involved in border decisions. For border officers called upon to implement many of the decisions produced by these instruments, the validity of data still counts. When it comes to the intelligibility of data, from whom it has been collected as well as how and by whom it has been analysed are matters debated at the frontline, where data knowledge can be met with suspicion.

In fact, another issue to arise regarding actionable intelligence in bordering concerns officers' trust in the reliability of the data and risk scores they see on their screens. Through comments that betray their scepticism towards the reliability of automation, preclearance and targeting, customs officers reveal themselves to be conscious of data-quality problems. On the one hand, if the operations of targeting scoring tools in predictive algorithmic security systems remain unknown to the general public, frontline border officers are similarly left in the dark. As a result, it is not uncommon for them to question the dependability of such analyses.

On the other hand, while none of my interviewees spoke of the normative and potentially discriminatory problems entrenched in the very design of predic-tive technologies, officers were acutely aware that much of the data that leads to risk-scoring and preclearance status designations is self-declared by private actors (travellers, importers, etc.) and not subject to verification. For instance, officers often insist that they have limited trust in the FAST and NEXUS programmes—the preclearance identity cards granted to those truck and car drivers deemed by US and Canadian border authorities to present a low risk. Information about card holders is updated only periodically, sometimes only after five years, while some updates are even left to card holders themselves.[14] Sarah, a young officer just out of her training at customs college, is sceptical:

> it shows that they've gone through criminal checks and everything. But, regardless, they're still subject to examination. (. . .) So, to me, or to most people, it doesn't matter if they have a FAST card. It just shows that they probably haven't done anything bad lately, or they haven't had any previous customs infractions. It doesn't mean that they're not smuggling anything. It just means that they haven't been caught.

Similarly inclined, Marie, an experienced officer we met in chapter 2, asked me somewhat rhetorically, if a truck driver obtained a FAST card two years ago, what guarantee do I have that he has not since been arrested for domestic violence, drug trafficking or driving under the influence? Given that these verifications are not made, she feels it is her responsibility to check people with preclearance cards, even though these have been developed to reduce such checks and facilitate border crossing in the first place.

This lack of confidence in low-risk evaluations generated from criminal, immigration and border-crossing data appears as a common thread throughout the interviews, so my interviewees might well be correct in their assessment. Delays for the inclusion or deletion of criminal records in CPIC (the main Canadian police database) can last up to two years. Further, the verification of a trusted trader status is undertaken every five years at the time of renewal of programme membership in FAST. Interestingly, the auditor general of Canada (2007) has come across similar distrust towards databases and encountered a selective appropriation of risk-management techniques by frontline border personnel. Interviewed for this audit, officers testified that they sometimes did not follow risk quotes on maritime containers established by automated systems and chose to inspect containers on the basis of their own discretionary reading of the data available, their knowledge of local specificities and their work experience. This conclusion is supported by Dekkers, van der Woude and van der Leun's (2018) findings in the case of internal roadside checks at Dutch borders where a smart camera system flagging potentially risky vehicles had "limited influence on the decisions made" by border guards—who at times even let go flagged vehicles because the guards did not find these cars and their occupants to be of interest. In any case, this shared caution confirms a pattern of distrust in relation to data and a preference for the use of discretion at the frontline in Canada and elsewhere.

Consequently, targeting is not always seen to be actionable by officers who may doubt the updated character of data and its validity and who may doubt analyses made by security professionals whom they do not know and whose recommendations they may believe show little understanding of local criminal trends and circumstances. At times, officers' distrust may lead them to pay lip service to targeting and automated inspection recommendations, especially when that which is targeted is contradicted by their experiential risk knowledges of what to search and when. If data-led decisions are the programmatic horizon in which the frontline must operate, the level of trust in delocalized data analyses shapes whether and how algorithmic decisions are enacted in practice, thus showing a significant point of friction in data-led bordering where discretion is still very much alive.

"Targeting in the future": untangling the feedback loop

As much as we assume that intelligence trickles down in security organizations, contemporary risk-assessment arrangements also ride on the hypothesis that unprocessed information will be recorded at the frontline and then circulated up the border chain for later analysis. In fact, while much has been said of the information that travellers and air carriers must now transfer to border agencies for analysis (such as passenger name records), the data-led border control model also depends on a continuous supply of information coming from street-level border officers. Indeed, border agencies do speculate that "data [is] dutifully fed into the system by border guards" (Andersson 2016: 34). The objective is not to make it to "real-time" analysis but to bring what is known about the latest criminal, security and immigration trends up to date.

Such updating involves recording officers' suspicions in databases and would thus spur investigations in border agencies' intelligence sections. Echoing Tazzioli (2018: 273), who argues that targeting is about "open[ing] up future spaces of intervention" as it archives data for analysis at a later date, Samuel, quoted earlier in this chapter, explains this aspect of the targeter's work in these terms:

> I'd say the role of the targeter is where they've done an examination at the back [inspection dock] and something just doesn't make sense and they say: "You know what? I don't know what was going on with that company but something doesn't feel right. I'd love to look at these guys again." So the targeter, probably working in a similar vicinity would say: "OK. I'll do some reports and I'll see what they're bringing in, and how often and so on. And, you know, do background checks on them, do a few more checks. And then, *we can target in the future* and see what there is."
>
> (emphasis added)

In the scenario privileged by targeting, secondary inspections become opportunities not only to enforce customs laws but for detailed information gathering. In fact, border officers are now required by internal policy to take more-detailed notes during their inspections for targeting purposes. Categories of relevant information include what has been found, the search method (e.g. random sampling of commodities or thorough search), how many boxes were opened, which commodities were found, and so on. Through these notes, and others taken following interrogations of drivers, officers can record their sense that "something does not feel right" and when they have "a knot in the stomach"—as some officers described their moments of doubt.

This is a significant departure from past practice, transforming the temporal reach of decisions made by border officers to record, or not to record, a piece of information for future use. Gilboy (1991) writes in her study of frontline work in airports—which she carried out before the use of information technologies in border control became standardized—that officers unable to substantiate a suspicion had to release the suspected traveller and hope to "catch him next time." Nowadays however, targeting allows officers to extend their influence beyond the border-crossing moment, thus bringing their legally enshrined "reasonable suspicion" to bear on future decisions made by other border actors. An officer now has the opportunity to feed another officer's misgivings in another port at a later date or to reach out to targeting authorities—who may, for instance, follow up by broadening their search beyond the sole truck driver and towards the carrier who employs them. In short, with targeting, an officer's doubt may not carry a direct investigative result, but it transforms release/refer decisions into moments of information gathering and offers the possibility to formalize suspicion into risk. It is in this sense that O'Connor and de Lint (2009: 50) conclude that "enforcement actions can be transformed into lookouts" at the border by passing on information about a cold hit (i.e. seizure accomplished without previous intelligence data) to intelligence staff.

However, a useful critique of information-based border interventions also requires unpacking data-recording practices on the frontline. Targeting assumes a new division of labour in border control, which involves a restricted but essential role for border officers who are now expected to record information they deem relevant for risk analysis. Yet I found variations in officers' recordkeeping practices, with consequences on intelligence-led border policing and, ultimately, for how we conceptualize anticipatory efforts in border control. In fact, border control agencies experience a variety of organizational and technical concerns that may affect this data collection model on the frontline. These concerns range from competing targeting priorities between headquarters and regions, overwork and lack of personnel (particularly in major airports), limited training with new information technologies and, as mentioned previously, widespread suspicion on the part of officers towards intelligence produced by delocalized analysts. Further, while they have knowledge of local trends, officers' capacity to include comprehensive narratives in their reports is reduced because they are limited by the "communication formats" built into databases (Ericson 2007).

As a result, whether border officers embrace this newfound data-entry role on the frontline remains uncertain given that this role comes without increased influence on data analysis or access to analysts. As Manning (2008: 71) suggests about policing, technologies that "decrease efforts in respect of valued routines . . . are used and praised; those that are associated with unwanted efforts or disvalued routines . . . are ignored, sabotaged, or seldom used."

Taken together, these concerns present the potential to distort the feedback loop in intelligence circulation between ports of entry and centralized targeting called for by upper-management echelons. The CBSA's 2016 evaluation of its targeting programme alludes to the Agency's worry on this matter:

> The regional intelligence and examining officers are also responsible for sharing information, local trends and risks with the NTC on an ongoing basis. Strengthening the information sharing and collaborative processes

would facilitate the decision-making process. Furthermore, a more effective *feedback loop* is expected to enhance the Targeting Program's ability to include regional trends, risks and realities in its analysis and, as such, be more responsible to the dynamic targeting environment.

(emphasis added)[15]

It seems that data circulation is not happening as "dynamically" as planned. A few years before the publication of this report, these plans were surmised by Mario, an experienced officer with much knowledge of the conception and implementation of the e-Manifest programme that integrates customs and risk analysis. Mario was quite critical of the centralization of targeting that was to follow e-Manifest. He also lamented that the programme failed to become "user-friendly"—that is, to directly connect officers to all border-related databases in order to support enforcement work in ports of entry, as he affirms it was originally planned. Because of operational and IT difficulties, as well as budget cuts, e-Manifest remained attached to the DOS-based ACROSS database, the main commercial database created in the 1990s, instead of being adapted to Windows.

Mario explained to me the debates within the CBSA about the centralization of targeting operations. At the time, upper management was considering organizing targeting in a series of regional hubs that included Windsor, Ontario, where the pilot project that led to the creation of a NTC in Ottawa was being tested:

> Until the debate between regions and Ottawa about targeting is closed. . . . It seems that for now, Ottawa is winning. In Windsor, anyway, they already have opened the National Targeting Centre. So they oppose regional or local targeting. (. . .) Regions fight to keep a part of their targeting responsibilities or at least maintain those they already have. (. . .) So, the local phenomena, Windsor won't be able to represent them well. Officers will probably have to note down local events, transmit these notes to Windsor, and it's Windsor that will do the targeting.

The operative word in this last sentence is "probably." How border guards handle their newfound "record discretion"—that is, the "capacity to identify and to document criminal and noncriminal events" (Nickels 2007)—remains open to inquiry. Research about variations in crime-recording practices among police officers shows them to be subject to a range of influences, including the geographical and temporal context of an infraction (Boivin and Ouellet 2014) and officers' perceptions of a crime's seriousness and over-recording as a union bargaining strategy—in this case, because over-recording raises crime statistics, thus giving a bad reputation to a city and its police department. In this sense, "officers hold a strategic role in the production of police-recorded statistics," deciding whether or not to record an incident and how to classify it (Boivin and Cordeau 2011: 187). Illustrating this issue in the area of border control, an officer indicated to me that although he believed it important to record his suspicions about local enforcement trends for further targeting analysis, he had stopped doing so because he did not receive feedback on whether the information provided was helpful and acted on.

In addition, in specific circumstances, the feedback loop can quickly become outdated and self-referential. As shown by research in policing and security, data collected by street-level officers is often parched, lacks thoroughness and is rarely updated (Piazza 2009). Border officers confirmed these problems for customs and, in one particular port, provided an illustration with the issues plaguing machine-release operations. We saw in the previous chapter that machine release permits the automation of discharge for low-risk cargo, thus limiting officer involvement in reviewing cargo manifests. In this particular port, an officer was at the time of research responsible for this system, keeping it updated with the latest evaluations of transporters and drivers. This officer was replacing someone who had stepped down from this role, overwhelmed by and unable to cope with the workload and technical abilities required by the system. During the tenure of this resigning officer, machine release operated on dated information, because exporter–importer files were not reviewed for months. This meant that a company found in compliance with and considered to represent a lower risk thus continued to be sent to less-random inspections and therefore had little opportunity to be found noncompliant. Meanwhile, inspection docks were overloaded with random truck referrals sent by the automated system on the basis of obsolete information and as a result of the difficulties experienced by this overwhelmed officer in adjusting random inspection referral rates. In this port of entry, the result was not border decisions taken in "real time" but the creation of a small-scale, self-referential system that bit its own tail.

In a nutshell, "targeting in the future" offers contradictory options for border officers. It potentially frees their discretion, extending it temporally by allowing fleeting doubts to persist beyond work shifts and potentially find a new life inside targeting's algorithmic combinations and intelligence work. Yet bordering technologies also transfer sections of borderwork towards delocalized data analysis while changing frontline work into data-entry positions. Border workers thus take "the mute role of a laboring body, while providing [management] with exclusive access to and control of the organizations' knowledge base" (Zuboff 1988: 284). Not only are the ensuing internal status struggles over who has access to and can manipulate data significant for unpacking recordkeeping influences on anticipatory bordering; more broadly, and as examined in Chapter 5, these struggles have also become collectively organized. In reaction to their demotion to the role of data collectors and to their loss of monopoly over the control of the border, these struggles have spurred officers' into embracing a more concrete and physical approach to bordering.

Conclusion

What conclusions can we now draw about these frictions over data circulation in border agencies? This chapter ran against the temptation to take upper-management echelons at their word as they dream of a neutral and flexible border and highlighted the blind spots in this vision. Taking border workers' points of view as my starting point, I examined various constraints to data mobility and the related debates in border agencies concerned with data access. As data moves through and gets stuck in a series of channels, obstacles and detours between discrete analysis and decisional levels, a different, more complicated story of data circulation emerges. This border interrupted story teaches us much about multiple interruptions within the purportedly fluid back-and-forth circulation of data in bordering; these disruptions deeply shape how "actionable" and "smart" intelligence can be.

Perhaps we should consider adapting to the realm of bordering Aradau's (2015) suggestion that the "pseudo-rationality" of big data analytics in security agencies bears resemblance to how astrology makes sense of the world—drawing correspondences between disparate elements that are given validity as they are translated into a seemingly coherent, truthful narrative. Similarly, Chan and Bennett Moses (2016: 24) point to the assumed "mythic qualities" of large data sets in predictive policing, where mass data supposedly "speaks for itself" and is seen to be in no need of further interpretation.

Similarly, the datafied border produces its own fragmentary truth about people and goods on the move. Among other disquieting findings, the injunction to anticipate upcoming border events presents the ever-renewed possibility to coin and act on alternative realities through feedback loops made up of old and new, incomplete and unverified data produced through less-than-systematic recordkeeping practices involving a range of actors and located in systems that often suffer from digital incompatibilities. In this sense, the seamless border tells us more about how, when deployed in these systems, the imaginaries of security are acted on in a self-referential manner, developing a virtual understanding of reality rather than an actual capacity to anticipate putative security threats and criminal trends that would exist beyond it. This particular manner of seeing border mobilities enabled by data is powerful and reigns despite deep organizational, infrastructural and technical problems with how this data has been collected, circulated and analysed. It is important to take these issues seriously because they carry consequences for those who cross borders. Truck drivers, travellers and migrants are questioned and searched (or not inquired into) on the basis of these virtual truths.

Noteworthy conceptual—but also equally important political—consequences ensue when we unpack the "seamless border" political fantasy, since this fantasy sustains border agencies in their legitimation work as they call for ever-larger budgets to fund more automation, more preclearance and more targeting. Undeniably, "the technical side of dataveillance . . . has become associated with the processes of policymaking on border security" (Jeandesboz 2016: 305). In this context, we need to continue investigating how border technologies are imagined, designed, adopted and deployed and raising questions about the accuracy and coherence of the data that they produce and the border decisions that are justified on their basis. Indeed, better objectivity and dependability are frequently mentioned in types of rhetoric that legitimate the recourse to intelligence-led security schemes. In the area of financial policing, Amicelle (2013: 196) has found that "the supposed reliability of financial policing intelligence is regularly highlighted. This premise is particularly prevalent in discourses of legitimation of the multiple measures advocated against terrorism financing."[16] Bringing to light the glitches in the sociotechnical arrangements in bordering and the everyday difficulties experienced by a variety of border control actors when it comes to the production and circulation of data contributes to destabilizing these discourses. It helps us to set our critique of high-level security professionals' "statistical objectivation" claims (Gautron and Monniaux 2016: 130) on firmer grounds, and it gives us additional tools to challenge the current depoliticization in the datafication of bordering and of security endeavours more generally.

Finally, this chapter reflected on the current neglect by studies concerned with borders of the most trenchant work-related features that shape the use of technologies. I suggested that the significance of the contested adoption of technologies by a range of security workers for theorizing the "smartness" of border control cannot be understated. The increased role taken by data in bordering impacts the daily work of officers who respond to this trend in unexpected ways. Technologies are introduced in bordering with the view that they will curtail the disorderliness of discretionary decision-making and transform frontline officers into data-entry workers and mere executants of intelligence-led policing decisions made elsewhere. This truly disrupts officers' everyday work lives. Abstracting borderwork, technologies make border mobilities less concrete and more difficult to seize.

There is no going back to the time of the independent port of entry only loosely connected to overall bordering. Yet as they voice their suspicion about the accuracy of risk-management procedures, as they insist on the effectiveness of their own assessments of drivers and shipments and as they assert their legally recognized discretion, border officers react to their increasing marginalization as decision makers. I argue in the next two chapters that this sense of losing their influence has paved the way for the turn to law enforcement and the enthusiastic adoption of low-tech policing tools in bordering.

Notes

1   Given the importance of the port, the high level of truck traffic and the high numbers of officers and overall employees working at the Windsor port, I state clearly that I have done fieldwork there and spent some time in this region. For anonymity reasons, no interview quotes will be attributed throughout this book to a Windsor port of entry employee.

2 The Peace Bridge (2018), *2017 Traffic Statistics Issued by the Bridge and Tunnel Operators Association*, www.peacebridge.com/index.php/media-room/press-releases-advisories/374-btoa-2017-stats (last consulted 25 Oct. 2018).

3 The ion scan can uncover drug traces on the surface of objects and body parts. It is also commonly used in airports and prisons.

4 See note 7 in Chapter 1.

5 As an indication of the privileging of cargo mobilities, the CBSA intended to inspect less than 1% of trusted trader shipments by 2017: CBSA (2016), *Part III: Departmental Expenditure Plans: Reports on Plans and Priorities*, www.cbsa-asfc.gc.ca/agency-agence/reports-rapports/rpp/2016-2017/report-rapport-eng.html (last modified 5 May 2016; last consulted 28 May 2019).

6 Both Deborah Cowen and Mark Salter have used sewing metaphors to go beyond the traditional representation of the border as a territorial line and offered heuristic conceptual tools illustrating the new spatialities of bordering. For Salter (2012: 738), the image of the suture "better represents this messaging, transition, implication between the inside and the outside" produced by externalized and internalized borders. Choosing the trope of the "seam" borrowed from a policy model proposed by a U.S. Army lieutenant, Cowen (2014: 83) discusses how supply chain security is envisioned by a range of logistics actors as a "space of transition" that "acknowledges the limits of a territorial model" in maritime bordering and the consequences of this model for remodelling the geographies of securitized logistics. In contrast, the notion of a seamless border, discussed in this chapter, is often deployed by border scholars and security professionals alike and concerns its putative expression in data-led bordering.

7 To be clear, there is no primacy of practice over technology design or policy discourse in the study of border control. It is as enlightening to unpack security discourses, political rationalities and techniques of legitimation, to critically examine the design of surveillance systems or to shed light on the complex realities that characterize border control as it is enacted. But generally, the most useful works distinguish between these registers and take time to think about how they are concretely articulated in sociotechnical arrangements.

8 The role of professional socialization in gaining interviewing skills and getting to behavioural "risk indicators" will be explored in Chapter 6.

9 The topic of information access at the frontline was understandably a sensitive one during research. Interviewed officers were of different opinions as to whether they could reveal the type of information to which they have access at the primary inspection line and for research ethics reasons, I did not insist. This hesitation gave me parched data on the topic, but my findings are confirmed by the following documents: Privacy Commissioner of Canada (2006), *Audit of the Personal Information Management Practices of the Canada Border Services Agency*, www.priv.gc.ca/media/1166/cbsa_060620_e.pdf; CBSA (2017), *Info Source: Sources of Federal Government and Employee Information 2017*, www.cbsa.gc.ca/agency-agence/reports-rapports/pia-efvp/atip-aiprp/infosource-eng.html; Eugenia Martin-Ivie v. Canada Border Services Agency (2011), *OHSTC 6*, www.canada.ca/en/occupational-health-and-safety-tribunal-canada/programmes/decisions/2011/ohstc-2011-006.html (all last accessed 13 Sept. 2018).

10 For an instance of the officers' union's strategic use of the media to demand more data access for their members, see S. Bridge and J. Lancaster (2015), Canadian border security: Travellers aren't fully screened, *CBCNews*, 25 May, www.cbc.ca/news/canada/canadian-border-security-most-travellers-aren-t-fully-screened-1.3082268 (last accessed 23 Nov. 2017).

11 CBSA (2017), *Info-Source: Source of Federal Government and Employee Information*, www.cbsa-asfc.gc.ca/agency-agence/reports-rapports/pia-efvp/atip-aiprp/infosource-eng.html (last modified 9 July 2017; last consulted 19 Oct. 2018).

12 See Privacy Commissioner of Canada (2006), idem.

13 See CBSA (2016), *Evaluation of the Canada Border Services Agency Targeting Program*, www.cbsa-asfc.gc.ca/agency-agence/reports-rapports/ae-ve/2016/tp-pc-eng.html?wbdisable=true (last consulted 1 Nov. 2018).

14 CBSA (2018), *Nexus. Updates to Personal Information*, www.cbsa-asfc.gc.ca/prog/nexus/contact-coordonnees-eng.html (last modified 13 May 2016; last consulted 15 Oct. 2018).

15 CBSA (2016), *Evaluation of the Canada Border Services Agency Targeting Program*, www.cbsa-asfc.gc.ca/agency-agence/reports-rapports/ae-ve/2016/tp-pc-eng.html?wbdisable=true (last consulted 18 Nov. 2017).

16 My translation.

References

Amicelle, A. 2013. Les professionnels de la surveillance financière. Le malentendu comme condition de possibilité. *Criminologie* 46 (2):195–219.

Amoore, L. 2013. *The Politics of Possibility: Risk and Security beyond Probability*. Durham, London: Duke University Press.

Andersson, R. 2016. Hardwiring the frontier: The politics of security technology in Europe's "fight against illegal migration." *Security Dialogue* 47 (1):22–39.

Aradau, C. 2015. The signature of security: Big data, anticipation, surveillance. *Radical Philosophy* 191:21–28.

Aradau, C., and T. Blanke. 2015. The (Big) data-security assemblage: Knowledge and critique. *Big Data & Society* July-December:1–12.

———. 2011. Pierre Bourdieu and international relations: Power of practices, practices of power. *International Political Sociology* 5 (3):225–258.

———. 2014. The (in)securitization practices of the three universes of EU border control: Military/Navy-border guards/police-database analysts. *Security Dialogue* 45 (3):209–225.

Boivin, R., and G. Cordeau. 2011. Measuring the impact of police discretion on official crime statistics: A research note. *Police Quarterly* 14 (2):186–203.

Boivin, R., and F. Ouellet. 2014. Space and time variations in crime-recording practices within a large municipal police agency. *International Journal of Police Science and Management* 16 (3):171–183.

Bourne, M., H. Johnson, and D. Lisle. 2015. Laboratizing the border: The production, translation and anticipation of security technologies. *Security Dialogue* 46 (4):307–325.

Broeders, D., and J. Hampshire. 2013. Dreaming of seamless borders: ICTs and the pre-emptive governance of mobility in Europe. *Journal of Ethnic and Migration Studies* 39 (8):1201–1218.

Chan, J., and L. Bennett Moses. 2016. Is big data challenging criminology? *Theoretical Criminology* 20 (1):21–39.

Cowen, D. 2014. *The Deadly Life of Logistics: Mapping Violence in Global Trade*. Minneapolis: University of Minnesota Press.

Davidshofer, S., J. Jeandesboz, and F. Ragazzi. 2016. Technology and security practices. In *International Political Sociology: Transversal Lines*, edited by T. Basaran, D. Bigo and E.-P. Guittet. London: Routledge, 205–206.

Dekkers, T., M. van der Woude, and J. van der Leun. 2016. Exercising discretion in border areas: On the changing social surround and decision field of internal border control in the Netherlands. *International Journal of Migration and Border Studies* 2 (4):382–402.

Dewerpe, A. 1994. *Espion. Une anthropologie historique du secret d'État contemporain*. Paris: Gallimard.

Douglas, M., and A. Wildavsky. 1982. *Risk and Culture: An Essay on the Selection of Technological and Environmental Dangers*. Berkeley: University of California Press.

Ericson, R. V. 2007. Rules in policing: Five perspectives. *Theoretical Criminology* 11 (3): 367–401.

Feldman, G. 2012. *The Migration Apparatus: Security, Labor, and Policymaking in the European Union*. Stanford: Stanford University Press.

Gautron, V., and D. Monniaux. 2016. De la surveillance secrète à la prédiction des risques: Les dérives du fichage dans le champ de la lutte contre le terrorisme. *Archives de politique criminelle* 38:123–135.

Gilboy, J. 1991. Deciding who gets in: Decisionmaking by immigration inspectors. *Law & Society Review* 25 (3):571–600.

Hall, A. 2017. Decisions at the data border: Discretion, discernment and security. *Security Dialogue* 48 (6):488–504.

Heyman, J. 2009. Ports of entry in the 'Homeland Security' era: Inequality of mobility and the securitization of transnational flows. In *International Migration and Human Rights: The Global Repercussions of U.S. Policy*, edited by S. Martínez. Berkeley and Los Angeles: University of California Press, 44–59.

Jeandesboz, J. 2016. Smartening border security in the European Union: An associational inquiry. *Security Dialogue* 47 (4):292–309.

———. 2017. European border policing: EUROSUR, knowledge, calculation. *Global Crime* 18 (3):256–285.

Linhardt, D. 2005. La "question informationnelle" éléments pour une sociologie politique des fichiers de police et de population en Allemagne et en France (années 1970 et 1980). *Déviance et Société* 29 (3):259–272.

Manning, P. 2008. *The Technology of Policing: Crime Mapping, Information Technology, and the Rationality of Crime Control*. New York: New York University Press.

Mawani, R. 2003. The "island of the unclean": Race, colonialism and "Chinese leprosy" in British Columbia, 1891–1924. *Journal of Law, Social Justice and Global Development* 1:1–21.

Mayer-Schöneberger, V., and K. Cukier. 2013. *Big Data: A Revolution That Will Transform How We Live, Work and Think*. London: John Murray.

Nickels, E. L. 2007. A note on the status of discretion in police research. *Journal of Criminal Justice* 35 (5):570–578.

Nolan, B. R. 2013. *Information Sharing and Collaboration in the United States Intelligence Community: An Ethnographic Study of the National Counterterrorism Centre*. PhD dissertation in Sociology. Philadelphia: University of Pennsylvania.

O'Connor, D., and W. de Lint. 2009. Frontier government: The folding of the Canada-US border. *Studies in Social Justice* 3 (1):39–66.

Orlikowski, W. J., and S. V. Scott. 2008. Sociomateriality: Challenging the separation of technology, work and organization. *The Academy of Management Annals* 2 (1):433–474.

Piazza, P. 2009. L'extension des fichiers de sécurité publique. *Hermès, La Revue* 53 (1):67–74.

Salter, M. B. 2012. Theory of the/: The suture and critical border studies. *Geopolitics* 17 (4):734–755.

Sanders, C. B., C. Weston, and N. Schott. 2015. Police innovations, "secret squirrels" and accountability: Empirically studying intelligence-led policing in Canada. *The British Journal of Criminology* 55 (4):711–729.

Sheptycki, J. 2004. Organizational pathologies in police intelligence-systems: Some contributions to the lexicon of intelligence-led policing. *European Journal of Criminology* 1 (3): 307–332.

————. 2017. Liquid modernity and the police métier: Thinking about information flows in police organisation. *Global Crime* 18 (3):286–302.

Tazzioli, M. 2018. Spy, track and archive: The temporality of visibility in Eurosur and Jora. *Security Dialogue* 49 (4):272–288.

Zuboff, S. 1988. *In the Age of the Smart Machine: The Future of Work and Power*. New York: Basic Books.

Chapter 4

Towards a police of the border
The virtualization of borderwork and a disrupted sense of self

Richard scowls; he is sceptical. Targeting is about to become centralized in Ottawa, where yet another layer of decision makers is being added to the patchwork of public and private actors involved in Canadian border control. Richard is not convinced this is such a good idea. He tells me that often targeters have never worked in the kind of port (air, maritime, highway) that processes the type of cargo he encounters every day in his region. Targeters simply do not have a realistic understanding of how decisions to inspect cargo are made in different contexts. It is only after searching countless loads and getting your hands dirty that you know whether a particular type of goods represent a low or a high risk. Targeters do not have that experience and therefore recommend useless inspections that Richard and his colleagues perform reluctantly, feeling that yet another aspect of their hold on decision-making is slipping away:

> You know you can't hold it against them [targeters], they don't know and this is how the department [CBSA] saw fit to change or shift this over, but. . . . At the same time . . . yeah . . . you feel for them I guess. And it's just not the best operation. Right? They keep more and more of that aspect away from us I find.

Richard is computer-literate, like many other officers, yet he laments that the interviewing and searching skills he has developed by examining countless loads, visa holders and drivers over the years are being made increasingly irrelevant by data-led bordering. In the previous two chapters, I have shed light on the conditions that brought about this increasing irrelevance of officers' experiential knowledge. They are now asked to enact risk and compliance recommendations made hundreds of kilometres away from their place of work by people whose skills they are unable to assess. They are expected, first, to accept that transporters have managed their own risks in their truck yards and on the road and, second, to provide exporters and importers with special low-risk treatment in order to ease trade flows. In short, officers have lost their sole charge of the border, and their influence has decreased as they come to share bordering with a growing number of actors in ever-more-complex sociotechnical arrangements. While I studied this in the realm of customs, we know that the trade facilitation paradigm pressures all border actors to enable cargo and human mobilities, whether they are posted in air, land or marine ports of entry. Accordingly, trends towards more automation and the centralization of targeting and decision-making impact all forms of borderwork. These trends emerge in tension with frontline border officers' efforts to maintain their hold on their authority as they witness their historical monopoly on decision-making slipping away.

This tension is closely tied to a more general sentiment expressed by officers: borderwork is slowly losing touch with reality. In this chapter, I pay particular attention to this feeling and what it means for officers' view of themselves as border workers. By doing so, my objective is to assess the effects of the growing immateriality of borderwork on officers' subjectivity. Border transformations progressively make that which is tangible and graspable through one's senses—that is, developing a sense of suspicion by seeing and talking to flesh-and-blood people and interacting with touchable and viewable objects—into secondary sources of knowledge in borderwork.

Border officers have long felt proud of the generous legal leeway that allows them to determine whom to arrest, search and question and what to seize or let inside the country—in short, how to make decisions and act in concrete situations at the border (Gilboy 1991, 1992). Here, I investigate the effects of the "progressive marginalization of the sensible" in borderwork (Sadin 2015: 127) on officers' view of themselves; how they apprehend the border and where it is located; and the role that they play in this transformed social space. Inquiring into these more intangible aspects of the current upheaval in bordering requires us to delve into the deeper experiential and subjective features associated with changing customs and overall bordering.

In particular, the chapter examines anew border officers' long-rehearsed discourse of helplessness in the context of these changes. Now mobilized by officers to critique the multiplication of border control players and the effects of technologies and preclearance in their work, this discourse is also an expression of their disorientation and sense of status subordination following the intensifying intangibility of their daily tasks. The tangible knowledge and sensory skills acquired during their professional socialization now enter into tension with algorithmic forms of knowing the border and with the facilitation logic that aims to speed up cargo flows. Computer-mediated borderwork requires a cognitive leap that not all are willing or able to take. Feeling deskilled and unappreciated for their work, abstract borderwork leaves officers uncertain about the purpose of their job. What is their role now that some of their tasks and responsibilities have been taken away, given to analysts or transferred to the transportation sector and other policing institutions?

These transformations disrupt their established professional identity and provide the foundation for testing novel strategies to affirm their continued significance at the border. I consider here three of these strategies: the first deploys a language that renders the more intuitive aspects of the job "scientific"; the second reframes discretion as a response to complexity in the wake of automation; and the third reinterprets discretion as a symbolic wage— for example, unpaid compensation in the form of pride in one's work, for officers who resist efforts that take decisions away from ports of entry. The chapter concludes by arguing that an increasingly reactive vision of borderwork emerges from these strategies—one that insists on the need to maintain a physical presence at the land border as a last line of defence. These strategies aim to re-establish concreteness in borderwork and to regain professional recognition for border officers and thus function as new "status claims" in frontline bordering (Bosworth and Slade 2014: 171). They set the stage for an altered sense of self to emerge, one of being a "police of the border."

Revisiting officers' "powerlessness"

My first encounter with officers' suspicious attitude towards national border management happened when a supervisor, apologetic, confessed that an officer had blatantly refused to be interviewed for my research, because he claimed I had probably been "sent by Ottawa." Throughout fieldwork, I have been exposed to a distrust—one generally unacknowledged in the literature but nevertheless obvious to border guards—that is based on the idea that the loyalties of the frontline do not lie with national management. Confirming this insight, officers often had qualms about their managers' location in the country's capital. They often complained about Ottawa's lack of appreciation for their work and their local needs. In fact, mentions of "Ottawa" were invariably tainted with a negative connotation. Portrayed as an unreachable realm, Ottawa's symbolic position was illustrated by frequent references to its elevated hierarchical situation through expressions such as "up there," the "powers that be" and "high management."

   In turn, officers then elevated themselves by insisting on (and even joking about) Ottawa's dearth of field experience and operational skills. Many interviewees expressed variations on this theme: "Ottawa, they don't know operations"; "Ottawa, they don't even know what customs is." Sometimes, officers even doubted national management's general know-how. Samuel, quoted in the previous chapter for his modulated risk-analysis method, added, "the expertise is very low up there. . . . They're making big decisions on things that they have little real-life experience with." Chuckling officers were particularly fond of telling the story of a colleague, or themselves, temporarily hired by headquarters on an assignment only to be constantly used as a resource by their Ottawa colleagues eager to obtain information about the daily reality and practices in ports of entry. Others expressed their repeated frustration at not being consulted on the practicality of changes in customs procedures. They often lamented not being appropriately trained to implement new programmes imagined by policymakers; they felt like guinea pigs when it came to new systems created by federal IT services.

That managers are not taken seriously by frontline workers who, in turn, insist that they feel disrespected and unacknowledged by disconnected "higher ups" is hardly news. Nevertheless, the discontent of street-level personnel is particularly significant at the CBSA. In surveys of federal employees, the border agency consistently ranks in the lowest echelon for overall satisfaction at work, along with employees of Correctional Services.[1]

It is useful to take a step back and examine how this growing sense of disconnect is expressed through renewed narratives of powerlessness.[2] These narratives constitute a particularly puzzling piece in the discussions concerned with how border control practices are framed and justified by policing actors. Border guards play a role in unaccountable machines of control that reshape global relations of privilege and exclusion by impacting how, and how fast (or slow), people and things move across borders. Numerous studies document the nefarious impacts of bordering on vulnerable migrants and travellers and speak to the humiliating effects of racial profiling and to the fear that immigration enforcement provokes in many (see, among others, Chacón and Bibler-Coutin 2018; Harrison and Lloyd 2012; Vecchio and Gerard 2015). In the interlude, I also indicated that customs officials' decisions can directly affect transport workers' livelihood and thus have significant disciplinary effects on truck drivers. In this context, how is it that state representatives with influence over peoples' mobility rights still see themselves as helpless? And why should we pay attention to these officers' feeling of being sidelined?

Expanding on these questions, I argue that street-level border officials' sense of helplessness in the context of technological changes, the centralization of decision-making and the multiplication of bordering actors has been instrumental in spurring the shift to a more reactive approach to bordering on the frontline. As reviewed in the next chapter, this narrative has even entered political rhetoric and labour campaigns demanding oppressive policing tools such as firearms. While acknowledging officers' complicity in daily transgressions against human rights and overall dignity in border spaces, I propose that we take this feeling of powerlessness—and its political manifestations—critically but seriously.

Utterances of powerlessness in frontline bordering have been well documented. These narratives sometimes touch on the purported weakness of the state in border spaces. For instance, in Mountz's (2010) study of Canadian immigration officers carried out before the creation of the CBSA, she heard frequent expressions of state vulnerability being repeated in combination with calls for more resources and expertise. A feeling of helplessness also arises when border officers attempt to contain heavier irregular migration flows. Casella Colombeau (2015: 489–490) describes how the *police aux frontières* stationed at the France–Italy border have become "fatalistic" because they are confronted with the "apparent uselessness of their daily work" in the context of EU limitations that rein in internal border controls over migration flows. Similarly, US border and immigration officials have long been exposed to the contradictions between projecting a public image of toughened enforcement towards irregular labour migration and the actual dependence of a range of industries on such migration (Andreas 2009; Heyman 1995). Such helplessness rhetoric can also be turned into what Infantino (2016: 71) refers to as a "bureaucratic strategy of blame avoidance," a valuable discursive resource for border officials in the wake of automation. Kalman (2016: 137) describes how officers use border technologies to their advantage during court proceedings as a way to deny responsibility for decisions to inspect: "Don't blame me," Kalman heard officers say in court, "blame the computer."

Building on these insights, I revisit the issue of border guards' helplessness by locating it in the context described in the previous two chapters. Accordingly, I suggest that this rhetoric points to the effects of a shift in the distribution of the power to decide in bordering. Such power not only refers to designating who and what may come into the country but also concerns decisions regarding what technologies should be acquired, the extent to which transporters will be involved in risk management, who will get to target or what type of decision will be automated. As we have seen, most of these types of decisions are new to bordering, and none of them is taken at the frontline. Here I am particularly attuned to how officers feel alienated from decision-making as a result of these changes.

Interviewing and searching: "the backbone of our job"

What does it mean to do borderwork when goods, importers and people have already been assessed when they show up at the border? Raymond, whom we met in the interlude, offers his perspective once again. Together with preclearance programmes, he believes electronic customs has made his job easier but also more tedious, he reports, because there is a lot less work to do. He estimates that he has lost roughly three-quarters of his daily tasks to automation and redistribution of cargo release between ports of entry since the end of the 1990s. He laughs and continues: "Inside the office, the work has changed. We used to need four people to screw in the light bulb, now we only need one!" This decrease in workload was unexpected. At first, Raymond continues, high management in Ottawa had promoted technologies by arguing that they would free up officers to perform more truck searches. But, as we have seen in the last chapter, this forecast did not become reality; inspections have not increased. I throw him a puzzled look, asking, "So what do you do?" His answer strikes me in its honesty: "We sit around, and we wait for a truck."

In other words, Raymond is bored. Some tasks have been transferred elsewhere; others have been automated completely or partially and are thus completed faster. As a result of these changes, customs officers such as Raymond also experience a growing intangibility in their work. To fully grasp how this experience provides an unaddressed but crucial background to understand the shift to enforcement in frontline border control, we need to start by inquiring into what makes borderwork "concrete."

Most of that sense of concreteness can be found in the sensory and embodied know-how that border officers develop over time. Officers derive a sense of occupational meaning from a range of activities that involve their bodies, senses and speech: asking face-to-face questions, reading body language, learning to catch people in a "lie," detecting nervousness, going through documents and receipts to find discrepancies in a border crosser story, kneeling to examine the underside of a vehicle and knowing where to look. Officers are proud of their ability to assess the credibility of a traveller's account of who they are and what they are doing. Their preferred method for doing so, even for those proficient with data systems, is interviewing. Richard is convinced that "the backbone of our job is that interview and those indicators you see of the client. That is the core of what we do." An experienced officer, Paul also reflects on the strategies he uses to distinguish between "good" and "bad" nervousness during his interviews: specifically, by playing with the line of questioning in order to reduce the nervousness felt by travellers when they approach uniformed security personnel; separating co-drivers for individual interviews; developing "people skills" and not "show up with a menacing face" while keeping a controlled attitude that refrains from triggering unnecessary nervousness. Paul is of the opinion that these embodied and affective dispositions take years to polish.

Paul would probably agree with Salter's (2007: 58) claim that eliciting speech at the border requires rehearsal: "It is this predisposition, this training toward unconditional, uninterrupted, and exhaustive confession of the traveller upon which the technique of listening at the border rely." From this perspective, learning how to interview has not changed much since Gilboy's (1991: 577) observation that airport border officers "chiefly learn how to make decisions by 'working the line.'" At the beginning of their careers, border officers work hard to hone these skills, acquiring them through formal training, exchanging tips with colleagues and trial and error. Slowly, they develop an experience-based know-how that becomes incorporated into what Lahire (2012) refers to as a "patrimony of dispositions" that becomes activated or not according to context; Bigo (2014: 210) has shown the usefulness of this concept for thinking about the shifting and plural practices of security professionals. Together with their great discretion, it is these acquired abilities to elicit revelation, to find that which is concealed and to read people that lies at the core of border guards' view of themselves—or what we can call (following the policing literature) their occupational identity.

An ethos of suspicion or making the intuitive "scientific"

An ethos of suspicion is readily espoused by officers. In fact, their narratives are replete with descriptions of how they differentiate between a border crosser who is "telling the truth" or "lying" to them. But as they are in the midst of new sociotechnical arrangements that marginalize their position in overall bordering, officers can rely on a first strategy to contest how their discretion is played down as merely subjective. By using a more "scientific-sounding" language that attempts to distinguish between truthfulness and falsehood, this strategy points to the emergence of more-"rational" configurations of discretionary bordering practices on the ground. If working the line means adhering to a suspicious occupational culture (Jubany 2017), a central aim of contemporary border interviewing is to have such suspicious sensibility rest on more-methodical approaches. In this sense, while relying on this strategy, officers are actually following more-general bordering trends working towards the standardization of decision-making.

My interviewees spend an important part of their professional socialization practising how to recognize what they call "indicators"—a shortened version of the official CBSA "risk indicators" taught in customs college. What exactly is an "indicator"? Pratt (2009: 468) details and analyses the categories of behaviour viewed by border authorities as constituting indicators: body related (sweating, rapid blinking, dress, alcohol smell), conduct based (fidgeting, avoiding eye contact, tapping fingers nervously on the steering wheel), verbal (tremor in the voice, stuttering), non-physical (bulky shirt as a sign of concealment) and narrative (inconsistencies in answers). These indicators, Pratt writes, are often "intertwined with moralistic and racialized knowledges" (462). Adding to Pratt's findings, my own research suggests that interpretations of what constitutes a useful indicator has long varied among officers. Richard's claim that "everybody kind of puts value into their own indicators differently" led me to consider whether indicators might well represent idiosyncratic understandings of risk and, as suggested by Pratt, whether this makes border decisions vulnerable to being overturned when confronted with evidentiary norms in the criminal justice system.

Although risk indicators can be weak bordering tools, since they give rise to multiple interpretations of that which represents nervousness, falsehood or dangerousness, they nevertheless offer a neutralizing language for the narration of one's suspicions that "something is not right" in ways more likely to be seen as legitimate and unbiased. As seen in the previous chapter, the CBSA is not blind to the significance of discretion in officers' occupational culture or to its contested reliability in decision-making. As a result, border enforcement techniques based on reading travellers' conduct are now taught in a standardized setting, that of customs college, rather than left to port-of-entry-based experiential learning, as they have been in the past. Illustrating this point in the case of police academies, de Lint (1998: 195) suggests that such training develops judgement habits and dispositions that focus on how one can interpret and categorize people and their behaviour. Importantly, while "smart borders" rely on the calculable character of risk (e.g. with algorithms that calculate on the basis of criteria such as nationality and travel itinerary whether someone is to be considered a threat; see Leese 2016), street-level border officers are coached into adopting evaluations of conduct that betray similar efforts towards formalizing the suspicion that arises from face-to-face encounters with travellers, migrants and transport workers. Of course, both of these areas are connected in practice. Hall (2017) has concluded that discretion remains active in the decisions taken in data analysis centres as to who and what is considered to present a risk. Additional research of this kind is needed to understand more fully the interactions in decision-making among risks that are deemed algorithmically calculable, the set of risk indicators acquired throughout border workers' professional socialization with risks readings apprehended through human judgement.

From this perspective, we can better understand the tendency among border officers to rationalize border categorizations and give their own indicators a scientific veneer. The search for untrustworthy border crossers now assumes that their putative fear of getting caught may be perceived in their movements, micro-facial expressions and verbal utterances and that these can be assessed by rendering officer perception less biased and more based on expert knowledge. Accordingly, frontline border authorities' reliance on "indicators" stems from an odd combination of teachings about how to read body language and forms of speech. Some of these lessons are taken from loose reinterpretations of social psychology findings. These involve a more or less essentialist sensitivity to difference—that is, a reading of the varied behaviours displayed by border crossers' from different countries premised on a stereotyped understanding of cultural variety in body language. Officers may learn these lessons and look for "how intent transitions into a visceral mode of anticipation" (Adey 2009: 281) that is coated in expert—yet typecasting—language.

A good example of this trend can be found in a short piece published in the border officers' union magazine by a "deception detection" trainer about "cultural interview training":

> Many years ago, when I first joined Customs, a senior customs officer told me that if people don't look into his eyes when he is questioning them, he automatically becomes suspicious of that person and is sceptical about their truthfulness. We've learned a lot since then. We have a much better understanding of cultural difference. We have research-based analysis that suggests that if eye contact is not made nor maintained, the person being interviewed may not necessarily be dishonest. Cultural interview training, as well as keeping up on more modern and scientifically researched interview techniques, keeps our officers up to date and gives them the ability to recognize *truly deceptive behaviour*.
>
> (my emphasis)[3]

The CBSA attempts to transform officers' "gut feeling" and "sixth sense" into a more formalized expertise through which decisions to search, interrogate and arrest could later be justified if politically called into question or appealed in court proceedings. Yet such expert language is not exclusively "Canadian"; it circulates globally among security personnel and between security organizations. One of my interviewees had been trained by American security professionals in behavioural observation and profiling, a set of techniques inspired by studies of micro-facial expressions to detect emotions and falsehood led by the psychologist Paul Ekman (whose work was the inspiration for the US television show *Lie to Me*). According to this officer, these trainers had themselves been taught by Israeli border control professionals known for their expertise in this regard in the transnational security community. Following these seminars, trainees reintegrate into their workplaces and are invited to share what they have learned, thus offering their own interpretations of these teachings to their colleagues. In short, discretionary powers and experiential know-how are increasingly combined with lay understandings of science that claim to produce objective and actionable facts about human behaviour, a set of knowledge inevitably remodelled in local security communities. This complex assemblage makes officers' decision-making problematic because it may legitimize such decisions as based on objective, science-based criteria taken from the latest psychological research on human behaviour.

An intangible job: living the virtualization of borderwork

Although commonly used in ports of entry, the adoption of a more technical language of risk indicators has not been sufficient to maintain officers' hold on borderwork. The preclearance and technological schemes, as well as pressures to facilitate the crossing of goods described in Chapter 2 and Chapter 3, alter established routines and introduce new modes of intelligibility that morph borderwork into a more disembodied set of tasks. As a result, the importance of familiarity with the borderland's inhabitants and its local economy, the peer-to-peer transmission of know-how through port-of-entry oral culture and the sensory skills developed by border officers over the years are eroding as legitimate bases for making decisions at the border. In turn, border agencies increasingly value more-quantitative and less immediately corporeal forms of knowledge developed through mass data collection, data analysis and detection devices (such as body scanners, X-ray machines, ion scanners).

We have seen in the preceding chapter that bordering is made more obscure by algorithmic and automated ways to "see" border flows through tools such as digital interactive maps and data-derived risk profiles. These are modes of visualization predicated on a more technical rationality that increasingly marginalizes officers' embodied techniques of listening (Salter 2007) and seeing that have long been at the basis of their decision-making. To paraphrase Sadin (2015: 127), computerized borderwork aims to "eradicate the sensible" in bordering—that is, to narrow down officers' flawed but discretionary capacity to deal with ambiguity and to come up with more-variable decisions that pay attention to context and then replace this capacity with forms of analysis that constraint decision via more uniform and data-led measurements of risk. This move away from a sense-based understanding of border crossers' identity and intentions can leave officers feeling deskilled.

At the same time, however, the datafication of bordering also brought about schemes to change border officers' role in tracking these flows. Zuboff (1988: 57, 2013) argues in her classic study of workplace technological trans-formations that "computer-mediated work" carries "pressures for a profound reskilling." Information technologies require reflexive actions that are cogni-tively more demanding, because they "symbolically render events, objects, and processes that become visible, knowable and shareable in a new way" (Zuboff 2015: 76). For instance, the type of modulated targeting theorized by Louise Amoore and its associated malleable understanding of risk reviewed in the previous chapter assumes a shift in frontline officers' cognitive abilities. This shift veers them towards a form of abstract thinking that is sustained by databases and takes them away from sense-based detection abilities. Zuboff (2013: 113–114) reminds us that we seem to have forgotten how this shift "in the nature of the effort from the realm of the body to the realm of thought," this passage to the cognitive work that comes with information technologies, can be "profoundly disorienting and disturbing" for those who experience it. Accordingly, I consider the effects of the shift towards computer-mediated borderwork and the corresponding reduction of officers' role in trade regula-tion on officers' view of their work as revealing that officers experience their work as more tedious and admit feeling increasingly powerless.

"We are used to having it visual, in front of us"

How are these pressures concretely experienced in borderwork? Jacob's vivid story of releasing air cargo manifests from afar illustrates this well. An offi-cer close to retirement who admits that he has considerable difficulty with computers, Jacob started evaluating airport cargo remotely about two years before we met and has yet to see one of those shipments. He speaks of his initial confusion and discomfort: "We found it difficult at the beginning to do this at a distance. We are used to having it visual, in front of us." Jacob is posted in a port of entry in the region where he grew up. He went through his career processing the same set of locally produced commodities and meeting the same truck drivers many times a week for years, some of whom he knows from childhood. Jacob is perplexed by this devaluing of local knowledge in remote decision-making and by the shift from seeing the border as a place anchored in a network of kinship and close social ties to a diffused, extended space of flows. As he remotely recommends the release of shipments for air-ports located far from his own port of entry, these decisions dissociated from their context of enactment fill him with a sense of unreality.

This growing abstractness also affects customs officers who worry about their capacity to enforce national regulations and avoid smuggling, because they are provided with limited information regarding cargo content and the means of transportation. Paul is well trained in the use of customs and border enforcement databases, and yet he articulates a feeling of powerlessness in his work. In the process, he expresses a critique of the market logics that preside over the automation of border control for goods:

> And the department gives little resources to this [implementing regulations]. Because it is proactive at the commercial level, it says: "If I slow down commercial activities with more law enforcement, it harms commerce." (. . .) So there are very few measures that are taken regarding containers. We have verifications to do by computers, but that does not tell us if there is a guy smuggled in with the shipment. That tells us approximately nothing. . . . We see the name of the company that imports, we verify what they give us as information, what the customs broker gives us, so the system releases automatically, a pre-release. It scans, all boxes are checked. But for us, working with this system, if you are not a targeter and you can't access taxation reports, well, the border officer is a bit helpless. (. . .) Nobody, certainly not higher ups, will talk about this.

Others echoed Richard's previous concerns regarding remote targeting. Marie expressed her doubts about the value of delocalized knowledge of cargo and transporters in data-led bordering but also spoke about what this meant for the organization of inspections in her port of entry. She reflected on the fact that while their wide discretion is legally sustained in Canada by their capacity to act on a "reasonable suspicion" (Pratt 2010), it has become more difficult for officers to do so in practice, especially for those working in cargo assessment: "Given that the inspection dock is so full with all kinds of things that have been sent randomly. . . . We don't send [to inspection] many exams recommended by inspectors that say: 'Well I have a doubt on this.'" She adds:

> It was better before. (. . .) There were less referrals from systems, it was more referrals from inspectors. You know, you see the person, you have doubts, you see it on the spot. It was . . . more tangible, whereas now, it is all random or selective. So they don't see the person, they just do random checks. In the end, those are examinations that take up time when we could spend it doing inspections that *we* detect.

In those cases, discretionary decision-making at the border is reconfigured as a moment of confirmation or ratification of decisions made elsewhere.

The intangibility in officers' work routines brought by the virtualization of borderwork has been further increased as some ports have lost their responsibility for electronic declarations processing to other ports—a 2008 policy prompted by cost-cutting measures. The effects of this redistribution of tasks can be observed in some ports found far from urban centres, such as regional airports or small and remote ports of entry. In these ports, officers may clear shipments crossing at ports located hundreds of kilometres away. In contrast, those who have lost their EDI responsibilities to other ports must find something to do with those free work hours. Taken together, these trends reinforce customs officers' separation from the information entering decision-making in border spaces while magnifying their sense that such decisions are increasingly made elsewhere.

These transformations in their work leave officers feeling delegitimized. As they lose some control over bordering processes that are becoming more intangible and less concrete, officers are reluctant to accept without discussion those decisions that are automated or made elsewhere. Yet these officers are not luddites. Like the Dutch border workers studied by Dekkers, van der Woude and van der Leun (2016), my interviewees expressed an "increased use of and belief in intelligence-based and technology-driven decision-making." This is especially true among younger officers. Nevertheless, in the case of Canadian customs officers, that belief is nuanced. On the one hand, customs officers express their unease at having to relinquish the tangibility of concrete visualization and their embodied intelligence of the border. On the other hand, even though many are not opposed to data analyses, they are still looking for renderings of that data that would include qualitative elements, combining computer-based analyses with experiential knowledge of local circumstances—an admittedly difficult feat in a 5000 kilometre-long country with more than 1200 ports of entry. Accordingly, and in contrast to generalizations that assume an enthusiastic embrace of technologies by border agencies, my findings reveal that the experience of computer-mediated borderwork has led many border officers to view automation and the delocalization of decision-making with caution.

Tediousness

A delicate issue emerges from customs officers' accounts of their experience with the virtualization of borderwork: boredom. Boredom has long been an essential characteristic of frontline bordering. Despite profound modifications in their work routines, officers confirmed the repetitive, lonely and monotonous character of booth work already noted by Gilboy (1991) in the case of airport-based US immigration officers. Depending on the length of shifts, customs officers spend between two and four hours alone at the primary inspection booth in one-hour-long segments. Thomas, a younger officer, says, "For sure, when it is your 50th truck driver who tells you: "Hey! Beautiful day," it gets boring. . . . It seems stupid, but an hour spent asking the same questions, that can be long. I don't know how they do it at the airport, they do it four hours straight." Notwithstanding electronic declarations, booth work remains labour-intensive because it requires that questioning, reviewing of paperwork and decision-making be completed in about 30-seconds.

Being bored can also serve as a synonym for being idle. While idleness might be unheard of in the case of border guards working in busy international airports, it is part of everyday work in land ports of entry, especially in customs sections of ports who have lost the responsibility for electronic declaration evaluations to other ports. Those facing the removal of some of their prerogatives and related tasks share their frustration at being unoccupied for long stretches of time. While it varied from port to port, this inactivity appears to be one of the most tangible effects of a reduced workload due to automation and preclearance. Phillips (2016: 581) argues in his study of boredom among police officers that having nothing to do may lead someone to make ill use of their time or experience "occupational stress and job dissatisfaction." Phillip found police officers use their discretion to fill downtime with other policing activities such as patrolling. Customs officers do not have this luxury. Confined to their port of entry, much of the activities that previously relied on their discretion have been eliminated or moved elsewhere. Earlier, I cited Raymond saying that as a result of many of his administrative duties being reduced, he and his colleagues "sit and wait for a truck." For my part, I saw officers in another port checking Facebook pages or sitting in the secondary inspection area, chatting and waiting for the odd truck to be sent for inspection. Arthur, an experienced officer, also told me, "So we do a lot less now. It's . . . actually boring sometimes. It's sad in a way that they took away a lot of work because you have a lot of downtime." He even confided that he now takes time to drive a few kilometres during his breaks to buy coffee at a local fast food establishment.

Critical border studies have been interested in examining what type of sociotechnical arrangements are created by data-led bordering, especially unpacking the rationalities involved in the creation of these arrangements. So far, I have pushed this type of inquiry into two new directions. First, I showed in the previous chapter that these efforts have transformed the actual tasks of bordering in unexpected ways, prompting impediments to the circulation of data in bordering. Second, I explored in this chapter how customs at a distance changes the affective experience of borderwork. It brings about an immateriality to an occupation that used to be defined by the capacity to physically assess travellers and goods. Taken together, the feeling of powerlessness, the sense of psychological dislocation brought on by new technologies and the occasional sense of boredom speak to the more intangible effects of disembodied borderwork. As I listened to officers trying to pin down the abstract character of their work and what this meant for them, it was difficult to shake the impression of meaninglessness that emerged from these narratives. The experience of customs at a distance could lead to a potential disengagement of border officers at the frontline. It probably does in some cases. But this is not the most significant reaction elicited in officers confronting this new state of affairs. Ultimately, bordering at a distance is accompanied by the need to redefine the occupational identity of frontline personnel; officers are in search of new ways of making sense of bordering and of their place in it.

Towards a police of the border

The professional identity of border officers has traditionally been intertwined with their discretion and a decisional scope to inspect, search, question and arrest wider than that afforded to all other street-level policing professionals in liberal democracies. As bordering becomes more abstract, this sense of professional identity afforded by discretion is shaken to its core. This is significant because how officers perceive how much discretion they are afforded by law and policy and by organizational practice impacts how they enact the border. In this section, I am less interested in producing a socio-legal analysis of how discretion is modified at the border as a result of the growing virtualization of borderwork and more interested in looking at the sociological consequences of these modifications for borderwork and how officers create professional identities. In this sense, after having reviewed earlier how officers make use of a pseudoscientific language in speaking to how they distinguish truth from falsehood, I examine two last strategies to which officers have recourse to keep their discretion alive. First, a more personalized discretion has come to present a response to complexity in customs work, a response that returns to a conception favouring officers' idiosyncratic assessments of people and goods. Second, I pay attention to how discretion has acted and still acts as a social wage. Finally, I examine how the experience of powerlessness at the border is accompanied by an emerging reactivity that ushers in a new trope of the border officer, henceforth associated with law enforcement.

Discretion as a response to complexity

In the area of immigration control, Sklansky (2012) tells us that border and immigration agencies started out as organizations with administrative law powers. However, in contemporary US border control, he observes the rise of an "ad hoc instrumentalism": "a manner of thinking about law and legal institutions that downplays concerns about consistency and places little stock in formal legal categories, but instead sees legal rules and legal procedures simply as interchangeable tools" (2012: 161). As underscored by Sklansky, this instrumentalist vision of the law raises "some important and underappreciated issues of accountability" (161). Here, I am interested in how this consideration of rules and regulations as interchangeable tools is illuminated in the case of Canadian customs by a peculiar situation. Following automation, there is a growing complexity in those decisions left to customs officers; this complexity bears significant effects on how officers make sense of their work.

Despite the loss of officers' monopoly over decision-making in customs release and border-policing decisions, the need for discretion has not been eliminated in customs matters. The transition to a technologized border control is tied up with the emergence of complex customs tasks. In fact, the partial automation of customs and risk management leaves out more-difficult cases that cannot be processed automatically. These cases necessitate a scope of technical, regulatory and quasi-legal knowledge that is difficult to assimilate. D-memos, those thick volumes of customs rules, make up thousands of regulations and directives that are applicable to imports to Canada. Officers also need to become familiar with parts of the international harmonized system—a system under the responsibility of the World Customs Organization, adapted for each country and outlining more than 10,000 codes that classify goods for taxation purposes.

The breadth of knowledge required from customs officers is vast and often changes: rules are added, removed or modified as a result of efforts to, for instance, facilitate trade or protect the environment and a particular agricultural sector. The resulting complexity is staggering and inaugurates the return to more idiosyncratic understandings of "indicators" and more personal uses of discretion. While preclearance, automation and the use of electronic declarations reduce the necessity for officers to review low-risk shipments, the need to cope with regulatory intricacies presents the possibility of metamorphosing the discretion of customs officers into a complexity-reduction strategy. Marie offers one explanation for this transition:

MARIE: For sure before . . . How would I say? I think we had more powers because we had the regulations in d-memos and we followed them. You know, we went by the type of commodity. There were laws and we applied them. (. . .) Today there are so many programmes that: OK, this company, you need to remember that it is a member of this programme, while this other one belongs to that other programme. Which ends up being not easy to follow. (. . .) So it does not make everyone all compliant and uniform. Before, it was more compliant and uniform. Today, well you make a decision with your client but the other officer beside you can make another decision (. . .)

KARINE: So it was not like that before, when you first started?

M: Well before, we started with the goods. Take trees for instance. We went to see in our d-memos, it was clear. Tree fell under the scope of Environment Canada, so you had to have this and that document. It was simple. Today, you have trees, but you also have the company. You check the company, well it's true, it is transporting trees, but it is also a member of this programme so it does not need to give x permit for the department. So it is so complicated, it doesn't even make sense!

So this is why it is confusing. The young ones [rookie officers], they try to ask us questions, we explain but it is not clear. So they ask another officer, and it won't be the same explanation. I find the change is going from people with experience and knowledge to being more of a generalist. It is not specific anymore, it is not specialized anymore. (. . .) So experience and knowledge are going away. The decisions we take are more personal, more individual.

Hawkins (1992: 12) suggests that discretion is "where the tensions, dilemmas, and sometimes contradictions embodied in the law are worked out in practice." What appears difficult in the cases described by Marie is how decisions must take into account how different regulations (relative to law) and programmes (relative to policy) should interact in concrete cases. Studies of police discretion suggest an answer to this conundrum: an abundance of rules makes it possible to pick and choose those likely to support previously made decisions in routinized accounts elaborated after the fact (Ericson and Haggerty 1997: 347). In other words, the sheer number of rules gives one flexibility to choose among them to justify decisions. In this sense, discretionary decisions would be legitimized through a set of "presentational rules" used post hoc (Smith and Gray 1985: 442; see also Dubois (2016) for a similar argument in the case of welfare street-level decision makers).

However, examining officers' discourse of discretion as a response to complexity speaks to a real problem: officers face a dearth of administrative tools to help them negotiate the contradictions in policy-related programmes that respond to a trade facilitation logic (such as preclearance and trusted trader border initiatives), and the myriad of national regulations over imports leaves officers doubtful about the legitimacy of their decisions and mindful of the lack of consistency in decision-making. Faced with such difficulties in weighting contradictory rules and policies against one another, officers developed a more individualized decision-making process for those cases too complex for risk-management technologies to handle.

Discretion as social wage

Discretion has been studied as a defining characteristic of all "street-level" bureaucratic work (Lipsky 2010), including visa and immigration offices (Infantino 2010), where the authority to decide on a wide range of everyday matters compensates for the clerical and uneventful nature of low-level frontline work. Writings on border control may not have fully taken into account the mundane, repetitive character of frontline borderwork and the experience, in some cases, of tediousness produced by the introduction of technologies. We can recall that there is little room given to discretion in low-risk cases as automation, preclearance and risk management schemes increasingly handle these scenarios.

Yet this feeling of tediousness helps make sense of customs officers' attachment to their discretionary powers. As mentioned earlier, discretion plays a particular role in border officers' self-perception. The assurance of autonomy has traditionally characterized border officers' occupational identity. However, commercial officers are losing sway over a wide range of border-policing decisions and over a significant part of the customs release process. This new context indicates a significant shift in how they conceive the purpose of their work and view themselves as security professionals.

As I listened to officers speaking about their work and power to decide, I became acquainted with the tensions and contradictions in officers' feelings with regard to their grasp on the border. If they commented on their influence over the border being diminished, they simultaneously insisted that they were the ones that had the last word on who and what can get into the country. This was an iteration repeated so many times (a variation on "ultimately, we are the ones who decide") that I came to see it more as a formulaic repetition than as an accurate depiction of the reality in ports of entry. In the words of Zuboff (1988: 248), such "ritualistic phrases" in the context of the technologization of a workplace are statements that serve to indicate both what workers think their work should be about (i.e. that they should be the main actors in border decision-making) and the fact that they know this is no longer a reality.

This is why I suggest that discretion in the commercial sections of ports of entry is becoming less a central feature of frontline borderwork than a "social wage" that customs officers continue to invoke to shelter themselves from organizational instability. Following Paap (2006), a "social wage" refers to a symbolic acknowledgement of someone's work through non-monetary advantages specific to an occupation, such as social status and discretionary power. This concept might be unfamiliar to students of borders given that it emerges out of the sociology of work. Paap (2006: 9) argues, in her ethnography of how American construction workers cope within a struggling industry with little union protections, that labour processes cannot be studied separate from "the social performances of workers' various identities." She suggests that although their salaries and working conditions are threatened, construction workers still find payment in symbolic advantages pertaining to their occupation—such as forms of domination emphasizing whiteness and hegemonic masculinity in the workplace (26). Paap's interesting insight applied to uses of discretion in borderwork sheds light on how officers can resort to symbolic rewards to maintain self-worth and protect their influence at the border.

In interviews, officers defensively invoked their formal discretionary powers; they insisted that despite preclearance programmes, intelligence-led policing schemes and automatically generated recommendations, they are the ones left with the ultimate moment of decision in the booth. Their pride in this aspect of their work—relying on their judgement, following up on

their "doubts" or proceeding to negotiated arrangements with local border crossers—confirms the continuing significance of discretion in customs
officers' view of themselves. However, how interviewees rationalized the intu-
itions and practical knowledge that enter their decisions tells only part of the
story. What also illuminates officers' narratives are the specifics of the institutional work environment in which they face a loss of clout at the border.

Despite institutional pressures for officers to reduce their discretionary
powers to uphold risk-management analyses and refer to data collection systems, officers continue to cling onto these powers, which for them define the
essence of their trade and for many continue to be seen as a more effective
border policing strategy. I suggest it is no coincidence that in one particular
port that had lost its EDI responsibilities, officers had heated debates about
whether they should "remove FAST cards" (preclearance cards) when truck
drivers were found in noncompliance—generally for smuggling the odd bottle
of alcohol or carton of cigarettes. Here, a major topic of discussion among
officers concerned their discretionary authority to confiscate cards that provided access to a risk-management programme, which, together with the loss
of EDI, had done away with much of the decision-making powers that officers
previously enjoyed. An officer at this port told me an officer's job was not to
collect taxes but to "keep people honest" and "uphold" the FAST programme
by taking away such cards. Another officer at another port commented that a
low-risk status could not be kept under these circumstances, thus effectively
converting a disregard for customs-related regulations into a security issue.[4]
What became clear to me in this port is how commercial officers' discretionary power increasingly stood for a social wage in a workplace that had effectively amputated everyday decision-making at the border of much of what
used to be its discretionary component.

Conclusion: becoming vigilant? Borderwork as reactive work

If officers attempt to maintain their occupational identity by invoking their
extended legal powers as a symbolic compensation for their loss of discretion,
they also increasingly view themselves as part of a reserve army protecting the
border. Interestingly, this topic emerged particularly from my conversations
with officers when boredom was mentioned. In such cases, officers followed
their comments by emphasizing their increased ability to quickly respond
to security emergencies. After telling me how much the recent technological, organizational and regulatory changes in their port's division of labour
diminished their influence on border decisions and the amount of work that
they were both required and capable of accomplishing, some officers spoke
of their capacity to be present and responsive at a moment's notice in times
of security emergencies. They insisted that their work was becoming more
and more about emergency response, "reaction" and enforcement. In a telling

instance of this narrative of borderwork as reactive, Raymond reflects on what he sees as officers' newly acquired capacity for quick reaction:

> Our truck exams have not gone up and we streamlined the movement of people and goods in the country. Everything has been streamlined. I think what has saved jobs and what has gotten people hired was the 9/11 threat and the enforcement part of the job and the [information] gathering part of the job has caused. . . . Not caused, that's not the word I'm looking for . . . has made Ottawa realize that we can't run at barebones. Because we never know when something could happen in the world. So we have to have our borders manned [*sic*] (. . .)
>
> That's the point that we're at. But, because of 9/11 and the constant threat that something could happen anytime in the world, . . . we're always going to be a potential target. You have to have the staff on. So, we've become. . . . We went from, I believe, an action job, because of all the documents we had to do, to more of a reaction job. And when you are in a reaction position, it's you know, a layman may say: "Ah, you guys all sit around and do nothing." Well, yeah, we do. But that's the nature of the job. But when stuff happens, you know [*he snaps his fingers*] at a moment's notice, we have to be ready. And you have to assume that anything can happen at a moment's notice.

For these officers, their work now depends on their ability to remain in a constant state of readiness. Perhaps there is an element of legitimating rhetoric in support of these explanations given by officers; after all, their livelihood depends on being acknowledged as significant security actors at a time when their influence in border policing is waning. But officers' reflections also announce a notable change in their occupational culture. The trend towards removing parts of the decision-making process from ports of entry undermines the traditional professional identity of customs, which was historically rooted in their assurance of broad discretion. These powers required the maintenance of face-to-face interactions, the significance of which is now reduced in customs compliance. In contrast, frontline customs officers now adopt an approach to their occupation that alters their identification with some of their traditional prerogatives and modifies how they assert their worth as security professionals. This transformation in self-representation is noteworthy. The interviewed officers were in the process of redefining their occupation as one of constant vigilance. Are we witnessing the emergence of officers who define themselves less by their ability to use discretion and more by their preparedness—their capacity to maintain themselves in a responsive position—as a "police of the border"? In this sense, a border officer is in the process of becoming a less busy but more patient and more alert policing actor. At the intersection of automation, the displacement of risk management operations and the partial devolution of border compliance to the industry lies a shifting conception of officers' function.

Acknowledgements

Parts of this chapter are excerpts from the following article:

Côté-Boucher, K (2016). The paradox of discretion, *British Journal of Criminology*, 56 (1): 49–57, reprinted by permission of Oxford University Press.

With many thanks to Oxford University Press.

Notes

1 Treasury Board of Canada, *2017 Public Service Employee Survey*, www.tbs-sct.gc.ca/pses-saff/ 2017-2/results-resultats/bd-pm/index-eng.aspx (last consulted on 29 Nov. 2018).
2 I thank Alison Mountz for pushing me to think further about this discourse of powerlessness.
3 D. Brown (2008), You have 30 seconds, *Customs Excise Union Douanes Accise Magazine*, Winter.
4 According to a CBSA official working at headquarters, FAST cards are seldom removed from truck drivers on a sole noncompliance matter. Current border authorities' efforts at increasing participation in trusted trader programmes probably explain this unwillingness to be rigid about programme requirements. If it is the case, then officers who recommend the suspension from the programme are likely to feel frustrated when they see a truck driver cross again with the same card.

References

Adey, P. 2009. Facing airport security: Affect, biopolitics, and the preemptive securitisation of the mobile body. *Environment and Planning D: Society and Space* 27 (2):274–295.
Andreas, P. 2009. *Border Games: Policing the U.S.-Mexico Divide (Second edition)*. Ithaca, London: Cornell University Press.
Bigo, D. 2014. The (in)securitization practices of the three universes of EU border control: Military/Navy-border guards/police-database analysts. *Security Dialogue* 45 (3):209–225.
Bosworth, M., and G. Slade. 2014. In search of recognition: Gender and staff-detainee relations in a British immigration removal centre. *Punishment & Society* 16 (2):169–186.
Casella Colombeau, S. 2015. Policing the internal Schengen borders: Managing the double bind between free movement and migration control. *Policing and Society* 27 (5):480–493.
Chacón, J., and S. Bibler-Coutin. 2018. Racialization through enforcement. In *Race, Criminal Justice, and Migration Control*, edited by M. Bosworth, A. Parmar and Y. Vásquez. Oxford: Oxford University Press, 159–175.
Dekkers, T., M. van der Woude, and J. van der Leun. 2016. Exercising discretion in border areas: On the changing social surround and decision field of internal border control in the Netherlands. *International Journal of Migration and Border Studies* 2 (4):382–402.
de Lint, W. 1998. Regulating autonomy: Police discretion as a problem for training. *Canadian Journal of Criminology* 40 (3):277–304.
Dubois, V. 2016. *The Bureaucrat and the Poor: Encounters in French Welfare Offices*. London: Routledge.
Ericson, R. V., and K. D. Haggerty. 1997. *Policing the Risk Society*. Toronto: University of Toronto Press.
Gilboy, J. 1991. Deciding who gets in: Decisionmaking by immigration inspectors. *Law & Society Review* 25 (3):571–600.

———. 1992. Penetrability of administrative systems: Political "casework" and immigration inspections. *Law & Society Review* 26 (2):273–314.

Hall, A. 2017. Decisions at the data border: Discretion, discernment and security. *Security Dialogue* 48 (6):488–504.

Harrison, J. L., and S. E. Lloyd. 2012. Illegality at work: Deportability and the productive new era of immigration enforcement. *Antipode* 44 (2):365–385.

Hawkins, K. 1992. The uses of legal discretion: Perspectives from law and social sciences. In *The Uses of Discretion*, edited by K. Hawkins. Oxford: Oxford University Press, 11–46.

Heyman, J. McC. 1995. Putting power in the anthropology of bureaucracy: The immigration and naturalization service at the Mexico-United States border. *Current Anthropology* 36 (2):261–287.

Infantino, F. 2010. La frontière au guichet: Politiques et pratiques des visas Schengen à l'ambassade et au consulat d'Italie au Maroc. *Champ pénal/Penal Field*, http://champpenal.revues.org/7864

———. 2016. *Outsourcing Border Control: Politics and Practice of Contracted Visa Policy in Morocco*. London: Palgrave MacMillan.

Jubany, O. 2017. *Screening Asylum in a Culture of Disbelief: Truth, Denials and Skeptical Borders*. London: Palgrave Macmillan.

Kalman, I. 2016. Framing Borders: Indigenous Difference at the Canada/US Border, PhD thesis in Anthropology, McGill University, Montreal.

Lahire, B. 2012. *Monde pluriel: Penser l'unité des sciences sociales*. Paris: Seuil.

Leese, M. 2016. Exploring the security/facilitation nexus: Foucault at the "smart" border. *Global Society* 30 (3):412–429.

Lipsky, M. 2010. *Street-Level Bureaucracy: Dilemmas of the Individual in Public Services (30th anniversary expanded edition)*. New York: Russell Sage Foundation.

Mountz, A. 2010. *Seeking Asylum: Human Smuggling and Bureaucracy at the Border*. Minneapolis: University of Minnesota Press.

Paap, K. 2006. *Working Construction: Why Working-Class Men Put Themselves-and the Labor Movement-in Harm's Way*. Ithaca: Cornell University Press.

Phillips, S. W. 2016. Police discretion and boredom: What officers do when there is nothing to do. *Journal of Contemporary Ethnography* 45 (5):580–601.

Pratt, A. 2010. Between a hunch and a hard place: Making suspicion reasonable at the Canadian border. *Social & Legal Studies* 19 (4):461–480.

Sadin, E. 2015. *La vie algorithmique. Critique de la raison numérique*. Paris: Éditions L'échappée.

Salter, M. 2007. Governmentalities of an airport: Heterotopia and confession. *International Political Sociology* 1 (1):49–66.

Sklansky, D. A. 2012. Crime, immigration, and ad hoc instrumentalism. *New Criminal Law Review: An International and Interdisciplinary Journal* 15 (2):157–223.

Smith, D., and J. Gray. 1985. *Police and People in London. Vol. 4*. Edited by P. S. Institute. Aldershot: Gower.

Vecchio, F., and A. Gerard. 2015. Surviving the politics of illegality. In *The Routledge Handbook on Crime and International Migration*, edited by S. Pickering and J. Ham. Milton Park: Routledge, 179–192.

Zuboff, S. 1988. *In the Age of the Smart Machine: The Future of Work and Power*. New York: Basic Books.

———. 2013. Computer-mediated work. In *Sociology of Work: An Encyclopedia*, edited by V. Smith. Thousand Oaks, CA: Sage, 113–117.

———. 2015. Big other: Surveillance capitalism and the prospects of an information civilization. *Journal of Information Technology* 30 (1):75–89.

Chapter 5

Gendered border politics

"Manning" the frontline, getting the gun

"The firearm is definitely one of the biggest changes . . . excuse me . . . *the* biggest change within the department in the time that I've been here." By now, you know Richard. Richard is not that different from many of his colleagues; he is proficient with databases and finds them quite useful. As seen in the previous chapter, he also thinks that interviewing "is the backbone of his job," a conviction that comes from considerable time spent at the traffic section doing immigration work before he started "working commercial." But what makes Richard stand out is his explicit and total enthusiasm for arming. While many officers I spoke to welcomed arming, Richard was the fiercest defender of the gun. He loved talking about guns. Richard was convinced that he needed to be armed because guns protected him and his coworkers. Guns were necessary for border enforcement. Guns completely transformed his work like nothing else before. As he expanded on the wonders of the gun, I listened to Richard with growing amazement. He had experienced the fusion of immigration and traffic divisions under the auspices of the new CBSA in 2003, seen the introduction of trusted trader programmes and pre-clearance cards and witnessed the increased importance of targeting in border decisions. At the time of our interview, Richard could see how the slow integration of customs and risk data analyses had already begun to alter his job in fundamental ways. Despite all of this, the change that struck him the most since he had taken his first steps as a border officer was the firearm. His insistence left me utterly confused. You see, at the time of our conversation, Richard was not armed.

Having found little mention in the border and security scholarship of this low-tech policing tool, I entered fieldwork with no expectations regarding arming. My interview schedule did not contain any question about firearms; I had completely neglected to consider the role of guns in borderwork. Despite my lack of interest in firearms and generally without prompting, officers could not stop talking about guns: the gun they carried or refused to carry, the gun they wish were trained for, the gun that changed everything. I was surprised to discover that officers considered the gun as meaningful as the technological changes discussed in the preceding chapters. What also astonished me was the fact that the significance that officers gave to firearms was not reflected in their everyday routines. There was an apparent disconnect between this insistence and how they described the largely administrative character of their work.

Why did so many border officers praise arming, even when, in many cases, they themselves were not armed, refused to be armed or could not be armed (for health reasons or because they were close to retirement age and were therefore considered unfit for gun training)? Why give such weight to a piece of equipment that most interviewees were not yet trained to carry? So far, I have suggested that we take seriously the decline of border officers' traditional hold on the border and that we pay attention to the impact that this had on how officers view themselves. As bordering is made increasingly intangible by the virtualization of decision-making and the multiplication of policing actors, firearms provide a sense of concreteness but also of renewed strength and command. Accordingly, this chapter treats firearms as low-tech devices that alter not only frontline bordering practices but also the symbolic nature of bordering.[1]

Against the backdrop of the social demotion of officers, I argue that arming is part of what Connell (2005: 39) refers to as a "project of masculinity," which brings into bordering the more conventional understandings of manhood associated with guns. In Canada, the officers' response to their demotion in status and authority has come to rely on one of hegemonic masculinity's most traditional and obvious symbols (Connell 2005: 212): the gun. This is significant because these legitimate means of violence (when employed by agents of the state) are embedded with potent gendered meanings. If the soldier has long been understood as embodying the virile nation (Cowen 2008), armed police and security officers are also closely associated. Yet the gun that preoccupies me is not the gun fired in war zones nor the one carried by the police in urban settings. In contrast, the gun we are considering here is actually found in a particular kind of socio-legal and political space: the land border.

As technical know-how is increasingly brought into border control, deploying forms of domination associated with the high-tech world and the knowledge economy, the firearm provides a different mode of legitimation for frontline borderwork. This legitimation has less to do with controlling at a distance the unimpeded flows of people, goods and money and more to do with reframing the border as a last line of defence to be protected against "bad guys" through sheer strength and firepower. To understand how borderwork as practice is inscribed in global relations of domination and subordination that mobilize a variety of means of control, we also need to examine how distinct bordering masculinities are emerging and coexisting in border spaces.

The story I tell in the following pages starts with how officers have come to adopt a gendered take on the recent history of bordering in Canada—citing not the computer but the firearm as an emblem of the transition that took them from a feminized past of bordering made of administration and taxation to a present of security and law enforcement. Particularly interested in the gendered representational labour involved in remaking officers into a "police of the border," I examine how this labour relies on what I term an *enforcement narrative*—one that emphasizes the investigative, oppressive and putatively dangerous aspects of officers' work over the administrative. By recasting as feminine the customs work and ambassadorial attitude that they argue was formerly required of them officers promote a view of the securitization of borders that is soaked in physicality and, at times, machismo.

Studying the enforcement narrative helps us appreciate how a small yet deadly weapon came to be the self-ascribed sign of worth for frontline officers struggling to maintain their grip on the border. In this sense, the firearm is not only a gendered narrative device favoured by officers espousing a policing sensibility. A weapon that has historically safeguarded state domination at home and abroad, the firearm also serves as a formidable emblematic resource for unionized border officers in their efforts to protect, maintain and improve their position. Through union campaigning, Canadian border officers have also claimed one of the most traditional tools of masculinist state violence for their own use.

In discussions of how frontline border workers carry out their work through discretion and their role in border policy implementation, we have neglected to consider how they collectively weigh in on the security agenda. If sociologists of policing have long recognized that the police are "street-corner politicians" (Muir 1977) and have studied the role of unions in policing, few works concerned with border control fully grasp the theoretical and empirical significance of the struggles of security bureaucrats, their impact on the definition and selection of border control and security objectives and the subsequent redirection of resource allocation to their benefit. Following Didier Bigo (see, among others, 2008), who aptly demonstrates how competition shapes the (in)security field, I further show that gender is an inescapable aspect of that rivalry. As an illustration of this argument, the final sections of this chapter present the unfolding of a political battle waged between border guards, a border agency and federal politicians. This battle covered the first decade of this century, and its effects are still felt today. The case of Canadian border officers' arming sheds light on how border politics are also gendered politics.

On the gendered politics of bordering

Before we get back to Richard, Nathan, Paul and their colleagues, I will explain the feminist approach to bordering that I take in this chapter. What happens when we look at the politics of bordering from a gender perspective? This is a fascinating question yet one that is often only alluded to by border scholars who generally neglect this aspect. The unending wars on terrorism and on undocumented migrants expose gender dynamics that are too often absent from our analyses (Hunt and Rygiel 2006; Pickering and Cochrane 2013). There seems to be a reluctance to inquire into bordering as a gendered project but also into how the agencies responsible for border control are currently restructured by gendered politics. Acker (1992: 568) argued in her classic articles published almost three decades ago that "Understanding how the appearance of gender neutrality is maintained in the face of overwhelming evidence of gendered structures is an important part of analysing gendered institutions." Of particular interest as we study arming at the border is Acker's (1990: 140) suggestion that we consider how masculinity becomes a "product of organizational processes and pressures."

Security and border organizations present a textbook case illustrative of Acker's insight. Young (2003: 2), in her essay on the logic of masculinist protection, brings our attention to security as a gendered endeavour:

> Viewing issues of war and security through a gender lens, I suggest, means seeing how a certain logic of gendered meanings and images helps organize the way people interpret events and circumstances, along with the positions and possibilities for action within them, and sometimes provides some rationale for action.

The politics embedded in the possibility to wield violence, assert state power and exert multiple forms of masculine domination (from datafication as male expertise to deploying the military in border zones) are becoming increasingly preponderant in bordering. This is recognized by Baird (2017: 199), who in a study of border security fairs—where the weapons and technologies that are used by border workers are sold and bought—suggests that border control is now a business where "the dominance of masculinities" shapes how "security knowledge is embodied." In this section, I mobilize conceptual tools that will help us reflect on how this dominance is asserted anew through firearms in a context where border officers rely on an enforcement narrative to reassert their place in contemporary border control. The symbolic worldview of border workers appears saturated with changing gendered meanings that remain open to investigation.[2]

At the last line of defence

In this chapter, I see armed bordering as a straight channel for what Brown (1995: 167) calls "the masculinism of the state"—that is, "features of the state that signify, enact, sustain, and represent masculine power as a form of dominance." States have long allowed overwhelmingly male actors to exert such dominance at borders with limited legal checks (Salter 2008). Recently, front-line border officers in Canada and elsewhere have seen such powers transform as borders have been extended beyond and inside geopolitical lines. As a result, as we have seen in previous chapters, their capacity to decide has been modified and partly transferred to a range of actors spread through discretionary chains (van der Woude 2017) that extend beyond the port of entry. This has also been seen in other countries among different types of frontline borderwork, including in the case of UK immigration prison staff, where status and job insecurity and limited decision-making power generate "considerable levels of ontological insecurity" (Bosworth and Slade 2014: 179). Frontline border workers in ports of entry, offices and immigration detention centres in many countries see their effective authority shrinking.

It is in this context that in both Canada and the US, armed and often white men[3] are currently populating the space of the land border. Researchers would be well served if we made sense of that fact and the part it plays in the localized mobilizations of firearms and military weapons in borderlands—especially as firearms are carried there by armed personnel and civilians drilled with military or police training. In the case of the militarization of the US border, "violence, not security objectives, guides border enforcement strategies . . . [which have] centered on the development of a militarized logic and a strategic plan for enforcement that emphasizes pain, suffering, and trauma as deterrents to undocumented migration" (Slack et al. 2016: 8). Both state and nonstate actors are involved in the coercive mixture that makes up border control at the US–Mexico border; among them are the Minutemen, a volunteer militia of former soldiers who task themselves with the armed defence of the border (Shapira 2013). In contrast, the Canadian case speaks less to a process of militarization than to a *programme*—in the sense given to the term by Foucault—that designs the border as a space in need of increased policing. Still, in both the Canadian and the US instances, arming is closely associated with gendered visions where the land border would require the shielding presence of armed men.

Borders are now seen in many countries to be too porous to flows of people and contraband. Border officers know this and, as we shall see later, exploit this anxiety to great effect. Paying attention to officers' call to arms therefore also requires investigating the gendered representations in depictions of the defensive role of the state at its borders—particularly when this call promises to bring about a strong, vigilant and armed presence at borderlines in order to stifle some of these flows. In this case, arming enables a particular unfolding of the masculine politics of protection where bordering appears less dependent on technological and distantiated security and more reliant on law enforcement activities that require staffing the border.

A weapon against social demotion

If the stage on which the drama of the gun is being palyed enacts the land border as a "manned" line of defence, the backdrop for this play is a gendered labour politics where the gun becomes a symbol restorative of officers' lost clout. The introduction of firearms in Canadian border control is therefore closely connected to perceptions of social status, themselves shaped by the changing registers of distinction characteristic of security and bordering practices.

It is no secret that guns promote empowerment through the threat of violence and lethality, but they also constitute a strong "marker of identity" (Cukier and Sheptycki 2012). In this sense, works on the "perceived meaning of guns" (Mencken and Froese 2017: 2) for US civilians offer an apt counterpoint to illuminate why and how border officers embraced firearms; gun owners "derive self-esteem" and "find guns morally and emotionally restorative." Particularly telling for our case is Mencken and Froese's observation that legislating against firearms can be taken as "an attack on [gun owners'] masculinity, independence, and moral identity." Similarly, and as developed later on at greater length, the prior refusal by the Canadian state at the beginning of the 2000s to grant the gun and thus acknowledge officers' desire to be viewed as enforcers was registered by border officers as a feminizing, thus offensive, gesture.

Further, guns grant their owners a sense of honour, tasked with the protection of others. Carlson (2015) found that predominantly white men from economically and socially disenfranchised US states have claimed the gun as a way of enacting what they perceive to be a protective obligation. This happens in a context of job precariousness where mistaken perceptions of increasing crime levels are exploited to legitimate gun ownership, allowing "men to assert social relevance by embracing a duty to protect" (388) and to reclaim their "position at the top of the gender hierarchy" (389). Interestingly, Carlson's (2012: 1114) work underscores the weight of these representations among US gun owners who associate firearms with a racialized politics of protection and civic duty and for whom guns are seen as the means to "resist emasculation by the state." In a similar fashion, the enforcement narrative related by Canadian border workers attests to their longing for a recovered masculinity in a tougher border politics.

Borders, security, masculinity: the enforcement narrative

A commercial border officer shift consists of inspecting trucks and cargo, sitting in booths asking routine questions and assisting truck drivers, importers and custom brokers with paperwork and administrative problems. Officers can also spend hours releasing shipments on computer screens. Most of their regular enforcement interventions concern small amounts of alcohol and tobacco smuggled in by truck drivers exceeding the legislated limit. Once a year, they may stumble upon a sizeable quantity of drugs, some smuggled firearms or counterfeit goods concealed in a truck.

Nevertheless, many of the officers I spoke to insist on the law enforcement part of their mandate. They fight drug trafficking and the smuggling of counterfeit money. They find abducted children and seize smuggled firearms.

If these arguments can feel self-aggrandizing, they should not be dismissed as a rehearsed public relations effort. This conviction is expressed in earnest: we used to collect taxes; now we are a police of the border.

By proposing the term *enforcement narrative*, I shed light on this tendency to emphasize the "policing" side of borderwork over more typical customs activities. This narrative fixates on the violent possibility of using force—thus calling upon a narrow view of policing that more resembles the image conveyed by popular culture than the more complex realities of the use of force, but also social regulation, order maintenance and individual conflict resolution in policing. This narrative presents a form of what Ugelvik (2016: 217) in the Norwegian case and Vega (2018) in the US case call legitimation work. Both have found that immigration and border officers come to terms with the moral quandaries and public criticisms raised by coercive practices (such as detention and deportation) through narratives that disavow the human dignity of migrants. Vega (2018) convincingly argues that border officers' efforts at legitimizing their morally ambiguous occupation thus "provide a normative foundation" to immigration control that justifies continued violations of migrant rights. I add to these reflections by proposing that legitimation work in bordering is also affected by labour politics. In the Canadian case, the enforcement narrative allows officers to project a more self-affirming and central image of their role in a time when those who design borders visualize them as virtual control spaces—a programme that leaves frontline officers on the sidelines.

A survey into the legitimation work performed through labour politics in bordering can begin with the apparent discrepancy between the enforcement narrative and the often-mundane character of officers' daily activities. A similar contradiction in the area of street policing has been studied by sociologists who have revealed it to be brimming with gendered connotations. Heidensohn (1992: 71) remarks on the rejection of the community-based, social service and administrative aspects of police work by officers who see these as feminizing tasks: "Indeed, there is much evidence of a resistance to this type of work from serving officers who recognize the tasks and their volume but resent them." It is a characteristic of professionals tasked with the protection of the public to adopt a glorified representation of their line of work as action packed, requiring a sense of mission, strength, valour and the occasional use of violence (Reiner 2010). In fact, those studying police work have time and again underscored how those serving in policing organizations are known to have a preference for "real" police and security work—for instance, crime fighting (Chappell and Lanza-Kaduce 2010). For Herbert (2001: 56), police officers looking for action "reinforce a robust form of masculinity, which encourages them to aggressively pursue 'bad guys.'"

Such resistance rests on inescapable gendered representations accompanying policing, public safety and security-related occupations. Beyond the already-quoted work of Pratt and Thompson (2008) and that of Prokkola and Ridanpää (2015) on the gendered politics of protection in Canadian and Finish bordering, other studies on the sociology of workplaces engaged in public safety confirm these insights. In revealing research on emergency care provision by Toronto firefighters, Braedley (2015, 2010) demonstrates that a great part of firefighting labour is related to care. If this alteration in their everyday work routines owes to improvements in fire safety, it is also due to the neoliberal reorganization of care provision. This new division of care labour positioned firefighters as first responders during medical emergencies, which, in times of austerity, also means caring for the disabled and chronically ill who have been abandoned by the healthcare system. Despite this daily occupational reality, the firefighters who participated in Braedley's research still hung onto a gendered and racialized portrayal of firefighting as an honourable and dangerous job done by strong white men fighting blazes and rescuing people. A narrative stressing the courage and heightened white masculinity of firefighters secures a positive view of themselves as workers grapple with an increasingly "feminizing" occupational experience and the gradual hiring of women and people of colour in fire halls. Importantly, this narrative was not exactly re-created by my interviewees. However, Braedley's research helps us uncover how masculinized representations of public safety occupations can help protect, and even enhance, the social recognition that these workers receive as well as, by extension, their generous salaries and working conditions in times of fiscal restraint—a feat that feminized care occupations such as nursing and childcare provision have not yet been able to replicate.

As we shall see in the next sections, there are parallels between narratives stressing the manly physicality of security-related jobs and the arming campaign led by the border officers' union. Through the symbol of the gun, the enforcement narrative emphasizes "a whole series of connotations to do with the use of force, self-presentation, authority, danger, and vulnerability" (Heidensohn 1992: 73), which were traditionally deemed to exclude women from policing work. Officers in particular mobilized these representations in union politics. The firearm as a masculine symbol was called upon in struggles for recognition between security agencies but also in struggles over resource distribution, pay and working conditions. My interviews, as well as the union's position on arming, suggest that this particular masculinization of the purpose, practices and material culture of borderwork is intimately linked to efforts to raise officers' occupational profile.

Gendered accounts of change: from tax collectors to armed border guards

As officers tell their accounts of what they see as the passage from tax collection to enforcement work, they do not so much emphasize their computing resources, biometric tools or scanning devices but instead offer multiple references to the recently acquired policing equipment they carry on their bodies. Officers frequently listed the enforcement tools added to their belts and mentioned their police-like, navy-blue uniform. Hired in the 1990s, Denis describes these tools: "It really changed a lot. When I got in, I was dressed in a pale blue shirt with regular shoes and a leather belt. . . . [Now] I have my bulletproof vest and all my tools. Handcuffs, baton and pepper spray and a radio." Experienced and mid-career officers also illustrated the transition towards enforcement with reference to the legal powers they gained in 1999—including being able to execute federal warrants. These new powers have introduced concrete modifications in work routines at ports of entry. Senior officers are particularly proud to mention they now have the capacity to arrest drunk drivers—the impossibility to do so being a source of frustration during their early careers.

Nevertheless, the adoption of firearms represents, by far, the most commonly invoked illustration of recent border control transformations. Like Richard, who was quoted in the introduction, many are convinced that the firearm represents one of the biggest changes that they have experienced during their years working as officers. Such insistence raises the question: why do border officers attach such significance to this particular piece of equipment? My conversations with Paul, Arthur and Nathan provide some important clues.

Leaving behind the feminized past of customs

Paul and I were having a discussion about what changed in his work since he started his career when the topic of 9/11 came up: "The events of 2001 have changed the world," he tells me. "At that moment, Americans decided that Canada would take its responsibilities. . . . Before that period, we were ambassadors. Welcome to Canada. We were there to greet people." Paul then surprisingly offers a gendered take on what kind of people were attracted to work at the border before this shift: "And then this transition has not been easy because the person, man or woman, who applied [to work at customs] in those times, well it was often people who were searching for a second wage. In Ontario, it was practically only women who were . . . they were clerks. People came and they did the clerical side a bit." Like other officers, Paul illustrates this evolution by referring to the gun: "But after 2001, it changed and we went towards enforcement. And then it was arming. But if you, you don't want to have it, the firearm, what do you do? The government requires you to carry it. So you have two choices: either you get in line or you quit. We are in that transition right now. I think it will last about ten years."

For Paul, the firearm epitomizes how border services gave up what he articulates as their former ambassadorial and clerical mentality. It is significant that Paul invokes the figure of the female clerk. In this story, she is not a bona fide border-policing actor but a second-rate administrative aide and a part-time working mother for whom bordering is not a vocation.[4] Paul's description is historically truncated: there were, and still are, clerks in the commercial sections of land ports of entry, and most of them are women. As further detailed in the next chapter, their numbers decreased in the 1990s, when the introduction of computers into bordering reduced paperwork requirements. Nevertheless, many of these women passed the tests required to become border officers, in order to remain employed; some of these women were still working for the CBSA at the time of research.

There is nothing innocent about this gendering of the recent past of customs as work accomplished by underpaid and part-time feminine clerical staff. Paul constructs clerks—and not border officers like himself—as representatives of a historical form of bordering characterized by administration. As a result of this construct, Paul creates a distance between border officers and the dull paperwork duties still occupying part of his days despite the recent securitization of the border.

Another conversation illustrates the efforts made by some border officers to dissociate themselves from what they portray as the feminized past of customs. An uncommon occurrence for experienced male officers, one of my interviewees, Arthur, started his customs career in a clerical position. He considers that by becoming an officer, he has "worked his way up." Many years later, he received with disbelief a check for retroactive wages owed after a positive pay equity decision was rendered on behalf of female federal employees. In contrast to his colleagues who had been clerks before they became officers and who willingly provided many details about that part of their career, Arthur spoke little of this period. It was as if he had not really been part of the clerical staff of his port of entry—even though he had held this position, been paid the same amount and worked under the same conditions. "*They* made little money when *I* was working there," he confided.

Both Paul and Arthur resist what they see as a feminized appreciation of their role, which they associate with an inferior social status. This resistance points to the sensitivity of mid-career and experienced officers regarding how their work is valued in the federal service. Reputed to be simple "tax collectors," they had previously encountered some contempt and marginalization; they are now pleased to receive the respect they think they deserve. In such gendered storytelling, the firearm becomes a clear symbol of this shifting tide towards a more prestigious appraisal of their job. My interview with another experienced officer highlights this dynamic particularly well. We have already met Nathan, who became a low-level analyst after an injury. Nathan and I were discussing the physicality of the training for "control and defensive tactics" when he broached the topic of the former symbolic feminization of customs work:[5]

NATHAN: The female officer I work with now, she just got back from it this week. She went all last week. She came back all limping and full of aches and pains.

KARINE: Yes. It's a tough job sometimes.

N: It's not at all like what it used to be.

K: No? What was it like before?

N: Pretty . . . Well, one of our ministers, Elinor . . . hum, Elinor, can't remember her last name, she called us "grocery clerks."

K: Ah! [Elinor] Caplan. Grocery clerks?

N: She said: "Well, Canada customs is just no more than grocery clerks" or "bank clerks" or something like that.

K: Why? Why would she say that?

N: Well, greet the travelling public and let them into Canada.

K: That was the job, or the way the job was described before.

N: We just collect duties and taxes. That's it. We don't do enforcement, drunk drivers, you just ask them not to drive. "Just park your car in secondary, we'll get you a cab" Now it's completely different. So . . .

K: Now it's what? How different is it?

N: Now? Well if they arrive drunk on your line, you arrest them for drunk driving, because we have the powers now.

K: So what changed the most since you started working?

N: Everything. Guns, pepper spray, baton, duty belt. We had nothing when I first started here. Computers. We had nothing. Computers in the office for doing B-15 for travellers, like when you go shopping in the States, they charge the duties and taxes. Those just came in when I first started here. Other than that, it was all . . .

K: . . . by hand.

N: Yes. So everything has changed since I've been here.

K: All computerized.

N: Computerized everything now, guns, duty belt, officer powers, powers to arrest drunks. Everything.

In these remarks, Nathan recalls a 2002 episode involving the then federal customs and revenue minister Elinor Caplan, under whose authority many of my interviewees worked at the time. In Chapter 2, I showed how bordering in Canada was at a crossroads in the early 2000s. Immediately after 9/11, security budgets exploded, as many enforcement and security agencies began to compete for a piece of the pie. The deskilling effects of the automation of customs were slowly being felt in ports of entry. Intelligence-led policing was taking on more importance in border control, while risk-management programmes were put back on the drawing table after having been tested but set aside at the end of the 1990s.

Minister Caplan's comments about bank clerks were made in the context of her directive to let armed and dangerous individuals into the country *since border officers were not armed* and thus considered improperly equipped to intervene in such situations. In her infamous quote reproduced in national media, the minister likens this eventuality to the reaction that bank clerks would have when confronted with bank robbers: "Frankly, it's a similar kind of situation as bank tellers." She adds, "You never want to put anyone in a situation where they are being threatened, where they will be in danger. So bank tellers will give a robber the money and call the police. We do exactly the same thing at the borders and it has worked effectively over a number of years."[6] Following these comments, the officers' union received "a deluge" of phone calls from angry members, complaining of being compared to simple clerical workers. The union president is cited in national media: "We were stunned when we saw that particular comment on her part. Obviously, customs officers can't begin to be compared to bank tellers. Caplan's comments show she doesn't understand what customs officers do or how many laws and regulations they have to administer."[7] For border workers, the minister's comments shed a derogatory and simplistic light on their work, a point publicly underscored by their union representative. It was also politically sensitive to insist on officers' inability to deal with the occasional extreme enforcement situation at a time when the union was leading a campaign to equip officers with guns.

The minister's observations generated outrage precisely because working as a bank teller is known to be a feminine occupation. Historically, women have long been groomed to take those clerical, lower-level positions understood as requiring limited skills. The trope of the bank teller exemplifies, in the minds of many, the clear gender segregation of jobs in the service industry (Acker 2006: 446–447). Such feminization of their job hurt the sensitivity of officers who felt diminished by this association just as they were collectively trying to shed their tax collector skins and put on their bulletproof vests.

Particularly worthy of attention in Paul's, Arthur's and Nathan's respective narratives, therefore, is how they partake in the production of a reworked masculinized ethos for border officers. This is a gendered distinction strategy taking place in a transforming work environment that is progressively staffed by women. In fact, at the same historical moment when women are being slowly integrated into border officers' ranks, the enforcement narrative symbolically transforms borderwork from a set of feminizing bookkeeping tasks into a masculinized border-policing project.[8] In those gendered narratives, the passage to enforcement and especially the adoption of its ultimate symbol, the gun, marks the transformation of the border from a soft and subdued taxation space into a strong and hard protective line where border officers argue that they should play a central part. Policing tools thus take on their full sense as symbols of a tougher form of border control that they aspire to embody. To quote Carlson (2015: 401), "what guns did protect against was a gendered threat: the threat of falling down the masculine hierarchy." In short, arming intended to recast the border officers' public perception but also their own, both in terms of a newly self-ascribed gendered subject position as "law enforcers" and in relation to their efforts to favourably project themselves as still-relevant border actors.

Guns affirm the relevance of frontline borderwork against a backdrop that made it politically vulnerable. In the first half of the 2000s, border officers and their union representatives saw the writing on the wall. Being likened to clerical workers when borders were increasingly seen as a security issue that should be dealt with by enforcement and intelligence agencies meant that they were being asked to surrender their historical control over the border. It was time to get it back.

"We are not second-class enforcement workers":[9] the fight for the gun

If you crossed the border in 2017 after driving through the Ambassador Bridge that connects Windsor to Detroit, you would probably have seen a billboard paid for by the Customs and Immigration Union (CIU-SDI): "We keep Canada's borders safe. We deserve to be treated better." Around the same time, the union president was quoted in local media praising border officers' role in law enforcement: "We're seizing drugs, we're arresting people crossing with illegal firearms. We are stopping people who have been drinking and driving. Basically, when you're crossing at any location, you are dealing with a law enforcement agency."[10] In this section, I chronicle the debates that led to the introduction of the gun, a low-tech artefact, at the Canadian border. These debates have been so fierce that some working at the CBSA today worry more about the public reception of this programme than about the agency's deportation record or accusations of racial profiling.[11]

"We keep Canada's borders safe": unions and conservative security politics

We know little about how border officers act collectively and strategically in a rearranged security landscape. It may be useful to take our cue from the limited literature on police unions, an issue still neglected according to Walker (2008), which first arose in the 1970s, when these organizations were getting stronger (Larson 1978). Street-level policing and security labour articulate "segmented market arrangements"—also characteristic of other labour markets—between a "unionized, high-cost sector" and a "non-unionized, low-cost sector" (O'Malley and Hutchinson 2007). While border officers are not the only street-level security workers in the country, they are the major unionized force involved in border control in Canada.[12] In contrast to the progressive union movement in Canada, the border officers' union and other law enforcement workers associations adopt a conservative outlook on their activities and mandate by privileging the promotion of their members' interests over other sociopolitical agendas pursued by the broader labour movement (Burgess, Fleming and Marks 2006; Finnane 2008). Such unions have a sociopolitical agenda of their own—one promoting a law and order approach that insists on channelling state resources away from social security, rehabilitation and prevention (matters that are generally placed out of their hands) and towards intelligence, security, policing and coercive approaches to criminal justice.

Unionized officers actively participate as stakeholders in the redefinition of their mandate, and they do so with relatively limited resources compared to those deployed by state authorities or the private security industry. In Canada, CIU-SDI represents all frontline border personnel (air, land, maritime and support staff) and those working in inland customs, investigation and immigration enforcement.

Beyond collective bargaining, the CIU-SDI regularly intervenes at senate and parliamentary committees on border matters. It lobbies political parties and the government to allocate more funds to frontline bordering and to include officers in pilot projects and collaborative enforcement teams. Their political impact is similar to that of police unions, as noted by Walker (2008). Because it advantageously comments in the media on border policy, the union also influences public perception of the border as a security issue. For instance, in 2012, CIU-SDI applauded a new initiative to "combat human trafficking" but shrewdly noted that its implementation might be difficult to achieve in a context of service and employment cuts.[13] Strategically deployed by the CIU-SDI, these public tactics display how such unions are aware of their capacity "to shake the appearance of a government's commitment to public safety" (Finnane 2000: 12)—especially when that government promotes a law and order governing platform, as had been the case in Canada between 2006 and 2015.

As shown by their campaign to obtain arming, the CIU-SDI mobilization comes with significant consequences on border policies. For the first half of the 2000s, in a time of significant policy-based, legislative, institutional, budgetary and technological change that made border control front-page news but threatened their members' influence on overall border control, the CIU-SDI lobbied and pressured all federal political parties for arming border officers. As we shall see later on, the union used, to great effect, a law enforcement rhetoric mixed with a concern for the safety of its members. These efforts were ultimately successful following the election of a Conservative government in 2006. Influenced by the union's campaign, the Conservative Party of Canada promised in its electoral platform to go through with arming land, inland and marine officers (the policy still does not include airport officers). It kept its promise once in power.

It is no coincidence that the firearm was introduced at the border by the Conservatives, whose government established a daunting record of masculinist and sexist policies that gave guns a place of honour. The Conservatives insisted on rebuilding the military and on fostering Canadians' knowledge of their military history in an attempt to "re-masculinize the nation itself"

(Cowen and Siciliano 2012). This government also abolished the National Firearm Registry, an important tool against domestic violence murders that had been adopted after years of social struggles by survivors of a misogyny-motivated shooting in 1989 at the Polytechnic school of the Université de Montréal (my place of work). The shooter killed 14 female engineering students for having dared to dream of a traditionally male career.

But the recourse by the officers' union to a masculine symbol and a lethal weapon to secure better working conditions and salaries for its members also deserves reflection. Such concerted efforts prompt us to investigate the interactions between organized security professionals, politicians and policymakers in the making of the border control agenda: How do unionized border workers negotiate their place as security professionals amid the multiplication of security actors? What does it mean for unionized officers to interact with policymakers and ministers as their employers and with politicians as potential allies? Which discourses do they strategically deploy to gain recognition for their work and a share of public funds? How do they use the willingness of state officials to spend in security and public safety to their advantage? How do they influence policy priorities?

The gun, this health and safety tool

For their proponents, guns are often seen as solutions rather than problems. Mencken and Froese (2017) have begun uncovering the representational politics that view guns as able to "solve social problems and make communities safer" rather than endangering those communities and their members. From the end of the 1990s onwards, border officers have integrated this logic into their assessments of their labour conditions. Arming is indispensable, many officers told me, *because it protects border workers.* Not everyone agreed, of course, but since this rhetoric has become key to their union's campaign for arming, it is worth unpacking.

My interlocutors often attempted to convince me that guns were "a necessary evil." Richard had given much thought to the topic: "I know I do take exception when people don't believe that we should be armed or don't believe that we should carry weapons or firearms. It's definitely a necessary evil, if you will, whether you believe in arms or not. It is something where, it's like OK, either you want enforcement or you don't." He then explained how arming was a natural follow-up to obtaining extended legal powers to question, detain and search:

> If you want me to enforce the law, if you want me to enforce the Criminal Code, if you want me to enforce criminal aspects of the Customs Act or Immigration Refugee Protection Act, then you know what? This is necessary. Once you get into a position where you're now removing people's freedom from them, putting them in cells, taking them out of their

element and placing them under arrest, it is something because it's . . . it's something that's going to be necessary because you never know how somebody's going to react.

Interestingly, from this point forward, Richard does not insist on law enforcement as much as on the need for self-protection that would arise from this increased capacity to enforce the law:

At the end of the day, I want to go home, you know? I have a wife, I have a family, I . . . you know I . . . I'm not saying that by carrying a gun you could never be shot, I'm just saying: give me a chance! Right? (. . .) I don't see the downside to it. People say: "Well you could have an unlawful discharge," well it's like . . . I'm not sitting here spinning a gun around on my finger like I'm Wyatt Earp or anything crazy like that. I mean, it's one of those things where you're saying, "Well cops can end up having an unlawful shooting, police could, so let's not arm our police officers." Well, you would tell me I'm nuts! Right?

This association between policing and arming is not a natural one. Regular police personnel in countries such as Iceland, most of the UK and New Zealand do not carry a firearm.[14] In 2016, only one year after having allowed its police officers to carry firearms, Norway decided to return to their original policy directive requiring officers to keep guns locked inside patrol vehicles.[15] But these diverse arming policies do not deter Richard. He concludes,

At the end of the day, there's bad guys out there and people will have guns. I mean . . . it's . . . same thing, even if it's not a gun, even if it's a knife. Lots of people carry knives, that's something that . . . we don't [know] about as much, but so many people carry knives. Especially truck drivers. Every truck driver carries a knife.

I ask, "Really?" Richard answers,

Absolutely, every single one of them. Now it makes sense, they cut seals, they have all their jobs for it. Every single truck driver. I never came across a truck driver that didn't have at least a folding knife of some sort, or I don't recall ever coming across one that didn't at least have a pocket knife, like a folding knife of some sort. And I get some who are just enthusiasts. Right? But again, I mean you're not drawing down on everybody just because he's got a knife, but there is potential there that has to be recognized, that has to be looked at.

In this defence of the gun, Richard deploys "the language of the gun," where "guns are perceived as dangerous yet attractive, necessary for aggressive, preemptive protection, powerful and power giving" (Harcourt 2006: 10). On the one hand, this language expresses an active notion of gun carrying, where guns are associated with a coercive view of policing and the capacity to intimidate civilians and subdue them if deemed necessary. Likewise, other officers equated arming with a hardened, more muscular form of border control that concentrates on displaying their potential for use of force. Richard expresses something akin to a desire for guns. A desire for the more active work life that guns suggest but also for the authority and command that they will ultimately give him in his interactions with border crossers. Yet if the increased powers obtained by officers at the end of the 1990s, combined with the introduction of the firearm, make possible a more extreme, potentially lethal form of control over border crossers' lives, it does so in a job that promises action but offers few opportunities to this end. Indeed, occasions to use force at the commercial section are few and far between, a fact acknowledged by many officers. Richard mentions truck drivers and their knives, but commercial officers work with a clientele that is unlikely to exhibit violent behaviour. As mentioned in the interlude, truck drivers comply with regulations and laws in order to both reduce time spent at the border (as they are paid by the kilometre) and protect their employment. Richard's mindset does not correspond with the daily realities of commercial work. Although he admits, "I know we don't get a lot of use of force instances back here in commercial," his approach to border control remains framed by concerns about the potential to exert violence.

On the other hand, and similar to what Harcourt has found in young offenders' relationship to firearms, Richard blends his wish to overpower potential adversaries and the perceived need for self-protection in an occupation where he might encounter weapons. This discursive mobilization of guns in relation to personal protection is not uncommon, but it is generally found in the "culture of high crime societies" where high crime rates are seen as "a normal social fact" and domestic protection is conceived as the domain of private individuals (Garland 2001: 367–368). While the proximity to the United States and its active gun culture certainly contributes to this sense of vulnerability felt by officers such as Richard, Canadian statistics regarding gun-related deaths (including suicides) are comparatively lower and have been happening in areas located far from the border. Gun ownership does, however, remain popular among hunters in Canada.[16] Springwood (2014: 460) suggests that the "enchantment" of firearms rests in the fact that the "embodied proximity to a gun provides psychological comfort" to gun owners. Richard's anxiety for his personal safety downplays the firearm's deadly potentiality and constructs the gun as a reassuring artefact.

We need to dig beyond these references to potential threats for a nuanced explanation of officers' attraction to handguns. Yet it would be inappropriate to underestimate officers' *perception* of the potential for hostile and violent encounters at the border. Some of my interviewees related vivid tales of life-threatening situations that generally occurred to a colleague in the traffic section. One such story concerned an officer who opened a car trunk only to find a man pointing his gun at her. A police officer was passing by at the time and disarmed the offender. During fieldwork, officers described other instances of intimidation on the part of travellers and told stories of finding hidden firearms in truck cabs. They recalled arresting criminally charged and armed individuals who attempted to cross the border to escape US authorities. Traditionally told informally by experienced officers as a pedagogical tool for informing rookies about "real" police work (Van Maanen 1973), these "war stories" took another turn in the interview context. They were important because they said something about the defencelessness that officers felt because of their being unarmed. This provides context to the need for "psychological comfort" that would be provided by guns.

But these stories were also part of a rehearsed repertoire of justifications that pro-gun officers and their union had been refining for quite a while. Similar to Richard's plea in favour of the gun, the officers' union adopted a health and safety language insisting that sidearms were required for officers' self-protection. This politicization of officer safety and its narrowing down to the acquisition of the firearm has been at the heart of an opposition between the CBSA management and the officers' union in a multi-year-long battle that started at the end of the 1990s and that is still ongoing.

This conflict was first waged on the battlefield of expertise. In early 2000, the CCRA (predecessor to the CBSA) commissioned an external analysis of work-related threats made against officers. The report concluded that arming was not necessary. Following this conclusion, the officers' union accused ModuSpec, the risk-management firm that had authored the report, of altering its recommendations to fit CCRA's decision not to arm officers—a charge repeated by the Senate Committee on National Security and Defence in 2005.[17] The union then hired a different firm, Northgate, to produce a counter study. The CBSA, however, refused to grant Northgate access to border facilities. Finding a sizeable number of research participants through the union and without acknowledging how its sampling bias might have skewed its results, the firm's 2006 study unsurprisingly concludes that officers working with the public should be armed.[18]

The battle was then brought to administrative tribunals and in the realm of labour pressures through refusals to work. The officers' union presented a series of cases before the federal Occupational Health and Safety Tribunal (OHST) involving traffic officers confronted, in reality or potentially, with armed individuals. Yet the tribunal overturned several work-refusal cases— when officers have refused to work for safety reasons—presented during the years of the union's arming campaign. These work refusals included short work stoppages by groups of colleagues in major ports of entry or by officers caught in "work-alone situations"—those seen as more likely to be endangered in conflicts with border crossers.[19]

Often, these appeals to the tribunal concerned the failure of CBSA management to provide officers with up-to-date information about "armed and dangerous lookouts." In one reported instance, US law enforcement had informed Canadian officials about armed bank robbers who could attempt to cross into Canada. Officials took more than three days to enter that information into the CBSA lookout databases that are accessible to officers in their booths (where they generally work alone). Significantly, this failure by CBSA management to communicate crucial information for the safety of its employees in a timely fashion has not been interpreted by the union as an opportunity for demanding improvements in IT and information management but rather as an additional argument in favour of arming. Those appeals, still pending in front of the OHST when the arming initiative was adopted in 2007, have for the most part been withdrawn—either by the union or by the CBSA. However, refusals to work have reappeared since 2014 alongside the union's campaign to bring arming to airports.[20]

Outcomes of arming

Despite these setbacks for border officers, the arming campaign has had several outcomes. First, through their cumulated efforts, the union has succeeded at associating health and safety concerns with arming. A sign of this success is that the CBSA has since performed a dramatic about-face on its former position that opposed the firearm. Violent incidents in ports of entry are now considered by CBSA high management as justifications for the acquisition of sidearms. A section of a 2009 internal review of the arming programme asks, "Is there an ongoing need for CBSA officers to be armed?" and endorses arming by presenting paltry numbers regarding threats of assault and bodily harm faced by officers. The results of a 2002 workplace assessment and indicates that there have been 106 "life-threatening encounters" on border officers over 26 years (between 1976 and 2002), which includes "being held hostage, being physically assaulted and being fired upon." Between 2006 and 2007, officers reported being assaulted ten times and threatened with bodily harm 13 times. Between 2007 and 2008, four assaults and 17 threats of bodily harm were counted.[21] Border officers seized around 500 firearms annually between 2005 and 2009 and more than 5000 other weapons between 2007 and 2008.[22]

Workplace aggression is a "surprisingly prevalent phenomenon" in jobs involving daily human interactions. However, a recent Cochrane Review protocol indicates that preventive and minimizing mechanisms already exist (Hills et al. 2015: 2; see also Guay, Goncalves and Jarvis 2015). Further, CBSA figures pale in comparison with statistics about workplace violence against healthcare workers in the same period. For instance, a third of Canadian nurses reported having been assaulted in 2005 alone, and nearly half admit having been victims of emotional abuse. Despite such a high rate of assault, no one has yet called for the arming of nurses.[23] I use the example of nursing, a profession located at the other end of border officers on the gendered occupational spectrum, to make a simple point: arming is not about health and safety. Claims that guns are needed to reduce incidents of workplace violence are considered rational and their taken-for-grantedness is left unchallenged because security and policing professions are socially coded as masculine. While it is to be expected that policing unions lobby for budgets to acquire the tools and resources to better protect their members when working in dangerous environments (Berry et al. 2008), the proof that firearms offer the most effective solution to real but infrequent occurrences of workplace violence remains to be presented.

That it is difficult to establish the usefulness of firearms in borderwork is a second outcome of the arming policy. Official statistics regarding the number of times that trained officers drew or fired their guns since the arming policy was implemented are few and far between. In 2017, it was reported that agents drew their firearms 299 times over a ten-year period, firing them 18 times; while 11 of those shots were accidental and six were meant to euthanize animals, we do not know the context for the remaining shot. Attempting to justify these numbers, the union president argued that guns served as deterrent to calm agitated and aggressive border crossers.[24] He did not provide any justification for the accidental shots, nor did he clarify whether harm had been caused. We also do not know why border officers felt compelled to draw their firearms in these cases and whether these situations could have benefited from conflict-resolution techniques that would have made pulling firearms unnecessary.

A third outcome of arming is that it is equally difficult to assess its total cost. We can assume that it has been significant, and yet this happened in a period of severe budget cuts in other governmental areas. In 2006, the federal government committed the impressive sum of Can$1 billion to the arming of 6700 border officers over a ten-year period.[25] This does not include the training costs and expenses incurred by the "doubling policy"—a welcome health and safety effort that came with arming and that eliminated work-alone situations in small and remote ports by hiring more officers for these ports. Together with the doubling policy, arming contributed to the creation of more than 700 new officer positions. This array of policy initiatives increased the number of full-time officers entitled to full-time wages, full benefits and pensions—expenses not accounted for by official cost forecasts. Nor were those wage raises accounted for that came with arming in the 2009 round of collective bargaining obtained in the middle of a recession, budget cuts and attacks on federal civil service unions.[26] In a 2008 letter to its members, then union president Ron Moran commended the high "level of access CEUDA currently enjoys with the present government."[27]

More than ten years after its inception, arming still provokes debate. As we shall see in Chapter 7, some officers (especially those mid career or more senior) refused to be armed or were prevented from doing so because of injury. This creates needs for accommodation—such as finding work that does not put them in face-to-face interactions with travellers—that have been met with difficulty. The possibility for career officers to avoid firearm training has been a significant point of contention between the union and management in the decade following the adoption of the policy. In 2017, the opening page of the union website welcomed visitors with two main issues: collective bargaining and the implementation of the arming initiative. The union continues to lobby for arming in airports—where officers have often received gun training but are not allowed to carry a firearm unless they belong to an armed task force.

A final outcome is directly related to my overall argument in this book regarding the recent shift to law enforcement in Canadian bordering. Arming has clearly affected self-selection in potential candidates for border officer positions, thus creating a workforce more inclined towards law enforcement and a coercive vision of border control. William, an experienced officer who was quoted in Chapter 1, told me that he now insists in his discussions with prospective candidates on the fact that they would have to get firearm training before being hired. According to William, firearms discourage many applicants. As a related issue, we need to investigate whether arming could partly explain the current gender imbalance at the frontline. Interestingly, the CBSA now participates in the Young Women in Public Safety Initiative; women make up only a quarter of frontline law enforcement personnel at the federal level.[28] In contrast to the last decades of the 20th century that brought in people of diverse walks of life, new recruits hired by the CBSA increasingly come from security, policing and even defence backgrounds. As we shall see in the next chapter, this insistence on law enforcement is evidenced by the new pedagogies of border control.

I have reviewed several outcomes of arming. While automation and the diffusion of border activities to other security actors should have seen a decrease in the number of border officers, especially in commercial sections of ports of entry, the union effectively countered the thinning of its ranks. Officers' fight to obtain their share of the growing state resources spent on security entailed relabelling their work through an enforcement narrative that insisted on the dangers they faced, putatively and in reality, and then deploying this narrative as a bargaining strategy. With the arming policy and its overall mobilization on behalf of its members, the officers' union strategically played a context politically favourable to security professionals that opened up in the decade following 9/11.

Conclusion

This chapter inquired into a series of puzzling questions. It examined officers' investment in arming to mitigate their sidelining from border control. My research uncovers the gendered dimensions of arming, by revealing how the arming initiative relied on narratives about a feminized past and a masculine present of borderwork, deployed a labour politics that returns to the traditional means of asserting the masculinism of the state and expressed a conservative take on issues of criminal justice, policing and security that was meant to enhance officers' professional status in their struggle to be regarded as legitimate security actors. Also, the arming challenge emerged when women began entering the border guard workforce.

Further, in a policing area where technological innovation is the bread and butter of many current analyses, this chapter demonstrates that low-tech devices such as firearms continue to be fantasized about and relied on in border control. This scenario calls into question the assumption often found in studies of security technologies that associate such devices with the past of security. Yet we have seen that the longing for guns *follows* the technologization of bordering rather than predates it. Relatedly, we can complicate this temporal opposition between low-tech and high-tech by unpacking the ways that gendered approaches to border control shape how the various technical objects of bordering are adopted, altered and resisted by border workers, and all of this happened when technical knowledge—another form of masculine domination (Connell 2005: 165) currently sweeping the security world with its imaginaries of automated and algorithmic bordering—challenged their traditional hold on the frontline. More research is needed to inquire into the coexistence and tensions between the competing gendered arrangements that make up border masculinities and how these arrangements recompose how state authority is experienced, embodied and imposed in border spaces.

Finally, this chapter contemplated why a border agency feels more open to public criticism over an issue that does not fall within the usual themes discussed by critical border and security scholars. The ongoing debates over arming and the still-contested status of border officers as enforcement workers teach us a lesson: border and security agencies perceive themselves to be politically vulnerable to issues that may have escaped our notice. Those of us who wish to put forth an effective critique of contemporary bordering that could translate into more social justice for border crossers should take note.

Fighting against their demotion in border control, officers repositioned themselves into a tougher "police of the border." While telling the story of the loss of influence by frontline border officials in a recomposed North American border space, I problematized the idea that security professionals have been passive in the context of these changes. Indeed, I demonstrated that by waging a gendered labour politics, they were actively and collectively engaging with these transformations, at times even placing themselves at the forefront of border control restructuring. In many ways, they were successful. By gaining the gun, unionized officers made frontline borderwork manly again.

Notes

1 In Chapter 7, we shall see in more detail that arming also alters bordering practices.

2 To be clear, my aim at this point is not to inquire into actual gender inequalities between officers or between officers and travellers. It is important to underscore that the gendered bordering I am writing about concerns conflicts between different valuations of where and how border control should be done. Consequently, this does not necessarily undervalue female border officers from a strict gender-equity perspective. Women who integrate into these work teams also materially benefit from this symbolic recasting through collective bargaining. Despite this caveat, we can also consider the possibility that by making bordering "male," women's recruitment and retention as border officers may become more difficult, therefore effectively limiting access to these benefits. I discuss this in the next chapter.

3 In contrast to the staff stationed in major Canadian urban airports, land border officers are generally white and a majority are men. During fieldwork, I have met only one non-white border officer. On the Canadian land border as a space of whiteness, see Helleiner (2016).

4 For non-Canadians, this reference to the social reproductive reality of provinces such as Ontario needs further clarification. Among other explanatory factors, recourse to part-time employment for mothers of children below school-age is higher outside Quebec because of the prohibitive cost of childcare and, in some provinces, because of more-conservative notions regarding mothering. See Bezanson (2010) and Uppal (2015).

5 Since they have been granted increased powers in 1999, officers receive CDT (control and defensive tactics) training. After these courses and a required recertification every three years, officers must demonstrate proficiency in handcuffing, weapon retention (if armed) and carotid control techniques and in the use of baton and OC (oleoresin capsicum) spray, aka pepper spray.

6 Elizabeth Thompson (2002), Customs agents chide Caplan, *Montreal Gazette*, 12 Apr. 2002.

7 Ibid.

8 Unfortunately, despite attempts to obtain numbers from the CBSA and from union officials, I was not granted access to statistics about the gender and age of frontline officers. However, my field observations indicate that the new cohorts of officers include many more women than those hired in the 1980s and 1990s. This entrance of women seems to have been stymied during the last years of the 2010s, in part because of the introduction of physical fitness tests little adapted to women's bodies. More on this in Chapter 6.

9 This was the Canadian border officers' union slogan for the 2012 campaign for the renewal of their collective agreement.

10 See picture by Nick Brancaccio accompanying the article: T. Wilhelm (2017), CBSA officers union erect billboards, threatens border "disturbances" after failed negotiations, *Windsor Star*, https://windsorstar.com/news/local-news/cbsa-officers-union-erects-billboards-threatens-border-disturbances-after-failed-negotiations (last consulted 29 Nov. 2018).

11 In February 2015, my master's degree student who did an undergraduate internship with the CBSA the previous year approached his former employer to inquire into whether he could investigate the "arming initiative" for his thesis. He wished to examine how the firearm is incorporated into the everyday work of border officers—a suitable topic since Canadian frontline officers are now trained to carry a gun. Yet the answer he received was unexpected: his former supervisors were happy to help him develop a research project as long as it did not concern the gun. It is too sensitive a topic. Why not inquire into "removals" (deportations) or perform an intelligence analysis about a particular (racialized) suspect group instead?

12 The obvious example remains Canadian airports, where the inspection line is staffed with underpaid, non-unionized security personnel employed by private security companies subcontracted by CATSA (the Crown corporation responsible for aviation security in Canada)—in contrast to American Transport Safety Agency (TSA), which employs unionized federal

workers. In the ports of entry I visited, I also found a similar division of labour, where employees of a local trucking carrier were subcontracted to unload trucks that were flagged for inspection.

13 CIU-SDI (2012), *Customs and Immigration Union Raises Questions for Minister Toews on Announced Anti- Human Trafficking Initiative*, 8 June, www.ciu-sdi.ca/?p=129071 (last consulted 3 Oct. 2012).

14 See the following articles: R. Noack (2015), 5 countries where most police officers do not carry firearms: And it works well, *The Washington Post*, www.washingtonpost.com/news/worldviews/wp/2015/02/18/5-countries-where-police-officers-do-not-carry-firearms-and-it-works-well/?utm_term=.9706026d9278 (last modified 8 July 2016; last consulted 7 July 2019).

15 A. Taylor (2016), Norway gave its cops guns: After 1 year, it's taking them away: What did it learn? *The Washington Post*, www.washingtonpost.com/news/worldviews/wp/2016/02/05/norway-gave-its-cops-guns-after-1-year-its-taking-them-away-what-did-it-learn/?utm_term=.7dbf29870e21 (last modified 5 Feb. 2016; last consulted 7 July 2019).

16 Statistics Canada (2018), *Juristat Bulletin: Quick Fact: Firearm-Related Violent Crime in Canada*, www150.statcan.gc.ca/n1/pub/85-005-x/2018001/article/54962-eng.htm (last modified 24 July 2018; last consulted 9 July 2019); S. Beattie, J.-D. David and J. Roy (2018), Homicide in Canada 2017, *Statistics Canada*, www150.statcan.gc.ca/n1/pub/85-002-x/2018001/article/54980-eng.htm (last modified 21 Nov. 2018; last consulted 9 July 2019); R. Fletcher (2018), Canada gun fact: Here are the latest stats on firearm deaths, injuries and crime, *CBC*, (last modified 31 Aug. 2018; last consulted 9 July 2019).

17 Senate Committee on National Security and Defence (2005), *Borderline Insecure*, www.parl.gc.ca/content/sen/committee/381/defe/rep/repintjun05-e.pdf (last consulted 10 July 2019), p. 30.

18 Northgate (2006), *A View from the Frontlines: Officer Safety and the Necessity of Sidearms*, www.ciu-sdi.ca/wp-content/uploads/2011/02/Northgate.pdf (last consulted 9 July 2019).

19 See Canada Border Services Agency *v* CEUDA, OHSTC 2006 049; Mike Coene *v* Canada Border Services Agency, OHSTC 2008 27; Tony Ferrusi *v* Canada Border Services Agency, 2011 OHSTC 28; Eugenia Martin-Ivie *v* Canada Border Services Agency, 2011 OHSTC 6. These archived decisions of this administrative tribunal may be found at: www.canada.ca/en/occupational-health-and-safety-tribunal-canada/programmes/decisions/archived.html

20 Airport CBSA officers temporarily refuse work over security concerns (2014), *Calgary Herald*, 25 Oct. 2014, www.calgaryherald.com/news/airport+cbsa+officers+temporarily+refuse+work+over+security+concerns/10325190/story.html (last consulted 19 Dec. 2016).

21 CBSA (2009), *CBSA Arming Initiative Evaluation Study*, www.cbsa-asfc.gc.ca/agency-agence/reports-rapports/ae-ve/2009/arm-eng.html (last modified 17 Feb. 2012; last consulted 26 Sept. 2012), p. 9.

22 Ibid., p. 10.

23 I thank Susan Braedley for bringing this comparison to my attention. Statistics Canada, *Factors Related to On-the-Job Abuse of Nurses by Patients*, www.statcan.gc.ca/pub/82-003-x/2009002/article/10835-eng.htm (last modified 15 Apr. 2008; last consulted 30 Mar. 2013).

24 K. Harris (2017), Border guards fired guns 18 times in a decade: Accidentally in most cases. *CBC*, 28 July, www.cbc.ca/news/politics/cbsa-border-guards-guns-1.4201882 (last updated 28 July 2017; last consulted 7 June 2019).

25 CBSA (2015), *Audit of Arming*, www.cbsa.gc.ca/agency-agence/reports-rapports/ae-ve/2015/arm-eng.html (last consulted 12 Dec. 2016).

26 Treasury Board of Canada Secretariat (2009), *Border Services (FB), Appendix A, FB-Border Services Group Annual Rates of Pay*, www.tbs-sct.gc.ca/pubs_pol/hrpubs/coll_agre/fb/fb08-eng.asp#toc223757315 (last consulted 27 Sept. 2012).

27 The former name of the officers' union, CEUDA, stands for Customs Excise Union Douanes Accise. R. Moran (2008, Winter), Word from the president, *CEUDA Magazine* (now unavailable online).

28 Public Safety Canada, *Young Women in Public Safety Internship Program*, www.publicsafety. gc.ca/cnt/bt/crrs/ywps-en.aspx (last updated 23 Apr. 2018; last consulted 7 June 2019).

References

Acker, J. 1990. Hierarchies, jobs, bodies: A theory of gendered organizations. *Gender & Society* 4 (2):139–158.

———. 1992. From sex roles to gendered institutions. *Contemporary Sociology* 21 (9):565–569.

———. 2006. Inequality regimes: Gender, class, and race in organizations. *Gender & Society* 20 (4):441–464.

Baird, T. 2017. Knowledge of practice: A multi-sited event ethnography of border security fairs in Europe and North America. *Security Dialogue* 48 (3):187–205.

Berry, J., G. O'Connor, M. Punch, and P. Wilson. 2008. Strange union: Changing patterns of reform, representation, and unionization in policing. *Police Practice and Research* 9 (2):113–130.

Bezanson, K. 2010. "Childcare delivered through the mailbox": Social reproduction, choice, and neoliberalism in a theo-conservative Canada. In *Neoliberalism and Everyday Life*, edited by S. Braedley and M. Luxton. Montreal: McGill-Queen's University Press.

Bigo, D. 2008. Globalized (in)security: The field and the ban-opticon. In *Terror, Insecurity and Liberty: Illiberal Practices of Liberal Regimes after 9/11*, edited by D. Bigo and A. Tsoukala. London: Routledge, 10–48.

Bosworth, M., and G. Slade. 2014. In search of recognition: Gender and staff: Detainee relations in a British immigration removal centre. *Punishment & Society* 16 (2):169–186.

Braedley, S. 2010. Accidental health care: Masculinity and neoliberalism at work. In *Neoliberalism and Everyday Life*, edited by S. Braedley and M. Luxton. Montreal, Kingston: McGill-Queen's University Press.

———. 2015. Pulling men into the care economy: The case of Canadian firefighters. *Competition & Change* 19 (3):264–278.

Brown, W. 1995. *States of Injury: Power and Freedom in Late Modernity*. Princeton: Princeton University Press.

Burgess, M., J. Fleming, and M. Marks. 2006. Thinking critically about police unions in Australia: Internal democracy and external responsiveness. *Police Practice and Research* 7 (5):391–409.

Carlson, J. 2012. "I don't dial 911": American gun politics and the problem of policing. *British Journal of Criminology* 52 (6):1113–1132.

———. 2015. Mourning Mayberry: Guns, masculinity, and socioeconomic decline. *Gender & Society* 29 (3):386–409.

Chappell, A. T., and L. Lanza-Kaduce. 2010. Police academy socialization: Understanding the lessons learned in a paramilitary bureaucratic organization. *Journal of Contemporary Ethnography* 39 (2):184–214.

Connell, R. W. 2005. *Masculinities (Second edition)*. Cambridge: Polity Press.

Cowen, D. 2008. *Military Workfare: The Soldier and Social Citizenship in Canada*. Toronto: University of Toronto Press.

Cowen, D., and A. Siciliano. 2011. Surplus masculinities and security. *Antipode* 43 (5): 1516–1541.

Cukier, W., and J. Sheptycki. 2012. Globalization of gun culture: Transnational reflections on pistolization and masculinity, flows and resistance. *International Journal of Law, Crime and Justice* 40:3–19.

Finnane, M. 2000. Police unions in Australia: A history of the present. *Current Issues in Criminal Justice* 12 (5):5–19.

———. 2008. No longer a 'workingman's paradise'? Australian police unions and political action in a changing industrial environment. *Police Practice and Research* 9 (2):131–143.

Garland, D. 2001. *The Culture of Control: Crime and Social Order in Contemporary Society*. Chicago: University of Chicago Press.

Guay, S., J. Goncalves, and J. Jarvis. 2015. A systematic review of exposure to physical violence across occupational domains according to victims' sex. *Aggression and Violent Behaviour* 25:133–141.

Harcourt, B. 2006. *The Language of the Gun: Youth, Crime and Public Policy*. Chicago: University of Chicago Press.

Heidensohn, F. 1992. *Women in Control? The Role of Women in Law Enforcement*. Oxford: Oxford University Press.

Helleiner, J. 2016. *Borderline Canadianness: Border Crossings and Everyday Nationalism in Niagara*. Toronto: University of Toronto Press.

Herbert, S. 2001. "Hard charger" or "station queen"? Policing and the masculinist state. *Gender, Place & Culture* 8 (1):55–71.

Hills, D. J., H. M. Ross, J. Pich, A. T. Hill, T. K. Dalsbø, S. Riahi, S. Guay, and B. Martínez-Jarreta. 2015. Education and training for preventing and minimising workplace aggression directed toward healthcare workers. *Cochrane Database of Systematic Reviews* 9 (CD011860).

Hunt, K., and K. Rygiel. 2006. (En)gendered war stories and camouflaged politics. In *(En)gendering the War on Terror: War Stories and Camouflaged Politics*, edited by K. Hunt and K. Rygiel. Hampshire, UK: Ashgate, 1–24.

Larson, R. 1978. *Police Accountability: Performance Measures and Unions*. Toronto: Lexington Press.

Mencken, F. C., and P. Froese. 2017. Gun culture in action. *Social Problems* 66 (1):3–27.

Muir, W. M. 1977. *Police: Streetcorner Politicians*. Chicago: University of Chicago Press.

O'Malley, P., and S. Hutchinson. 2007. Converging corporatization? Police management, police unionism, and the transfer of business principles. *Police Practice and Research* 8 (2):159–174.

Pickering, S., and B. Cochrane. 2013. Irregular border-crossing deaths and gender: Where, how and why women die crossing borders. *Theoretical Criminology* 17 (1):27–48.

Pratt, A., and S. Thompson. 2008. Chivalry, "race" and discretion at the Canadian border. *The British Journal of Criminology* 48 (5):620–640.

Prokkola, E.-K., and J. Ridanpää. 2015. Border guarding and the politics of the body: An examination of the Finnish Border Guard service. *Gender, Place & Culture* 22 (10):1374–1390.

Reiner, R. 2010. *The Politics of the Police (Fourth edition)*. Oxford: Oxford University Press.

Salter, M. 2008. When the exception becomes the rule: Borders, sovereignty, and citizenship. *Citizenship Studies* 12 (4):365–380.

Shapira, H. 2013. *Waiting for José. The Minutemen's Pursuit of America*. Princeton: Princeton University Press.

Slack, J., D. E. Martínez, A. E. Lee, and S. Whiteford. 2016. The geography of border militarization: Violence, death and health in Mexico and the United States. *Journal of Latin American Geography* 15 (1):7–32.

Springwood, C. F. 2014. Gun concealment, display, and other magical habits of the body. *Critique of Anthropology* 34 (4):450–471.

Ugelvik, T. 2016. Techniques of legitimation: The narrative construction of legitimacy among immigration detention officers. *Crime, Media, Culture* 12 (2):215–232.

Uppal, S. 2015. Employment patterns of families with children. *Statistics Canada*, www150. statcan.gc.ca/n1/pub/75-006-x/2015001/article/14202-eng.htm (last consulted 18 Nov. 2019).

van der Woude, M. 2017. *Chain Reactions in Criminal Justice: Discretion and the Necessity of Interdisciplinary Research*. Den Haag: Eleven International Publishing.

van Maanen, J. 1973. Working the street: A developmental view of police behaviour. *M.I.T. Working Paper #681–73*, https://dspace.mit.edu/bitstream/handle/1721.1/1873/SWP-0681-14451100.pdf

Vega, I. I. 2018. Empathy, morality, and criminality: The legitimation narratives of U.S. Border Patrol agents. *Journal of Ethnic and Migration Studies* 44 (15):2544–2561.

Walker, S. 2008. The neglect of police unions: Exploring one of the most important areas of American policing. *Police Practice and Research* 9 (2):95–112.

Young, I. M. 2003. The logic of masculinist protection: Reflections on the current security state. *Signs: Journal of Women in Culture and Society* 29 (1):1–25.

Chapter 6

Becoming a border enforcer

A changing apprenticeship

Remarking that most of his recently hired colleagues have earned a post-secondary degree in a security-related field, Steeve reflects on how officer selection at the CBSA favours recruits who wish to pursue careers in law enforcement:

> That's the mindset. And then the people who are being attracted to the work are definitely folks who wanted police work. Whereas, I can tell you, of the ten people I worked with when I was hired [in the early 2000s], none of us wanted to be police officers.

In fact, since its inception in 2003, the CBSA has been overhauling its recruit-ment process. While the Customs Act affirms security and trade facilitation as its twin mandates, Steeve's observations suggest that this agency privileges the first half of the equation in its recruiting. In the following pages, I delve into the respective merits of the old and new pedagogies of border control as they are described by officers who work together and have the same job title yet had in mind different careers when they first stepped into their officer shoes. Highlighting the dynamics that brought about what I term *generational bor-derwork* in this book, this chapter looks into what changed (and what did not) in the selection and training of Canadian border officers.

Since border organizations are transforming at a rapid pace, I follow Chan's (2003: 20) invitation to pay attention to instability and variability in policing actors' professional socialization—that is, to how border officers are recruited and how they apprentice into their new job. Like her, I decided not to "assume the existence of a relatively homogeneous and stable organizational culture into which newcomers become acculturated." As the previous chapters began to demonstrate, the ways of doing and thinking borderwork in ports of entry are shifting. For more than a decade now, the CBSA's most recent training schemes have been marked by an enthusiasm for enforcement. Accordingly, this chapter and the next unpack the more fundamental transformations in the professional socialization of Canadian border officers that accompany the movement towards arming, the dual policy emphasis on security and trade facilitation and the increased use of surveillance technologies at borders. They also ask whether officers are properly prepared for enacting these various—sometimes contradictory—policy trends.

Returning to Bourdieu's and Lahire's terms first evoked in Chapter 1, it is through early professional socialization that border officers first acquire their dispositions and a "feel for the game" of borderwork. Accordingly, I make a number of arguments regarding the changing professional socialization of border officers. I first draw attention to the CBSA's attempt at removing local ports' influence in officer appointment by standardizing the hiring process. In spite of these efforts, however, my research reveals that the choice of a career in border services and officers' apprenticeship in ports of entry continue to be shaped, at least in part, by local influences. The chapter then goes on to investigate the remodelling of training at customs college following the police academy template. Its curriculum now emphasizes developing enforcement skills at the expense of many other skills—such as commercial regulations, conflict resolution and legal knowledge of human rights. Training also places stressful pressures on future recruits, indicating that the informal aspects governing life at customs college also contribute to the emergence of an enforcement orientation in rookie officers, one that remains even after contact with experienced officers in the field.

Nevertheless, we will see some continuity between experienced, mid-career and rookie border officers' experiential learning. A significant part of on-the-job training remains focused on acquiring better interviewing techniques and mastering "risk indicators" and customs regulations. In this chapter, I explore how officers learn to adapt to the bureaucratically dictated demands of their role and exert themselves to perform authority. I pay particular attention to the gendered nuances involved in this experiential learning process and to the lessons that it suggests for investigating the potential effects of including women in security professions.

In short, the chapter begins untangling the relationships between training and reform efforts in border control. I am convinced that such examination is necessary. On the one hand, looking into what knowledge and behaviours are fostered in recruits expands our understanding of the register of variables arguably at work when border and security organizations consider how to enact their priorities. On the other hand, an inquiry into how the very selection and preparation of future officers turns them into a generation of border enforcers also gives us insight into how such processes could be amended to produce another kind of border worker. In fact, our lack of interest in professional socialization within security and bordering organizations undermines the possibility of tackling the various ethical, political and democratic challenges aptly underlined by specialists of security and policing (Sheptycki 2007; Huysmans 2014; Wood and Dupont 2006). These challenges are closely related to whether and how security professionals remain accountable to and compliant with human rights. As we shall see, there is unfortunately little in the current selection and training of Canadian border officers that addresses these issues.

Choosing borderwork: motivations and expectations

In contrast to studies that begin with the immediate training of officers—for instance, in research on UK Immigration Services (Jubany 2017)—I start by taking a look into aspects of prospective officers' lives that lead them to borderwork. Before hiring, these recruits do not evolve in a sociocultural vacuum; as is the case for all of us, the mechanisms that socialize future border officers are plural (Lahire 2012). Accordingly, I follow Lahire's (2013: 126–127) suggestion to start with what Merton called anticipatory socialization and take note of the social conditions of possibility of career entry into a security profession. In a world where surveillance technologies and intelligence production in risk analysis centres seem to have taken over bordering, it is nonetheless true that personal networks and kinship, media narratives, local folklore and political-economic factors continue to bear on the choice of an officer career.

Borderland folklore

The sociology of policing and the military notes that such institutions assume that recruits favour a law and order agenda as proxy for social stability and that they prefer *esprit de corps* to personal freedom (see e.g. Chappell and Lanza-Kaduce 2010: 190). As shown later, the novel screening and gun-carrying certification requirements and the current length of overall training suggest that recruits who agree to undergo a more stringent selection process are more receptive than their predecessors to a coercive take on bordering. However, prospective officers present a variety of motivations and expectations for entering border services.[1] Interviewees spoke of reasons that neither contradicted nor precisely mirrored the official description of ideal candidates provided by border authorities.

Some officers mentioned the influence of cultural narratives emphasizing traits associated with hegemonic masculinity, such as courage, strength and risk taking, on their decision to become an officer. Smiling, they offered familiar tropes describing a workday spent on the streets at the sacrifice of one's personal life and characterized by a mix of honourable conduct and occasional rule bending for the common good. Sarah reminded me of the role taken by such tropes in inspiring law enforcement careers. When I met her, Sarah was a rookie who had recently completed her customs college training. With a father in the military, she grew up and studied in the region where she now worked. Thinking about her long-held wish to join a law enforcement corps, Sarah confirms the influence of the crime-fighting mythology characteristic of North American contemporary visual culture:

[Law enforcement] was something I was just always interested in when . . . even when I was little. You know the [television] show *Cops*? As crazy as it may seem, I just loved watching it. Absolutely loved watching it! And I thought it would be so cool to be a cop one day!

Nevertheless, the anticipatory socialization of border officers goes beyond the symbolic force of media representations of policing. Chan (2003) found in her research with Australian police recruits that personal connections and previous information gathered among police officers were as likely to influence the choice of a profession in policing—thus confirming earlier and similar results obtained by the criminologist John van Maanen in earlier studies. My interviews with officers, as well as my conversations with borderland residents, extend these findings to borderwork while adding to them the influence of local folklore. Gossip, folk tales and regional news construct the border as a smuggling haven and provide prospective candidates from border regions with insights into their future occupation.

Given the long history of cross-border smuggling at the Canada–US border (Farfan 2009), everybody in border towns has come across accounts of alcohol and tobacco smuggling; I heard many variations on this theme. A truck driver in a small border community told me of exchanging tips with neighbours and friends on how to avoid paying taxes on tires brought back from the US. Someone else confided that she smuggled a survivor of domestic violence across the border two decades earlier. Others recall the heydays of Quebec Gold, a marijuana strain frequently sneaked across the border for smokers in the state of New York. Local newspapers in borderland communities also publish front-page articles about the last major seizures at the local port of entry. One such article had been laminated and hung on the wall in the main office of a port I visited. These stories draw a picture of borderwork as constantly concerned with the taming of illicit traffics. Raymond, the experienced officer we met in the interlude, told me, "You know [when I started as an officer] I truly expected that every day there was going to be a big drug seizure." Raymond then reacts to my smile at hearing his confession: "I just did! . . . You always would hear stories about people smuggling 50 bottles of alcohol and selling them and stuff."

Elizabeth, a mid-career officer whom I will properly introduce at the end of this chapter, also had to re-evaluate her expectations after a few months on the job: "You know, I did not know much about customs. . . . So I thought that it was more law enforcement than what I figured out it was when I started. So, I said, in the end, it's a lot of client services." Asked what made it different from what she anticipated, Elizabeth answered:

There is a lot of documentation. (. . .) Before I worked for customs, I would have never thought that all these government departments could be involved. (. . .) Because, in the end, customs, it's full of laws and regulations. It's not as much "customs" as the Criminal Code, health, agriculture, environment. . . . It's so varied. We touch on everything that comes into Canada.

Officers quickly realize that these stories do not exactly match their ordinary working life, but these stories have already played their role: it made people interested in borderwork.

A good local permanent job

As important as it was, an interest in security and law enforcement was not the most-cited reason for becoming a border officer. In this sense, my interviews confirm the results of the CBSA's 2011 internal survey of recent graduates from customs college, according to which only 11% of recent recruits joined the CBSA for the enforcement aspect of the job. In comparison, 33% of respondents cited job security as their principal motivation for becoming border officers.[2] Such importance given to stable employment is not surprising; it was cited by the majority of my research participants as an important reason to have chosen their current job. Despite vigour returning to the North American job market during the mid 2010s, structural economic insecurity has been increasingly prevalent in Southern Ontario industry towns facing deindustrialization and those who are employed work for less money and fewer social benefits. Meanwhile, the rural areas of Southeastern Quebec have been experiencing years of recurring crisis in the forestry industry compounded by a perpetual trade conflict between Canada and the United States over lumber. Borderland mills have reduced their activities, villages are shrinking and local businesses are closing. We will see in the next chapter that experienced officers in these regions reflect on these difficulties and are more likely than younger officers to envision their work as guided by economic protectionism as a result.

In this context, federal service positions are coveted; they offer stable employment, social protections and a comfortable public service pension. Of course, officers' working conditions can be demanding on one's health and social relations. The constant rotation of the day/night shift schedule disrupts sleep patterns and general health, especially for ageing officers. This shift rotation also makes it challenging for parents to organize day and night care for their children; in fact, as is also the case for police work, it is likely to constitute a barrier to entry, retention and promotion for mothers (Martin and Jurik 2007).[3] Yet the perks associated with the job are hard to beat in a North American and global labour market that increasingly offers contract-based, temporary, non-unionized and underpaid employment without social benefits (Vosko 2006, 2010). Many of those interviewed acknowledged their fortunate position. This was particularly the case for those who had grown up in working-class or farming families, those who became employed with border services after being laid off from their former workplace or those still living in communities hard hit by the economic downturn and closures in the manufacturing sector—in short, the majority of my interviewees.

Beyond employment stability, my research uncovers a unique dimension of the professional socialization of border officers: their attachment to place as a prime motive to enter the profession. As explained later in more detail, the CBSA's hiring policy now requires prospective officers to accept a posting anywhere in Canada. Therefore, it is not surprising that internal CBSA surveys do not inquire into officers' interest in maintaining kinship and friendship ties. Yet I found that all of the long-term employees I spoke to were born and raised in the vicinity of their workplace; in fact, most of the officers I interviewed (including rookies) still came from the immediate region or up to an hour drive away from the port of entry where they worked. It still remains true that proximity to home and family was a major reason cited for applying to border services. Born and raised in the region where she works, Catherine, an experienced officer, explained her need for close family ties in a job that can be socially isolating. She moved back home after some years spent at a port of entry a few hundred kilometres away:

> Well, family support is a big deal, especially when you're in a business or have a job where a lot of the public don't . . . aren't necessarily that friendly because of what you do. You tell somebody where you work, the first thing they do is get on the defensive.

Despite the CBSA's recent policy of distancing officers from their place of residence, fieldwork reveals that local placement still remains the norm. Therefore, the recent standardization of hiring procedures and the CBSA's search for enforcement-related aptitudes reviewed in the next section should not distract us from continuities in the expectations and motivations held by recruits, including the importance that they place on economic security, kinship relations, family obligations and their attachment to their region.

Standardizing hiring

Back then: home, family and a touch of nepotism

In contrast to the current CBSA practice that attracts postsecondary criminal justice as well as law and security profiles, past recruits before the standardization of hiring in 2007 came from a variety of educational backgrounds. It would have been quite exceptional in the 1980s for a new hire to have a university degree. Most career officers I met had a high school or college diploma. Beyond education, different factors presided over officer selection throughout Canadian Customs' history. In general, past practice favoured regional, even nearest-village appointments. Most experienced officers were hired as revenue employees directly through their port of entry after answering an advertisement in the local newspaper. At different times in customs history, policy also favoured the hiring of war veterans. The practice of distributing customs positions as a form of status recognition and income-generation reward for military service was first used by the British nobility during colonial times (Mcintosh 1984) and later revived after World War II. I interviewed three experienced officers who had worked with veterans at the start of their careers in the early 1980s. While respectful of their service, William thought that these veterans did not do much. Janette, a former customs broker who joined the border agency in the early 2000s, referred to these former veterans as "grocery police."

Hiring could also be a matter of nepotism and kinship ties. Many experienced officers mentioned that at the time of their hiring at the end of the 1980s, most of their coworkers had fathers, uncles, cousins and brothers working with them. Nowadays, if not a result of nepotism, borderwork can still be a family business. Some officers told me that they had a brother employed by the CBSA in their region, thus confirming the continuing significance of kinship networks at the land border even if standardization in hiring has taken effect. Local border crossers in the regions I visited often knew officers, because they or their children had grown up together.

Now: promoting enforcement

Things have significantly changed since the CBSA began standardized hiring by using a model borrowed from the federal police. Because of modifications to the Public Service Employment Act in 2007, which legislated on a "national area of selection for officer-level jobs," recruitment at the CBSA was made national. This tendency towards hiring and training standardization is not uniquely Canadian. Frontex also offers common border guard training in the hope of developing more-consistent bordering practices at Europe's external borders (Horii 2012).

For Canadian border workers, having recruitment respond to national criteria represents an important shift. Since then, candidates must apply in nationwide competitions, and following the deployment model of the RCMP, they must be willing to accept a position anywhere in the country. Interviewed officers told me that posting is established through a lottery system that takes into account recruit preferences, and it must be accepted for a minimum of two years, after which time one can file for redeployment closer to home. This new policy is intended to prevent favouritism by detaching hiring from kinship and local interdependencies. However, this neutralization of locality has carried perverse effects in its wake. Where former hiring policy promoted "flexibility at a local level," Kalman (2016: 112–113) shows that the national hiring policy tends towards the "depersonalization" of the relationship between officers and border residents, as it succeeded in bringing border agents from afar. This relationship had been central in reducing local conflict and in generating mutual understanding, especially when it came to unceded Indigenous territories such as Akwesasne (Cornwall–Massena at the Ontario–New York state border) where the bordering activities of both settler colonial states present complex jurisdictional issues while denying Mohawk sovereignty on these lands (Pratt and Templeman 2018). Kalman connects this depersonalization to the crisis that followed the Mohawks' opposition to the presence of armed border officer in their communities and to the subsequent relocation in 2009 of the port of entry as a result.

What does recruitment look like nowadays? Currently, officer enrolment makes plain the belief that border control requires a set of attitudes, capacities and skills more aligned with law enforcement and different from those previously held by customs officers. At the most visible level, change includes the willingness to wear policing equipment and to be trained in the use of enforcement tools. Further, the standardized hiring process is thorough. Candidates can be eliminated at various stages, which include an evaluation of bilingual abilities, an interview, physical fitness testing, medical and psychological evaluations and security clearance screening (including fingerprinting, employment and address history and even details about family members). Not unlike the truck drivers and travellers they assess, prospective Canadian border officers are now carefully vetted. As underscored by Loftus (2009: 19) in the case of the police, such changes in hiring are fundamental in altering the "ingrained dispositions" and "the entrenched values, beliefs and assumptions of officers."

To illustrate this overt promotion of enforcement attitudes and abilities in hiring, let's spend some time on one aspect of this selection process: physical fitness tests. The recourse to such tests is worth analysing not only because they enable a gendered reshaping of officers' embodiment but also because they shed light on the structural conditions that preside over this reshaping at the early stages of officer selection. The test used by the CBSA is adapted from RCMP material. The physical requirements of the test, such as muscular strength and endurance, are justified by the fact that to "effectively employ control and defence tactics in full uniform requires a significant level of muscular strength" as does "wearing a fully loaded duty belt throughout a shift." The case is vaguely made for cardiovascular capacity to foster "the ability to sustain a high level of work over an extended period of time" and for skill-related fitness to improve "accuracy, speed, balance, agility, and coordination."[4]

Physical fitness tests have been problematically used for a number of years in many North American public safety jobs, such as firefighting and policing. These occupations have "well-earned reputations as white, heteronormative masculinist labour forces" (Braedley 2019) that devalue and exclude subordinated masculinities and femininities from these forces while encouraging the assertion of dominance and encouraging ruthless and adversarial conduct on the part of their members (Burdett, Gouliquer and Poulin 2018; Johnston and Kilty 2015; Prokos and Padavic 2002). Physical fitness tests have long introduced a masculinist bias that acts as a sexist barrier to entry into these professions (Cordner and Cordner 2011; Lonsway 2003; Seklecki and Paynich 2007). They are an integral part of the employment inequities experienced in Canada by women, LGBTQ2S people and people of colour in these occupations, including instances of discrimination, harassment and barriers to promotion.[5]

In the US, police forces that use such tests have been found to hire fewer women (Schuck 2014). In Canada, these tests have been successfully challenged in court. In a 1999 decision, the Supreme Court of Canada concluded that workplace standards such as selection criteria must take into account physical differences between men and women from the outset (Cox and Messing 2006). Further, doubt has been cast over these tests' ability to "accurately reflect the physical requirements of common police work" (Batton and Wright 2019). In fact, there is

> little empirical evidence that these tests are (a) reflective of the most common tasks that officers are expected to perform, (b) predictive of performance when coping with hostile or noncompliant citizens, and (c) associated with fewer negative organizational outcomes, such as the cost of employee health care or absenteeism.
>
> (Schuck 2014)

Undoubtedly, borderwork involves physical effort. Crawling under trucks or cars does require some agility and flexibility, and yes, an experienced officer complained to me of back pain caused by wearing his tool belt every day. But countless other occupations involve physicality, often at more-demanding levels. We have also seen that much of officers' equipment is barely relied on every day. This brings legitimate questions as to the actual usefulness of such tools beyond the symbolic and masculinized performance of state power at the border. These tests constitute another piece of the puzzle in the shift towards law enforcement in bordering, conveying to potential applicants an image of borderwork as a heavy, potentially aggressive and corporeal duty.

Early training

I now turn my attention to the formal and informal aspects of officers' early training. In the words of van Maanen (1973: 408), whose classic work on police professional socialization remains a point of reference, "early organizational learning is a major determinant of one's later organizationally relevant beliefs, attitudes and behaviours." During their initial learning period, aspiring border officers develop the basic skills required by their workplace. They acquire technological, administrative and investigative skills; learn about the laws and regulations they are required to apply; and are made aware of their employer's main policy objectives. But recruits also begin to shape new generational dispositions and learn to engage with their profession's changing mindset.

Fostering local habits: when officers were hired by their port of entry

After being hired by their port of entry, officers used to be trained by their new colleagues in search-and-seizure procedures but also in a wide range of administrative responsibilities. Much of that training taught them to consider borderwork as concerned with the regulation of cross-border trade, tax collection and the protection of the Canadian economy. Their apprenticeship was characterized by on-the-job learning, the informal passing of colleagues' know-how and skill sets and the adoption of behaviours prioritized by officers and management in their particular port. The professional socialization of officers was mostly experiential and local; their behaviour, attitudes and know-how had already been firmly established well before attending customs college.

Such localized transmission of knowledge allowed for a strong port subculture to develop, a sense of how bordering was to be done at that particular port. It shaped how discretion was to be used—for instance, influencing the port's preference for "helping" the local economy by enforcing national regulations on imported goods more severely, adopting an anti-smuggling focus or being more emphatic about the payment of duties. Local management thus put a specific colour on their port's reputation through hiring and training. These port-based attitudes still linger. In fact, truck drivers are aware of US and Canadian port-of-entry subcultures and will willingly discuss where they prefer to cross, depending on the reputation of a port for being fair or for treating people more severely.

After being appointed, officers worked from three to ten years before being sent to customs college. The length of this in-class training varied according to the cohort, from 9 to 16 weeks, depending on the year when my interviewees attended the college. The course divided officers' time between what was called international and what was called commercial—that is, between the rules pertaining to the regulation of travellers at the land border and in airports and those controlling importations and exportations through air, marine, train and highway modes of transportation. Given the fact that immigration enforcement responsibilities lay with Citizenship and Immigration employees before the creation of CBSA in 2003, there was little immigration-related training at the time. Hired in the first half of the 1980s, Jacob recalls his 14-week stay at the customs college in Rigaud, near Montreal, at the beginning of the 1990s:

> First week was immigration, the rest was all customs. That's all. We got one week in immigration because, when you process the travellers on the

line, you have to know some of the rules in immigration. (. . .) But there was no use of force, there was no handcuffs, nothing, when I was there. It was basically learning the tariffs and regulations.

Those who attended Rigaud under that model all pointed out that attendance had required a lot of time away from their families. But they also recall that this part of their training was not as stressful as the one experienced by current recruits. When career officers were sent to the Rigaud campus until the first half of the 2000s, they had the certainty that they would keep their employment regardless of their academic results and that they would be fully paid during the duration of their in-class training. The stakes are now much higher. In contrast to past practice, recruits must now undergo unpaid in-class training for weeks at the CBSA's college, with their employment dependent on their successful completion of the course.

All full-time officers are now required to repeat their use of force training at customs college every three years. For a few days, they review restraint techniques, handcuffing and legal procedures regulating arrest. During these short sojourns, older officers interact with recruits undergoing their initial academic training. Jacob speaks of the ambiance at Rigaud compared to the ambiance from when he attended:

> You see the new ones who are there. Holy cow! You go in the cafeteria and they are sitting at the table beside us and they speak only of the training. They are really concentrated on their studies. For us, let's say it was lighter than that.

Rigaud boot camp: socializing enforcers

When we attend university or a postgraduate technical school, and when we start working, we are resocialized; that is, we learn new habits and ways of seeing the world that we had not been in touch with through our family, social networks or early schooling (Darmon 2016: 75). This resocialization process is particularly acute in security, military and public safety professions. For instance, military pedagogies profoundly reshape soldiers' embodiment, sensory experience and identity formation (Lande 2007; Hockey 2009; Woodward and Jenkings 2011). Nolan (2013) describes, in her study of the CIA, how intensive this "acculturation" process can be in the elite intelligence world, where resocialization strategies for recruits include fostering a deep identification with the agency and enforcing secrecy and a strict separation from civilians and other non-CIA security personnel. Of course, CBSA training is not that demanding, and its goals are not geared towards a complete resocialization of aspiring border officers. Yet some aspects of this training speak to a higher degree of intensity than that previously experienced by senior officers.

A major indication of the turn of officer training to law enforcement has been its remodelling along the police training model. Before attending Rigaud, recruits must first quickly dispose of matters such as "values and ethics" as well as "diversity and race relations in the workplace" during a four-week period of online preparation.[6] Such an expedited review of fundamental matters related to human rights and accountability indicates a lack of proper training to prepare Canadian border officers for what will become an essential part of their daily work: interacting with border crossers (Lalonde 2019). Prospective officers are then sent to customs college for four and a half months of intensive training, followed by an on-the-job training period of 12 to 18 months. The curriculum includes a substantial enforcement component that was previously absent from past training. Indeed, three of the six main stated objectives of the curriculum are now related to enforcement (including classes on firearm skills, use of force, seizures, detention, search and arrest), and attendance to physical fitness classes has become mandatory. Further, the CBSA follows renewed police training curriculums that have been developed internationally since the 1990s, which emphasized "cognitive and decision-making domains" (Haarr 2001: 405) and "formal training in 'subjective' features of policing" (de Lint 1998: 290). This part of the training aims at developing the successful resolution of simulated scenarios where students must show their capacity to apply their newly acquired regulatory knowledge to concrete situations. At contemporary police academies, "problem-based learning" often emphasizes conflict resolution and community policing with the view of fostering a more democratic approach to public safety (Werth 2011). At customs college, however, it relates to the acquisition of enforcement and interrogation skills. For instance, rookie officers that I interviewed were tested on their ability to recognize "risk indicators" of nervousness in travellers (played by professional actors).[7]

More than changes in curriculum, it was the modification in the *experience* of training that caught my attention as I talked with officers. In addition to the official academic programme, the college teaches recruits a set of unofficial lessons, or what Chappell and Lanza-Kaduce (2010) call the hidden curriculum of police-type trainings. Two informal features of police training appear to be duplicated at Rigaud: the fear of stigma and shame that accompanies failure and the stress experienced by recruits. Nicknamed by Sarah with tongue-in-cheek humour "Rigaud Boot Camp", in-class training was described by all interviewees as being more rigorous and nerve-racking than in the past. On the model of the police academy, recruits are exposed to high levels of stress. Whenever they are asked about their experience at CBSA's college, rookie officers insist on the psychological and emotional dimensions of their academic training rather than its actual content.

Officers described in detail the fear of failure at Rigaud. A clerk, Victoria had wished to become an officer but failed her formal training despite her knowledge of customs regulations. She went back to being a clerk. Her case illustrates the high requirements held by the border officer training, even for those with previous work experience at the border. Sarah recalled that two people failed in her class of 15–20 people, and a concurrent class lost five students. As an indication, from 2006 to 2010, the pass rates at Rigaud have fluctuated between 77% and 88%.[8] Evaluations are an especially stressful time. Thomas, a rookie officer who had completed the training two years before we met, recalled a "panic" moment related to these evaluations:

> You always doubt yourself, and then it starts turning in your head, like a hamster in its wheel. I give you an example: during the second part of the training, we had questions about immigration, and . . . I remember, there was a wind of panic about a simulation test in our group. Everyone was asking the same question. "No, it's not that!" So the group was divided [about the answer] and we were one day before the test and there was no teacher because it was over the weekend.

The theatrics of failure is particularly humiliating and contributes to a general atmosphere of anxiety for remaining recruits. Candidates who fail tests are immediately sent to their room, required to collect their personal belongings and escorted out of the building. This whole process is witnessed by the remaining participants. The fear of being kicked out runs high and keeps trainees on their toes. Sarah was extremely apprehensive of expulsion: "There's so much pressure on you. (. . .) You are so afraid to mess up because you don't want to get kicked out."

All of the officers who went through the overhauled CBSA training kept vivid memories of their experience. Thomas perceived the training to be not academically difficult but instead mentally challenging:

> It is not difficult in terms of studying but there is the psychological level, the stress. They get all over you to see if you will break. (. . .) I watched a lot of documentaries about army training but . . . I wouldn't say that it is the same. . . . It is more about whether you will break at some point, saying, "I can't do this anymore." (. . .) Rigaud, it's something (. . .) you get completely out of. . . . You become a different person during these nine weeks. You are beside yourself.[9]

As a testament to the life-altering quality of this resocializing experience, Thomas broke up with his girlfriend after his college training ended.

Contrary to Jubany's (2017: 113) findings on UK training of immigration officers, which is done in a relaxed atmosphere where "storytelling and sharing" predominate, Canadian border officers describe their academic training as demanding and evolving in a high-pressure environment. Such intensification through anxiety-driven practices generates stressful inner group dynamics while working through the dispositions of aspiring recruits, teaching them more than a simple curriculum of border regulations and policies. Conti (2009) reflects on how humiliation in early officer training simultaneously functions as "status degradation" and "status elevation"; it is through those types of experiences fostered by police-type trainings that recruits become acquainted with the dynamics of authority and subordination that they are expected to reproduce in their interactions with civilians. At Rigaud, the combination of an enforcement-based curriculum with stress, fear of failure and the spectacle of shame offered by trainee expulsion contribute to the production of a policing sensibility that prepares officers to exert authority at the border.

Changing pedagogies of border control: accounting for the generation gap

A key area of discussion regarding professional socialization concerns the role that early training plays in changing police practice and culture in the long term. Most researchers highlight recruits' motivation while training and as they begin working (Devery 2003; Pruvost and Roharik 2011). Yet studies also note that the early dispositions fostered at police academy can be altered by the realities of police work, as recruits are pressed to adapt their dispositions to fit into their new workplace.[10] The literature reveals that while cultural change does happen in contemporary policing, traditional views in police organizations still persist. As they become acquainted with police bureaucracy, budget cuts, legal constraints on action and complex relations with the public, the disillusionment experienced by policing actors, then and now, has been associated with officers' "shifts in ethical standpoint" and isolation from the public (Alain and Grégoire 2008). Van Maanen's (1975) argues in his classic account of this disillusionment that street-policing training requires a consistency in dispositions displayed at work regardless of police academy training. This consistency would ultimately elucidate the intergenerational stability of police conduct: "In large measure, the flow of influence from one generation to another accounts for the remarkable stability of the pattern of police behaviour" (222).

Against this backdrop of understanding, the critical attitude shown by the rookies I interviewed towards their senior colleagues is all the more intriguing. Why do they give so much weight to what was learned in Rigaud over knowledge accumulated over years of field experience? In contrast to what the literature tells us about police officers, when faced with the realities of their daily routines, newly appointed officers do not seem to change their understanding of what "real" borderwork should be about—instead, challenging their experienced peers (a theme that I will return to in the next chapter).

When looked at through the prism of reform efforts in security and policing agencies, reaching some degree of continuity between the attitudes that training aims to foster and those held at the border is no small feat. The CBSA has been successful in promoting a generational change in occupational culture that many other policing organizations in the world would envy. The CBSA's success with a project to replace the set of normative understandings held by officers is especially noteworthy given the current international context. Policing and security organizations everywhere face difficulties in the promotion of reforms going against the grain of traditional police or intelligence culture as well as of established power struggles between agencies—as has been shown to be true in the case of community policing, and better recognition of diversity as well as in the case of promoting intelligence cooperation (Loftus 2009; Nolan 2013). What accounts for this success? I suggest this project gained traction precisely because it *embraces* dominant elements of traditional policing culture.

The previous chapter gave an account of firearm promotion as a strategy to limit officers' loss of influence in bordering; it is now possible to add to this analysis the finding that a configuration of expectations, hiring policy and training also participates in the making of an enforcement-based vision for borderwork, one that insists on the characteristics of policing most associated with the potential to harness the state's legitimate means of violence. Ultimately, officers' early professional socialization makes it clear that borderwork is no longer about preparing Ministry of Revenue employees to apply Canadian regulations and collect taxes but about becoming part of a "police of the border." This representation reflects entrenched popular and gendered stereotypes about policing and security work as action-packed occupations. While the discrepancy is growing between this image and the daily reality of borderwork, including the fact that it still involves time-consuming clerical, trade facilitation and regulatory components—especially in maritime (Thibault 2019) and highway commercial work—officers' early professional socialization is now more aligned with their prior expectations. It is on this point that the generation gap between approaches to borderwork begins to appear.

In the field: learning the ropes

We have reached the moment when officers take up their posts. From this point on, recruits' professional socialization unfolds into a variety of experiences that depend on where they start their careers. This involves learning interview skills and recognizing "risk indicators" (those aspects in behaviour, speech or documentation that arouse doubt in officers about a border crosser) but also acquiring the more specialized knowledge that comes with working "commercial."

Learning to work commercial: a specialized knowledge

Whether an officer begins their career in traffic or in commercial depends on the approach taken by local management. Traditionally, the traffic section is viewed as the unofficial training school for rookies, and this is still the case in many ports. Here, they learn the basics of interviewing travellers, searching their belongings and applying basic customs regulations. After a few years and depending on seniority, officers may apply to transfer to the immigration or commercial sections if positions open up. But in ports where local management prefers developing a specialized workforce trained in the particulars of customs and trade compliance from inception, rookies are hired directly as commercial border officers.

To work at the commercial section, a border officer must acquire an impressive amount of knowledge. First, trainee commercial officers are taught onsite to search trucks, trailers, truck cabs and merchandise in order to find hidden compartments, concealed drugs, illicit merchandise and firearms. In some ports, they also learn how to operate a VACIS truck, an X-ray vehicle that rapidly scans a truck trailer's contents without emptying it. In other ports, they train to inspect small commercial shipments imported by courier companies in a warehouse attached (or close) to the commercial section. In addition to adapting their enforcement skills to customs work, officers must familiarize themselves with customs forms and learn to release shipments electronically. They get acquainted with a number of trade, environmental, agricultural and health regulations for which they verify compliance on behalf of a variety of federal ministries and agencies. They become skilled at recognizing counterfeit goods, the lumber species that necessitate a permit to enter the country or the diet pills prohibited from importation. Diane, a seasoned officer for whom everyday commercial work "is an adventure," recalls an anecdote that speaks to the complexity of this regulatory knowledge that she had to learn throughout her career:

> Sometimes we have to refer back because they change policy and procedures. So sometimes there are certain things . . . you want to ensure the direction you're taking is correct, so you go back to your d-memos.[11] And we have a huge volume of directives so . . . It's funny! A lady had come down one time from Transport Canada (they were doing a project with us), and so she says, "I brought all my directives with me" . . . and it was just a volume! We have 21 . . . well actually 22 like that!

Officers also learn about the harmonized system nomenclature (HS codes), an international customs tariff classification scheme overseen by the World Customs Organization that links each legally traded commodity to a ten-digit code.[12] 98% of all international trade is classified through this system. Canada's classification system includes about 10,000 HS codes.[13] Beyond accumulating trade-related statistics, this classification system designates countries of origin for imported products to apply appropriate duties and taxes or to establish preferential treatment in cases where Canada entered a free trade agreement with the country of origin. While customs officers do not memorize every HS code, they familiarize themselves with those applying to the type of commodities that cross their port most regularly.

Despite such complexity, the rookie officers I met had received no commercial-based training during the time they spend at customs college—with the exception of basic food, plant and agricultural inspection. As Sarah explained, the first months on the job can be "overwhelming" for those officers appointed to a commercial section just after graduating from the college:

> Rigaud was great. However, it doesn't teach you about commercial operations. So, this is a completely different job from what I learned in Rigaud. So, all of the paperwork was completely new to me, the computer system was new, everything was new.

Diane agreed: new officers like Sarah are ill-prepared and have not received enough training to orient themselves in commercial, where "things change pretty quickly."

Most of those whom I spoke to had learned their trade by working the line and through their more experienced colleague's teachings. William, whom I mentioned in the introduction, speaks of those moments when enforcement-trained rookies stare blankly at their senior colleagues, wondering what to do with a challenging customs case. He adds that:

> Older officers are a safety net when rookies are confronted with a situation. So, when it is not related to law enforcement, they wonder: "OK, but how do we treat this?" That is when the older officer, with more experience, is able to say: "Look, I'll show you. Those are horses. Horses, they can't come in for more than 72 hours." Oh, wow! All of a sudden, they found that older officer interesting. They listen to him religiously, because they had no idea.

Experienced officers find themselves providing guidance with databases, mentoring rookies in their inspection and interviewing skills, answering queries about trade regulations or correcting the occasional mistakes made by their rookie colleagues in filling in customs forms or releasing shipments electronically. Those teachable moments create a multitude of occasions for transmitting knowledge but also, as seen in the next chapter, for intergenerational discussion about what borderwork should focus on.

Interviewing at one's discretion: an uneven learning terrain

Like many of my interviewees, Thomas (a rookie) opined that custom college's instruction to "risk indicators" is rigid and lacks the nuances found on the job. Thomas and his colleagues thus call them "Rigaud indicators":

"When a border officer makes decisions, it's every time . . . discretionary. How they teach it there, it is more set in stone." Richard, the officer whom I mentioned in Chapter 5 who was convinced that arming had "changed everything" in borderwork, agreed that a wide range of interpretations of people's behaviours are made possible by looking for indicators:

> It all depends. Everybody kind of puts value into their own indicators differently. And that's kind of the key. No two officers are really the same. Something that you might think is a big deal: Hey, this guy's pulling his ear, this guy is answering a question in a manner that they don't find fitting, he's maybe overly nervous, or overly chatty, right? That's one you see often: This driver is overly chatty! Why are they overly chatty? Well, they've been driving by themselves for about three days. (. . .) They haven't talked to anybody. (. . .) It's just sometimes . . . [they] just want to talk to anybody! (. . .) And again, some people say that's a great indicator. And some people say . . . well, excuse me, that's not a great indicator.

In Chapter 3, I demonstrated that borderwork produces a variability in taxonomies of risk. This variability also rests on officers' professional socialization once in the field and on the particular career path taken by officers throughout those years. Learning to balance one's suspicions about travellers and truck drivers evolves. Richard explains:

> If I look back and see myself now compared to seeing myself back then, well the experience. . . . You obviously feel better about how you handle situations, but I just think . . . just a little more responsible, and not that I was really negligent or reckless but back then it was like OK, you'd fire in anybody who was even remotely suspicious. But when you first start, everybody's suspicious because you're like. . . . You don't trust anybody! Right? And eventually, you kind of grow and learn and eventually. . . . I guess you'd say you evolve, your skill gets honed, you learn about . . . how to categorize people from people and do better risk assessments.

It is useful to compare Richard's thoughts on how he tended to be more distrustful at the beginning of his career with Sarah's thoughts. Sarah exemplifies well what Richard himself described as his early experience, still relying on "Rigaud indicators" in her assessments:

> Maybe [the truck driver] is a little nervous, but nervous could be something for contraband as well, like, you know, just those. . . . You can hear it in their voice, they're stuttering, or they're shaking a little or they just look nervous or doing those repetitive motions like, you know, tapping on their steering wheel and all those things that you learn in Rigaud.

In Chapter 4, I argued that the ability to elicit speech from travellers and to recognize signs from which suspicion arises is the basis of the professional identity of border officers. Here, I actively engage with Salter's (2007) suggestion that examination at the border is an acquired practice. Learning how to conduct face-to-face evaluations of travellers is a gradual process; techniques are transmitted by formal training and between colleagues exchanging tips but also in the form of an experiential know-how with its own logic of practice. We will see in the next chapter that investigative techniques such as using databases and interviewing and reading "risk indicators" receive different generational valuation at ports of entry. However, there is a continuity in the way experienced officers, mid-career officers and rookie officers testify to having learned these skills. Examination is seen as a craft that has to be honed and refined for years in the field in order to be fully incorporated into the habits of border guards.

When examining differences in risk taxonomies, we would also be wise to reflect on the variations within security officials' learning experiences. With the irregularity experienced by rookie officers in field training opportunities, officers are not all created equal when it comes to their interviewing abilities. The port of entry offers an uneven terrain for acquiring the range of knowledges that influence interviewing as well as behavioural risk assessments. Officers may be hired by a small port of entry in a remote region or by a major port in an urban area. They may work close to home and thus be acquainted with the region, its residents and frequent border crossers or be relocated for their first assignment. Similar to airports, those who start at the traffic section learn the ropes of interviewing after encountering travellers with diverse backgrounds during repetitive hours of booth work. Later, they might spend a few years working immigration, exploring a wide-range of interviewing techniques. But those officers starting their career at the commercial section directly after their customs college training might not become as proficient at these skills. This can happen for a number of reasons. On the one hand, shipments and carriers are often precleared, reducing opportunities for inquiries about the commodities that are about to enter the country. On the other hand and as seen in the interlude, truck drivers show predictable patterns of travel; they are generally familiar with border regulations and willing to respect them in order to keep themselves employed. This routine is less likely to produce the variety of interviewing situations encountered by officers at the traffic and immigration sections.

This uneven learning terrain affects how border decisions are made and eventually can expose these decisions to legal action, especially in cases where they are submitted to the evidentiary norms of criminal justice. As recruits differentially learn interviewing skills and how to recognize that which putatively indicates risk, they may not be able to make strong cases for immigration admissibility decisions and criminal court proceedings. In fact, in an internal audit about its training programmes, the agency reports that "poor note taking, inadequate interviewing skills and poor evidence handling by BSOs [border services officers] have resulted in the CBSA being unsuccessful in admissibility hearings and criminal investigations as the evidence provided was not able to withstand legal challenges."[14] As seen in chpater 4, examinations blend years of experiential learning with interpretations of scientific findings and formal technical teachings about how one can access the meaning of human behaviour, affect and speech by reading a person's body and voice. However, differences in field-training experiences and individual officers' development of idiosyncratic interviewing techniques indicate the vulnerability in interpretations of signs of deception, truth and nervousness during face-to-face interactions between officers and border crossers.

An apprenticeship in dominance: gender, age and displaying authority

Having earned the right to represent the state at its borders by successfully passing the test of customs college, border officers still need to master a series of strategies for self-presentation and demeanour to embody their authority convincingly. Before I turn to how Marie, Elizabeth and Thomas have learned to embody authority, I reflect on why an examination of what I call the apprenticeship in dominance is important for our wider investigation into the shift to law enforcement in border control.

A staple area of discussion in the sociology of policing concerns the mechanisms that invest the police with the authority to enforce the law and concerns the limits to such authority.[15] As Sheptycki (2017: 4) argues, beyond acquiring formal policing skills, "primary police socialisation concerns the mastery of a set of tactics that are about asserting authority, taking control." Displaying authority thus depends on an "effect of demonstration" productive of "truth effects as important as the means on which it rests" (Chauvenet and Orlic 1985: 462). Such projection of authority involves the development of an "asymmetric and hierarchical relation with their 'clients'" (Alain and Pruvost 2011: 268). Accordingly, making these asymmetric relations possible depends partly on how those wearing the uniform will learn to bring state authority to life.

Conveying such authority takes on a particular twist in border spaces, as it is based on a less legally constrained, more crude form of state power. Writing of border *performativity*, Salter (2011), following Butler, theorizes borderwork as a "stylized repetition of acts of sovereignty." While the term *performativity* might be better applied to matters relative to individual self-expression and resistance to social scripts and institutional demands than to the requirements of bureaucratic settings, the main idea behind Salter's proposition remains worthy of attention. Through repeated daily gestures (interrogating, searching), motions and postures (carrying oneself wearing a bulletproof vest) and acts (allowing or refusing entry into the country), security professionals enact the state's authority at its limits. Adopting an authoritative attitude, learning to speak in ways that can be simultaneously imposing and distant and building the confidence to always keep eye contact with travellers in order to both impose respect and "detect deception" are all embodied dispositions that take time to develop. These "techniques of the body" (Mauss 1934) are crucial to the successful display of state authority at the border. Yet authority at the border also entails the work of *legitimation*. In the world of scholarly debate about the normative valuations that sustain borderwork in the exercise of such power—such as what is seen by officers as doing a good job or what kind of decisions they think are justified—Vega (2018) invites us to ponder how border officers also legitimize the "uncritical performance" of problematic official mandates at borders. In short, Vega (whose work is located at the Mexico–US border, where border workers arrest, detain and deport daily) finds that as they talk about and do their job, border workers legitimize not only their own actions but also what the state does at its borders through them.

Building on these observations, here I look into another modality in the apprenticeship of dominance that requires learning how to display authority at the border and that has been neglected thus far: how gender and age enter the performance, justification and *perception* of authority at the border. In fact, I have found that officers, especially women and younger officers, work hard to conform to expectations that come with being tasked to protect borders. Authors interested in the integration of women into police forces have long underlined the demands made on female officers regarding their disciplined conformity to masculinized codes of conduct (Heidensohn 1992). However, women entering security occupations live an especially contradictory experience as a result of such expectations: "their peer groups require them to behave in accordance with organizational norms, whereas society does not expect them to drift from gender role stereotypes" (Poteyeva and Sun 2009: 513). For Diphoorn (2015), "masculinized body capital . . . is a key source of [street-level officer] sovereign power," and some have to labour at acquiring this capital in order to be taken seriously by their peers and the travelling public. In fact, the "belief in the legitimacy of male and white privilege" (Acker 2006: 454) found in all organizations is pivotal to successful enactments of authority in security, border and police organizations.

Whether representatives of the state exert coercion (or threaten to do so) and whether this results in compliance from border crossers entails heavily gendered, racialized and age-related features. This creates intricacies around privilege and subordination in border spaces that are not always acknowledged in all their complexity. Learning to display authority happens not only because of peer pressure and the organizational structure of security but also, and in large part, because of travellers' attitudes, expectations and social positionality: whether they are citizens, white, male and with means will have an impact not only on how border crossers are treated at the border but also on how they expect to be treated.

The uniform does not make the officer

The combined state of being required to display self-confidence and a modicum of experience in your 20s, fresh out of Rigaud, and dealing with impatient travellers (many of whom are older than you are) certainly presents some teachable moments. Thomas was one of the officers I met who showed the most respect for truck drivers and their difficult work lives. He had friends in transportation. Thomas came from a working-class family (his father was employed in construction) and was actively involved in his union. Yet he recalled a recent unwarranted altercation with a driver:

> Two weeks ago, I got a bit confronted by a 51-year-old man. There were two normal vehicles that entered into the commercial section because they were commercial vehicles. So, for security reasons, I could not see the person because of [the location of] my booth, so I told the gentleman, "Could you tell the person who follows you to back up?" So he said, "Yeah, really?!" And then it went downhill: "Idiot! Listen, young man: I am 51 years old, I won't get shit on by a young punk." And I said, "OK. What does age have to do in this story? I have a job to do, I have my work methods and I have to respect them."

Thomas' uniform did not prevent this driver from insulting him without fear of repercussion. But young officers are not the only ones subjected to such treatment. Women of all ages are likely to see their authority questioned. For instance, a senior traffic officer I met while on a tour of her port of entry told me that the previous evening, a traveller had refused to comply with her instructions, arguing that he would not take orders from a woman.

Altercations between officers and border crossers present a strong gendered component. Arthur, a tall and muscular senior officer, proudly described how he came to the rescue of a young female officer who faced some difficult travellers. Arthur described a situation where his helpful but paternalistic intervention was enough to transform a situation of noncompliance into one of consent to authority:

> But they know that I'd be there for them [young officers] also, so. . . . If I see them getting in trouble, I'll say: "Excuse-me, can I help you?" and that stops the confrontation. (. . .) Yeah. Out front [in traffic] there were officers so bad, we had students. . . . They'd make the students do every car while they sat down on their . . . behinds and did nothing. I'd watch this young student, maybe 20-year-old young blonde, go to a car surrounded by six guys [travellers] and she'd be backed over in the back seat trying to find if they got bottles and all six guys were [looking] down [at her behind] and, "Hum, ah . . ." I walked over and said [*he raps on*

the table]: "Get up here now!" and the young lady said, "Thank you very
much." She was frightened to death.

Predictably, instances of prejudice from border crossers involve not only
youth and gender but also race. Denise, a young officer of colour, confided
that she was processing paperwork at her booth one day when a driver said
she was beautiful "for a woman of colour."

These descriptions of occasional sexist and racist conduct (as well as
instances of intimidation and harassment) directed at young, racialized and/
or female officers by travellers who feel entitled enough to question these
officers' authority point to a seldom-explored dynamic. On the one hand,
we generally assume that power relations in border settings favour security
professionals and immigration authorities. This assumption has been verified
time and again. Security professionals at every level on the border-policing
hierarchy remain widely unaccountable for their actions. As further explored
in the conclusion to this book, security politics, the interdiction of refugees
(Kaushal and Dauvergne 2011), powers of detention (Silverman 2019), illegalization and deportation (Villegas 2015 and the accumulation and exchange
of personal and biometric data on travellers and the establishment of no-fly
lists by security authorities (International Civil Liberties Monitoring Group
2010) are among the practices that support the thesis of extensive state powers in ever-swelling border spaces in Canada and elsewhere, and they shed
light on the few remedies offered to those caught in this expanding net.

On the other hand, border officers remain street-level bureaucrats who
occupy low-level positions within the overall security field. Consequently, during concrete, everyday situations involving travellers and border officers at the
land border, social status classifications (age, race, citizenship, gender, ethnicity
and class) intersect in ways that can (but do not necessarily) privilege border officers. As illustrated by these stories, the uniform does not always bring
about deference from border crossers; border infrastructure and the spatial
arrangement of ports of entry, however impressive, do not automatically create
compliance with border regulations. As a result, the effective display of authority by officers is rigged with uncertainty. To tilt the balance of power in their
favour, border officers have to sharpen the affective dispositions associated
with their position. During their first years in the field, border officials, and
especially female officers, cultivate a series of informal gendered strategies that
help them look the part. While we tend to take for granted the performance
of authority by uniformed state representatives, my interviews with Marie and
Elizabeth highlight the slow and demanding process that it entails in practice.

Authority as a gendered apprenticeship: Marie and Elizabeth

The female officers I met can be counted among the first cohorts of women to
have entered Canadian border services. Like Marie, many were hired as clerks

for the commercial section of their ports of entry at the end of the 1970s or during the following years, only to find their position jeopardized a decade later. As detailed in Chapter 2, commercial operations became increasingly computerized after 1989, thus lessening clerical labour needs at customs. Canada Customs and Revenue proceeded to cut administrative staff, which was historically overwhelmingly female as a result of an explicit gendered division of labour in ports of entry where border officers were male and clerks female. These clerks were told that they needed to apply for officers' positions if they wished to remain employed. Marie joined the traffic section as a trainee officer, like many of her colleagues in the same position, after a hiring procedure that required qualifications and tests.

A senior officer close to retirement when we met, Marie was pleased to have escaped the "monotony" of clerical work. But she was shocked by the year she spent doing traffic work; the regular confrontation with travellers contrasted with common practice at the commercial section, and she asked to be transferred back to commercial after a year spent in traffic. In her comments, she spoke comparatively about her gendered experience, believing that the "clientele is much more aggressive" in traffic: "They are mean and not easy to work with. (. . .) And in those years, I did not have enough character, so with the first clients who were quite aggressive, I had tears in my eyes quite easily. But we develop a character." Marie added that she found truck drivers "much more pleasant to work with . . . because we see them again, and I did not have. . . . Anyway, I am not an officer who is really, really severe and mean. I am quite polite, and I say "vous" [*formal address in French*] to everyone. . . . I never had problems. (. . .) Even though these are men who sometimes have criminal records and all, but it goes well."[16] Marie returned to her experience in traffic and to how she constantly had to assert herself:

> What I found really lame in traffic is that because you are a woman, you always have to prove everything, prove your authority. . . . You don't have that on the truck drivers' side. For sure, they are "tough" and "rough," but if you keep your authority. . . . You do your job, you don't have to be friendly with them. You don't. . . . You do your work, that's all. I don't have problems with anyone.

Then, Marie elaborated further on what she has to do to remain in control:

> For sure, you stand up for yourself, and for sure, if you start buying into their stories . . . it would be easy, you know, that a truck driver starts flirting with you, but if you remain respectful and stand your ground, you won't have any problem. Don't get into friendships or anything of the sort. You have to keep . . . your . . . your position. (. . .) At work, I am at work, but outside, I am. . . . Look, I have fun, and we can. . . . We laugh a lot, I am even teasing. But at my job, this is how it works. You know, I will be very polite with people if they tell me jokes, I'll laugh but

it stops there. I don't deviate and become friendly with them. I am also very respectful of the clientele.

I asked Marie whether she thought that this experience was different from that of her male colleagues:

At first, it is probably more difficult. But I shaped my own personality that way. And now, this is who I am. And since I learned lots of psychology when attending CEGEP [the postsecondary college system in Quebec], I am able to approach the majority of people by looking at them and starting to talk to them: "OK, this one, I have to talk to him this way, I have to be careful with this particular aspect." (. . .) Even with other employees, I get along with everyone because I know how to approach people.

Whereas Marie had been hired as an officer in the 1990s, Elizabeth started her career at the beginning of the 2000s. She grew up in the region where she now works and had experimented with superintendent work at some point. Elizabeth viewed enforcement tools and arming as symbols of a "new mentality" in borderwork, even though, and in contrast to Richard, for instance, she believed that arming has "not changed much" in her everyday job. According to this young, mid-career officer with gentle manners and a soft voice, working at the border makes female officers more firm and exacting. She described a typical encounter at the border:

You are in a booth and there are two booths open, but curiously, there are more truck drivers on one side than on the other. That's because truck drivers all say to each other [on their CB radio] "Ah! There's a nice little girl!" So now, you have a line-up and it's the female officer who has it! [*She laughs*]. So, you are wondering: "Why do I have more?" And suddenly you hear a comment in a truck driver's radio.

I asked Elizabeth, "Is it because you are supposed to be friendlier?" Elizabeth concurs: "Yes. That's it. That is the only reason why: 'She is nicer, this one; she makes you cross faster.'" Listening to Elizabeth, I wondered: "Are you nicer?" She replied: "No. If there is something, I think that women, we are stricter than a man can be, I think. We don't want to be taken for fools and we do not wish. . . . One should not necessarily trust physical appearance."

Both Marie and Elizabeth work in a masculine environment. We have seen that borderwork is culturally marked masculine. A majority of their colleagues and even their "clients," truck drivers, are overwhelmingly male. This situation generates gendered expectations as to who should be the bearers of authority at the border and how they should handle this state-sanctioned capability. Seeing a woman in this position does not usually fit those expectations.

Accordingly, as Marie and Elizabeth reflexively discussed how they perform their authority, they illustrated how women in security professions learn to develop a number of gendered strategies for imparting their presence at the border with a commanding quality. If Elizabeth wants to avoid "being taken for a fool" (as do all her colleagues), she has to be intentional about it, shaping her conduct to surpass in severity the manner of her male colleagues. Having to work against gendered stereotypes that cast her as softer, more flexible and "nicer" means having to overcompensate and be "stricter."

Not wishing to adopt the commanding behaviour favoured by some of her colleagues and use her prerogatives too forcefully, Marie chooses another route. After all, she "is not too mean or too severe." Nevertheless, Marie also had to readjust her conduct in order to avoid being harassed or challenged. Experience at traffic quickly taught her that being an authority in customs, importation rules and tariffs did not mean that her directions would be followed by border crossers. Marie first looked for ways to remove manifestations of familiarity from her behaviour. She believed that they could be interpreted as a display of vulnerability or flirting, that being familiar would generate from border crossers sexist and sexualizing responses to which women are often subjected in their everyday lives but which, in the context of borderwork, would also reveal that she is no longer in control. Beyond language tools such as the use of *vouvoiement*, her explanations were filled with distancing strategies that she improved on over the years to affirm such control: "not getting involved in friendships," "keeping your authority and your position," "stand up for yourself and stand your ground," "remaining polite," "be respectful of the clientele" and "not getting involved in their stories." She even relied on psychological knowledge learned during her postsecondary education in order to assess how to best approach truck drivers and her own colleagues.

Listening to Marie and Elizabeth, I realized that the performance of sovereignty relies on being effective at embodying competence and on authority over the travelling public and that this constitutes an ongoing gendered labour. Accordingly, of concern here are not those reticent border crossers who legitimately call into question the wide range of powers granted to border officers when they realize with dismay that their privacy and dignity are reduced at the border.[17] In contrast, at issue is the fact that female officers somehow appear "out of place" in bordering because they are women in a position of authority working in a masculinized security environment.

The significance of women's apprenticeship in security professions

What light does the contested and limited presence of women in borderwork shed on the contemporary transformation of bordering practices? In a fascinating article, Cowen and Siciliano (2011) examine the reincorporation of underemployed men of racialized and working-class backgrounds in the private security and paramilitary industries in the UK and the US. Such reconfiguration of the labour market points to the securitization and militarization of the social in a struggling economic context. These authors see in this trend the redeployment of traditional forms of masculinity characterized by "machismo, strength and physicality" that had recently rescinded socially and the construction of femininity as unsuitable to these securitized institutions (1518). Similarly, I showed in Chapter 5 how the push to adopt the firearm speaks to a general shift towards a policing sensibility that privileges an understanding of borderwork as a reactive, strenuous and dangerous activity and that deploys traditional hegemonic tropes of masculinity.

At the same time as border organizations such as the CBSA integrate this shift to law enforcement, building on risk-management schemes and intelligence sharing while arming their frontline workers, these organizations are nonetheless attempting to hire more women. In the case of borderwork, women's presence problematizes the taken-for-granted masculine character of the state's authority at the border. In this sense, Marie's and Elizabeth's reflections regarding how they learned to perform authority at the border are particularly significant given the relative historical novelty of women's presence in policing and security institutions *as enforcers*—lest we forget that women have long worked in these areas in a subordinated, clerical capacity. While some work exists on the difficult integration of women into the police and the army, there is currently little empirical research, either ethnographic or survey based, that concretely examines this gendered shift in security and intelligence professions and, most importantly, that studies its potential impact on the practice of security. Consequently, together with a study of the re-emergence of hegemonic masculinities in security practices, analyses of gender relations in enforcement organizations should further investigate the tensions created by the interactions between the revival of such traditional conceptions of police and security work and efforts to increase the number of women employed in security organizations.

Conclusion

This chapter shed light on how security professionals are selected and actually become skilled at policing people and goods circulating in border spaces. Having explored the essentially uncharted terrain of border officers' professional socialization, it provided an original angle into the dynamics of border control transformations and into how hiring and training are integral to enacting shifts in border policies—such as the shift towards law enforcement. It would be useful to study how recruitment policies impact the practice of bordering in other contexts. For instance, the US has been actively recruiting veterans for its Customs and Border Patrol, even expediting their hiring. How are this recruitment policy and the militarization of the Mexico–US border related?[18] In fact, examining how aptitudes, skills, norms and language are transmitted, acquired and converted allows us to illuminate anew dynamics of change in various areas of policing and security. By comparing the hiring and training experience of experienced officers and mid-career officers with that of rookies, my findings demonstrate the continuities, transformations and unique features in the contemporary professional socialization of Canadian border officers, including the continuing attachment to place and politico-economic considerations entering officers' choice of career.

I have also outlined how officers are now exposed to the shift towards an enforcement mentality when training at customs college, where they acquire a generational view of borderwork that they hang onto as they join ports of entry—a point I examine further in the next chapter. Given the sociology of policing literature on professional socialization showing that field experience often undermines the academic training received by recruits, we have seen that this surprising finding can be explained by the alignment between officers' prior expectations about their work and the novel enforcement orientation of their hiring and college training. The chapter also underlined how border officers' professional socialization remains dependent on field training. By individually testing different investigative and interviewing strategies, rookie officers build up a regulatory knowledge and a series of skills that only experience can sharpen. A final issue of professional socialization that particularly confronts female and young officers is the distancing strategies that they develop throughout their career as a way to establish their authority, not only because their workplace is characterized by increasingly masculinizing features but also because of border crossers' expectations regarding the gender, age and race of state power.

This chapter painted the background for examining the current generational shift to border enforcement. While experienced officers were trained for trade compliance and tax collection tasks and were expected to pay attention to local economic needs, rookie officers are taught to focus on risk management and enforcement work. I now turn to young and career border officers' narratives about how their respective professional socialization produces generational tensions in ports of entry. These narratives illustrate the depth of the change lived by border officers while enthusiastic and enforcement-minded recruits integrate into close-knit work teams where officers have accumulated up to 35 years experience.

Notes

1 This finding is shared by Pruvost and Roharik (2011) in the case of French police recruits.
2 Canada Border Services Program Evaluation Division Internal Audit and Program Evaluation Directorate (2011), *Evaluation of CBSA Officer Recruitment and Port of Entry Recruit Training*, www.cbsa-asfc.gc.ca/agency-agence/reports-rapports/ae-ve/2011/poert-forpe-eng.html (11 Apr. 2012; last consulted 1 Aug. 2019), p. 10.
3 See *Jonhstone versus Canada* where a border officer contested the rotating schedule as discriminatory on the basis of her childcare needs and those of her partner (also an officer):

http://decisions.fct-cf.gc.ca/en/2007/2007fc36/2007fc36.html (10 July 2012; last consulted 1 Aug. 2019).

4   CBSA (2018), *Physical Evaluation: Preparation*, www.cbsa-asfc.gc.ca/job-emploi/bso-asf/pare-tape-eng.html (last modified 18 May 2018; last consulted 15 July 2019).

5   Canadian Press (2017), Canada's spy agency reaches settlement in discrimination and harassment lawsuit, *CBC*, www.cbc.ca/news/canada/toronto/csis-spy-agency-harassment-lawsuit-settlement-1.4452118 (15 Dec. 2017; last consulted 31 July 2019); R. Houlihan and D. Seglins (2018), Unofficial RCMP 'sissy' memo a sign of toxic work environment, women say, *CBC*, www.cbc.ca/news/investigates/unofficial-rcmp-sissy-memo-a-sign-of-toxic-work-environment-women-say-1.4511804 (31 Jan. 2018; last consulted 31 July 2019); Reuters (2018), Canada military survey finds 960 victims of sexual assault in a year, *The Guardian*, www.theguardian.com/world/2016/nov/28/canada-military-sexual-assault-survey (28 Nov. 2018; last consulted 31 July 2019); R. Schmunk (2019), New $100M settlement reached in RCMP sexual harassment case, *CBC*, www.cbc.ca/news/canada/british-columbia/rcmp-sexual-harassment-lawsuit-100-million-settlement-1.5203683 (8 July 2019; last consulted 31 July 2019).

6   Canada Border Services Agency (2016), From recruit to officer trainee: Training and development programmes, www.cbsa-asfc.gc.ca/job-emploi/bso-asf/training-formation-eng.html#a2 (modified 08 Oct. 2018; last consulted 18 July 2019).

7   For more details on risk indicators, see Chapters 3 and 4.

8   Canada Border Services Program Evaluation Division Internal Audit and Program Evaluation Directorate (2011), *Evaluation of CBSA Officer Recruitment and Port of Entry Recruit Training*, www.cbsa-asfc.gc.ca/agency-agence/reports-rapports/ae-ve/2011/poert-forpe-eng.html (modified 11 Apr. 2012; last consulted 5 May 2017), p. 22.

9   The length of training at customs college has been revised many times over the years. When Thomas completed the training, it was kept shorter, at nine weeks.

10 For illustrations of this argument for Brazil and the US, see Albuquerque and Paes-Machado (2004) and Haarr (2001).

11 All customs regulations, policies and procedures are reviewed and explained in d-memoranda, enclosed in more than 20 thick volumes of detailed customs regulations. Designed primarily for commercial officers, "d-memos" explain customs regulations relating to topics such as warehousing, couriers, imports and taxation. The complete list of customs-related d-memoranda can be found at www.cbsa-asfc.gc.ca/publications/dm-md/menu-eng.html (last modified 29 May 2019; last consulted 1 Aug. 2019).

12 The first six digits are internationally recognized classifications for commodities; the next two digits itemize the object; and the last two are for statistical purposes. These four last digits are specific to the importing country. World Customs Organization, *What is the Harmonized System (HS)?* www.wcoomd.org/en/topics/nomenclature/overview/what-is-the-harmonized-system.aspx (last consulted 1 Aug. 2019).

13 Statistics Canada, *Canadian Export Classification*, www150.statcan.gc.ca/n1/pub/65-209-x/65-209-x2017000-eng.htm (last modified 12 Dec. 2016; consulted 1 Aug. 2019).

14 Canada Border Services Program Evaluation Division Internal Audit and Program Evaluation Directorate (2011), *Evaluation of CBSA Officer Recruitment and Port of Entry Recruit Training*, www.cbsa-asfc.gc.ca/agency-agence/reports-rapports/ae-ve/2011/poert-forpe-eng.html (modified 11 Apr. 2012; last consulted 1 Aug. 2019).

15 See Chapter 4 in Brodeur (2010).

16 Marie's comment about criminal records concern the 1990s and early 2000s. Nowadays, truck drivers with criminal records are less likely to cross the border in either direction because both Canada and the US have started strictly enforcing interdictions to entry for travellers with criminal records since the mid 2000s.

17 As per an oft-quoted 1988 Supreme Court of Canada decision that acknowledge a lesser expectation of privacy at the border. See *R. v. Simmons*, [1988] 2 S.C.R. 495. https://scc-csc.lexum.com/scc-csc/scc-csc/en/item/377/index.do (last consulted 10 Aug. 2019).

18 US Customs and Border Protection, *CBP Hires Veterans*, www.cbp.gov/careers/veterans (last modified 4 Mar. 2019; last consulted 1 Aug. 2019).

References

Acker, J. 2006. Inequality regimes: Gender, class, and race in organizations. *Gender & Society* 20 (4):441–464.

Alain, M., and M. Grégoire. 2008. Can ethics survive the shock of the job? Quebec's police recruits confront reality. *Policing & Society* 18 (2):169–189.

Alain, M., and G. Pruvost. 2011. Police: une socialisation professionelle par étapes. *Déviance et société* 35 (3):267–280.

Albuquerque, C. L., and E. Paes-Machado. 2004. The hazing machine: The shaping of Brazilian military police recruits. *Policing and Society* 14 (2):175–192.

Batton, C., and E. M. Wright. 2019. Patriarchy and the structure of employment in criminal justice: Differences in the experiences of men and women working in the legal profession, corrections, and law enforcement. *Feminist Criminology* 14 (3):287–306.

Braedley, S. 2019. Equity shifts in firefighting: Challenging gendered and racialized work. In *Working Women in Canada: An Intersectional Approach*, edited by L. Nichols and V. Tyskka. Toronto: Women's Press.

Brodeur, J.-P. 2010. *The Policing Web*. Oxford, NY: Oxford University Press.

Burdett, F., L. Gouliquer, and C. Poulin. 2018. Culture of corrections: The experiences of women correctional officers. *Feminist Criminology* 13 (3):329–349.

Chan, J. 2003. *Fair Cop: Learning the Art of Policing*. Toronto: University of Toronto Press.

Chappell, A. T., and L. Lanza-Kaduce. 2010. Police academy socialization: Understanding the lessons learned in a paramilitary bureaucratic organization. *Journal of Contemporary Ethnography* 39 (2):184–214.

Chauvenet, A., and F. Orlic. 1985. Interroger la police. *Sociologie du travail* 4:453–467.

Conti, N. 2009. A Visigoth system: Shame, honor and police socialization. *Journal of Contemporary Ethnography* 38 (3):409–432.

Cordner, G., and A. M. Cordner. 2011. Stuck on a plateau?: Obstacles to recruitment, selection, and retention of women police. *Police Quarterly* 14 (3):207–226.

Cowen, D., and A. Siciliano. 2011. Surplus masculinities and security. *Antipode* 43 (5):1516–1541.

Cox, R., and K. Messing. 2006. Legal and biological perspectives on employment testing for physical abilities: A post-Meiorin review. *Windsor Yearbook of Access to Justice* 24 (1):23–53.

Darmon, M. 2016. *La socialisation (Third edition)*. Paris: Armand Colin.

de Lint, W. 1998. Regulating autonomy: Police discretion as a problem for training. *Canadian Journal of Criminology* 40 (3):277–304.

Devery, C. 2003. Learning at the academy. In *Fair Cop: Learning the Art of Policing*, edited by J. Chan. Toronto: University of Toronto Press.

Diphoorn, T. 2015. "It's all about the body": The bodily capital of armed response officers in South Africa. *Medical Anthropology* 34 (4):336–352.

Farfan, M. 2009. *The Vermont-Quebec Border: Life on the Line*. Charleston: Arcadia Publishing.

Haarr, R. N. 2001. The making of a community policing officer: The impact of basic training and occupational socialization on police recruit. *Police Quarterly* 4 (4):402–433.

Heidensohn, F. 1992. *Women in Control? The Role of Women in Law Enforcement*. Oxford: Oxford University Press.

Hockey, J. 2009. "Switch on": Sensory work in the infantry. *Work, Employment and Society* 23 (3):477–493.

Horii, S. 2012. It is about more than just training: The effects of Frontex border guard training. *Refugee Survey Quarterly* 31 (4):158–177.

Huysmans, J. 2014. *Security Unbound: Enacting Democratic Limits*. London: Routledge.

International Civil Liberties Monitoring Group. 2010. *Report of the Information Clearinghouse on Border Controls and Infringements to Travellers' Rights*. Ottawa, https://iclmg.ca/documents/reports/r-clearinghouse-border-controls/

Johnston, M. S., and J. M. Kilty. 2015. You gotta kick ass a little harder than that: The subordination of feminine, masculine, and queer identities by private security in a hospital setting. *Men and Masculinities* 18 (1):55–78.

Jubany, O. 2017. *Screening Asylum in a Culture of Disbelief: Truth, Denials and Skeptical Borders*. London: Palgrave MacMillan.

Kalman, I. 2016. Framing Borders: Indigenous Difference at the Canada/US Border, PhD dissertation in Anthropology, Montreal: McGill University.

Kaushal, A., and C. Dauvergne. 2011. The growing culture of exclusion: Trends in Canadian refugee exclusions. *International Journal of Refugee Law* 23 (1):54–92.

Lahire, B. 2012. *Monde pluriel. Penser l'unité des sciences sociales*. Paris: Seuil.

———. 2013. *Dans les plis singuliers du social. Individus, socialisations*. Paris: La Découverte.

Lalonde, P. C. 2019. Border officer training in Canada: Identifying organisational governance technologies. *Policing and Society* 29 (5):579–598.

Lande, B. 2007. Breathing like a soldier: Culture incarnate. *The Sociological Review* 55 (s1):95–108.

Loftus, B. 2009. *Police Culture in a Changing World*. Oxford: Oxford University Press.

Lonsway, K. A. 2003. Tearing down the wall: Problems with consistency, validity, and adverse impact of physical agility testing in police selection. *Police Quarterly* 6 (3):237–277.

Martin, S. H., and N. C Jurik, eds. 2007. *Doing Justice, Doing Gender (Second edition)*. Thousand Oaks: Sage.

Mauss, M. 1934. Les techniques du corps. *Journal de Psychologie* 32 (3–4).

McIntosh, D. 1984. *The Collectors: A History of Canadian Customs and Excise*. Toronto: NC Press, Revenue Canada, Customs and Excise, Canadian Government Publishing Centre, Supply and Services Canada.

Nolan, B. R. 2013. Information Sharing and Collaboration in the United States Intelligence Community: An Ethnographic Study of the National Counterterrorism Centre, PhD dissertation in Sociology. Philadelphia: University of Pennsylvania.

Poteyeva, M., and I. Y. Sun. 2009. Gender differences in police officers' attitudes: Assessing current empirical evidence. *Journal of Criminal Justice* 37 (5):512–522.

Pratt, A., and J. Templeman. 2018. Jurisdiction, sovereignties and akwesasne: Shiprider and the re-crafting of Canada-US cross-border maritime law enforcement. *Canadian Journal of Law and Society/Revue Canadienne Droit et Société* 33 (3):335–357.

Prokos, A., and I. Padavic. 2002. "There oughtta be a law against bitches": Masculinity lessons in police academy training. *Gender, Work & Organization* 9 (4):439–459.

Pruvost, G., and I. Roharik. 2011. Comment devient-on policier? 1982–2003. Évolutions sociodémographiques et motivations plurielles. *Déviance et société* 35 (3):281–312.

Salter, M. 2007. Governmentalities of an airport: Heterotopia and confession. *International Political Sociology* 1 (1):49–66.

———. 2011. Places everyone! Studying the performativity of the border. *Political Geography* 30 (2):66–67.

Schuck, A. M. 2014. Female representation in law enforcement: The influence of screening, unions, incentives, community policing, CALEA, and size. *Police Quarterly* 17 (1):54–78.

Seklecki, R., and R. Paynich. 2007. A national survey of female police officers: An overview of findings. *Police Practice and Research* 8 (1):17–30.

Sheptycki, J. 2007. The constabulary ethic and the transnational condition. In *Crafting Transnational Policing: State-Building and Police Reform across Borders*, edited by A. Goldsmith and J. Sheptycki. Oxford: Hart.

———. 2017. Liquid modernity and the police métier; thinking about information flows in police organisation. *Global Crime* 18 (3):286–302.

Silverman, S. J. 2019. What Habeas Corpus can (and cannot) do for immigration detainees: Scotland v Canada and the injustices of imprisoning migrants. *Canadian Journal of Law and Society/Revue Canadienne Droit et Société* 34 (1):145–161.

Thibault, D. 2019. L'espace portuaire à Montréal: Entre sécurité et commerce, Master's paper in Criminology. Montréal: Université de Montréal.

van Maanen, J. 1973. Observations on the making of policemen. *Human Organization* 32 (4):407–418.

———. 1975. Police socialization: A longitudinal examination of job attitudes in a urban police department. *Administrative Science Quarterly* 20 (2):207–228.

Vega, I. I. 2018. Empathy, morality, and criminality: The legitimation narratives of U.S. Border Patrol agents. *Journal of Ethnic and Migration Studies* 44 (15):2544–2561.

Villegas, P. E. 2015. Fishing for precarious status migrants: Surveillant assemblages of migrant illegalization in Toronto, Canada. *Journal of Law and Society* 42 (2):230–252.

Vosko, L. F., ed. 2006. *Precarious Employment: Understanding Labour Market Insecurity in Canada*. Montreal, Kingston: McGill-Queen's University Press.

———. 2010. *Managing the Margins: Gender, Citizenship and the International Regulation of Precarious Employment*. Oxford, NY: Oxford University Press.

Werth, E. P. 2011. Scenario training in police academies: Developing students' higher-level thinking skills. *Police Practice and Research* 12 (4):325–340.

Wood, J., and B. Dupont. 2006. *Democracy, Society and the Governance of Security*. Cambridge: Cambridge University Press.

Woodward, R., and K. N. Jenkings. 2011. Military identities in the situated accounts of British military personnel. *Sociology* 45 (2):252–268.

Chapter 7

Dobermans vs hush puppies

Generational frictions in ports of entry

Not long before I met Catherine, she had attended a CBSA-led seminar about "how to deal with people from the other generation." Having learned her trade with officers who were war veterans at the end of the 1970s, Catherine has worked all her career at the border. She found her early mentors "more cordial" than her current younger colleagues, who, she believes, are too heavy-handed with border crossers. Catherine simply does not recognize herself in how they speak of their job: "You're working in the wrong thing. . . . If you're going to deal with people like that, you should be a policeman." As I hope to have made clear throughout this book, border officers do not make up a single, cohesive "culture" but rather bring a host of competing and conflicting perspectives on how one should define, speak about and do border control. Perhaps the most important of these disagreements concern what I have come to term *generational borderwork*. Officers were surprisingly forthcoming in how they discussed bordering through generational lenses and acknowledged deep-seated differences between younger and older officers. They frequently associated work methods, use of bordering devices and the relative importance of their security and economic mandates with the past, the present and the future of border control. Such temporal grounding clearly broke down borderwork into "old" and "new" ways, and officers valued one or the other depending on whether they saw themselves as belonging to the old or the new generation.

The chapter supports one of this book's contentions: the shift to enforcement is experienced through generational borderwork—where practices, dispositions and outlooks on the purposes of bordering are shaped by distinct generational experiences that are anchored in distinct patterns of hiring and training that now favour a more peremptory, oppressive and regimented take on border control. Accordingly, generational borderwork represents a unique dimension of officers' divergent perspectives on their work, thus expressing the oft-silenced differences among views that shape border control on the ground. In this chapter, I concur with Vega (2019: 7), who, in the case of US immigration enforcement, argues that to understand and reform border control, we need to pay attention to the "variation in how agents with different social locations, years of experience, and level of expertise perceive immigration phenomena, understand their role, and carry out their mandates." In this chapter, I explore how these variations have played a role in the shift of Canadian border control towards law enforcement.

I am chiefly interested in how officers' generational views betray conflicting classifications of border control methods. Much has been written about categorizing in bordering where those on the move are ranked along risk scales that become articulated with judgements on citizenship, ethno-cultural membership and differential treatment relative to overall social status (see, among others, Parmar 2017; Barker 2013; Pickering and Ham 2014). These classifications answer to their own temporal logics. As argued by Mezzadra and Neilson (2013: 132), categorizing things and people through borders creates "borderscapes where the compression, elongation, and partitioning of time exerts effects of control, filtering and selectivity" that differentially impact how travellers, migrants and goods may be permitted to cross borders— quickly, slowly or not at all. But, as I have argued elsewhere (Côté-Boucher 2018), whether it insists on the significance of anticipation to contemporary security or interrogates the centrality of pre-emptive logics to security practices, current scholarship disregards some unique dimensions of the temporalities in which security professionals locate their action—and those of their colleagues—on an everyday basis. Thus, this scholarship often takes for granted that bordering and security are concerned with anticipating future criminal or security threats and with pre-empting migration that is deemed undesirable. I show in this chapter that the temporalities of security are much more varied than they were previously thought.

Particularly unexplored by the border and security literature is how classifications internal to security agencies (e.g. generations) make possible, promote or dismiss specific security practices and knowledge and enter how border crossers are categorized but also treated—thus painting a picture of what a "job well done" looks like. Yet such categorizations shed a unique light onto the regulation of mobilities through borders. They may influence whether, when committing a customs infraction, a truck driver will receive a penalty that will go on record or be given a mere warning. They can also have bearing on whether information contained in databases about a driver, a shipment or an importer will be considered essential or partly disregarded in favour of an officer's skill at establishing an interview that facilitates disclosure. Or again, they may influence how thorough officers might be with a search recommended by a coworker, depending on how they value this colleague's abilities as passé or current. Border officers belong to the same "universe" of border control (Bigo 2014), but they also envision their work differently, depending on when they were hired and how they were trained.

When we follow the development of these internal classifications, we also get a foothold into how dynamics of change affect security professionals' prestige. Given the assertion that use of force represents an important but not defining aspect of policing (Brodeur 2007), Proteau and Pruvost (2008: 8) argue that the everyday practices of security professionals "are less marked out by . . . physical violence than by a variety of registers of distinction, conscious or unconscious, which allow [one] to impose oneself—or to attempt to—as a 'real' professional." Generational tensions over classifications of work methods mobilize such registers, producing informal rankings called upon in generational competition over status, resources and legitimacy—who from old timers or rookies best understands what bordering is all about. By studying the policing of mobilities as a generational endeavour, we can consider the renewal of the patterns of competition that make up border control.

Accordingly, by presenting an investigation of generational borderwork in the commercial sections of Canadian land border ports of entry, this chapter tells the story of the marginalization of tax collection understandings of borderwork and of the downward social mobility of officers associated with these roles. Such sidelining is echoed by narratives oozing with nostalgic reminiscence about an imagined past of a simpler and more commendable form of border control based on good old interviewing and customs work. The chapter then sheds light on the promulgation of new internal categorizations of recognition and esteem—those favouring academic credentials over work experience and insisting on officers' capacity to coordinate technological aptitudes with interviewing skills—and of the everyday consequences of these transformations upon border officers' work routines, relations with colleagues and promotional prospects. The chapter thus identifies the dynamics of ageing pertaining to bordering as revealed by security professionals' changing outlook on their own practice. The chapter finishes with the most evident illustration of generational change according to border officers: carrying a firearm. Firearm training involves concrete modifications in officers' bodily dispositions, affecting work routines along generational lines. By fostering a more distantiated and suspicious attitude, firearm training makes possible the advent of a policing sensibility in those who are armed, ultimately altering the relationship between the travelling public and those who have now become border guards.

William and his generational problem

While commented on by many, nowhere were generational frictions between officers more clearly laid out than in the words of William, whom I introduced in the first sentences of this book. Without any prompting to that effect (we had just been discussing his retirement plans), this experienced border worker broached the issue himself, an indication that he took it seriously. He even suggested that if I could reflect on and provide solutions to these generational tensions in ports of entry, my research would be particularly useful. Allow me to spend some time on this part of our conversation, since this chapter (and this book, if I am being honest) has been inspired by William's reflections:

WILLIAM: But I would tell you that the challenge of the coming years, what I find difficult is the whole human relations aspect. (. . .) I think we are not adequately tooled to deal with three generations of workers together. (. . .) I understand, they [older officers] are close to retirement, they wish the river to flow more calmly. And [there are] the Dobermans. They bite every-thing that's around them, it's not moving enough for them, not enough fighting. You know, not enough action.

KARINE: The Dobermans are the new officers?

W: Yes, the new ones. In a way, that they show themselves to be willing, that's one thing. That they undermine the old generation, that, it's a pity, I find it pathetic. . . . Now, the young ones, here, they say to the others, "You should think of leaving, that wouldn't be a bad thing. You know, the new ones are coming in, that would give them some room." You know, it is very disrespectful. (. . .)

K: What are the differences of philosophies between these generations? So, for instance, the new generation is just fresh out of Rigaud. They get here, they are newly trained. How do they approach their work compared to the older generation?

W: They are more law enforcement. They see the gun coming. They see themselves as the police of the border. The old generation, they were hired as public servants. They collected duties and taxes, customer service and, when the situation required it, they did oppressive interventions. Whereas today, the oppressive side is much more put to the fore.

K: In their training?

W: Yes, and also because our mandates are drugs, missing children, firearms, pornography, money laundering and all that. So, the principal mandates concern organized crime, concern people of real bad faith. Whereas before, they said to people, "Well, listen, this is a tourist clientele who comes for a ride and once in a while, you will find someone who will tell you an unbelievable story."

   The young ones tell the old ones, "You are not on board anymore for enforcement matters. You are preventing us from doing a good job." And the old generation says, "Yes, but look, for us, public service is impor-tant." And, for sure, it takes a big thing before they start taking measures against a person. They will rather give warnings and say: "You shouldn't have done this." But the young one, he wants it now: "He lied to me. We intervene, we seize the goods." You know, they do mini-contests between themselves, to see who will catch the most [infractions].

K: The young ones.

W: The young ones. So, if you are young and you are paired with an old officer who doesn't want to do too much, well, he's hurting you in your competition with the other. I mean two young officers together. You see the picture?

K: Yes, yes.

w: (. . .) And in contrast, there are paperwork cases that are a bit more complicated. So the newbie doesn't know how to do them. So, he says: "You, Dave [*experienced officer, fictive name*], are you aware why . . ." And then Dave feels like saying, "Hey, smarty pants, you who wants to see me retire, figure it out by yourself if you're so clever when you just get out of Rigaud."

(. . .) But the young officers to whom I speak of economy, they don't give a damn. (. . .) When I tell them: "Well we need to protect the Canadian economy," they answer, "Hey, it's so expensive in Canada." They don't see their interest. So, the young ones, they will say, "We do law enforcement. We catch bad guys, that's what we do." And the collection of duties and taxes, the economic protection aspect of our work: "Let's leave that with the old hush puppies, you know, they don't feel like running after the ball anymore, we'll leave them that."

k: Hush puppies are going to retire.

w: So we will be left with the new generation. So, I said, "Let me ask you a question. You are my little Dobermans. You are good, it is true that you have flair. You work well. Can you swear that in 30 years, you will have the same determination, the same motivation, with all that we went through here: to ask for, to want things and to be told no, to be snubbed. In 30 years, if I visit you, you will be the same as what you are now, all fired up? Let me doubt that. Let me doubt that." So, we left it there, you see. It is all suppositions. But it is part of the conversations that we have to have between generations who live together.

Exacerbating intergenerational strain between colleagues, the specificities of the small port of entry where William works certainly do not help him with what he calls his human relations challenge. In this port, officers are responsible for clerical work and learn to perform both traffic and basic commercial tasks. In contrast, all of the other ports of entry that I visited have separate commercial and traffic/immigration sections and benefit from having their own clerks who deal with paperwork and trade statistics while being responsible for some of the front desk services provided to importers and truck drivers.

In this small border crossing, rookie officers and experienced officers (there are few mid-career officers) are constantly required to interact. Since each shift need few officers, the port lacks both the softening impact of a larger work team and the possibility, on any given shift, of forming groups sharing work habits acquired during their career. This situation is not improved by the compactness of the facilities. On each of my visits, officers profusely apologized for receiving me in a workspace where everyone steps on one another's toes, and many dreamt aloud of the day when calls for infrastructural investments to remodel and expand the port would actually be heard in "Ottawa"—this is where William thinks his port is being "snubbed."[1]

Furthermore, remoteness from urban centres and national hiring procedures create a high employee rotation rate. In contrast to past practice, whereby rookies were hired from a local pool of applicants, young officers often leave after two years—the minimum period stipulated in their contract—and apply to be relocated in ports of entry or offices closer to home. Consequently, the irritation of experienced officers at constantly having to repeat in-port training with new recruits was evident. I heard similar echoes of frustration in another mid-size port.

The inclusion of new officers disrupted the habits of this tightly knit port of entry made up of officers who grew up in the same region, trained each other and worked together for a number of years. Recruited from cities and suburbs, ready to carry firearms, rookies show up in ports of entry with college and university degrees in hand and their heads filled with the enforcement-based training they received at customs college. As William puts it, these young officers are "willing": they turn up at work prepared—and expecting—to find missing children, seize drugs and find concealed weapons. But what they encounter in this small port makes for quite a shock. They mainly perform routine administrative work, processing a limited number of local truck drivers who cross the border five times a day and locals coming back from a trip across the border. These rookies expected action and are ready to "bite," but they find themselves in a quiet community reliant on their port of entry for cross-border work, business, reception of US parcels and occasional shopping.

Furthermore, and in contrast to their more experienced colleagues, these rookies do not share kinship ties in the region, nor do they have decades-long relationships with locals. Villagers comment on seeing these new young faces in town and readily discuss whether they are friendly or whether they "overstep" their powers. But the cherry on the cake for rookie officers is their realization that they cannot be armed like their colleagues in bigger land ports of entry, because their port is too small to accommodate a safe storing space for firearms—a situation similar to that of Canadian airports, where, as we have already discussed, officers are not armed. These circumstances create the need for many adjustments on the part of both outsider rookies and insider seniors; it is not surprising that tensions sometimes arise between the two groups. Next, we will see that some of these tensions concern contrasting valuations of customs officers' responsibilities. These valuations appear in nostalgic reminiscence about the good old days of border control, when tax collection and economic protectionism were not seen as a remnant of the past but as a most honourable duty.

Border nostalgia

Amid these generational tensions, nostalgic narratives offer a grounded critique of how room has been made for more antagonistic bordering at the expense of economic protectionism and of a more "ambassadorial" attitude. Running against, or at least across, this trend are the unachieved reforms of border control that officers reveal; generational narratives become a resource through which officers reflect on the consequences of these official choices. Officers' nostalgic evocations thus activate assessments that do not whole-heartedly embrace contemporary security trends in bordering. Accordingly, as we take into account the restructuring of border agencies, we can shed new light on the temporalized forms of self-understanding—such as officers' yearning for abilities they think are disappearing—that arise from these novel contexts. Whether we encounter "chivalrous" attitudes (Pratt and Thompson 2008), humanitarian approaches (Aas and Gundhus 2015; Pallister-Wilkins 2015) or contemporary outlooks on discretion (van der Woude and van der Leun 2017) at the border, it is fruitful to inquire into the historicity of these ordinary forms of self-understanding.

Generational narratives show up in some interviews in the form of nostalgia for an imagined, more respectable past of border control. As nostalgic officers recall how things used to be, they offer comparative moral judgements about what border control has become. As in the cases of Catherine and of William mentioned earlier, these officers reflect on the sometimes-aggressive attitude displayed by younger colleagues eager to find opportunities to enforce the law and "catch bad guys." In contrast, their memories evoke a time when visitors were greeted with "Welcome to Canada"—a blessed epoch without batons, guns or handcuffs, when training in conflict resolution facilitated disclosure and when travellers used to thank them for their professionalism. Such nos-talgic recollections have also been found in police research with patrol officers who reminisce about simpler times when "there was 'no need' for technology to do good police work" (Tanner and Meyer 2015: 389).

What are seen as "new ways" of doing borderwork are contrasted unfavour-ably with times before computers and risk management, when officers had full control of the border, knew their paperwork, fostered trust with locals, made complete use of their discretionary powers and knew how to get truth out of a border crosser. In these nostalgic moments, officers long for the nobility of a modest work life committed to the protection of Canada's borders. These grievances disapproved of recruits' supposed unwillingness to display the dedi-cation that experienced officers believed they had shown throughout their own respective careers, associating their desire for a swift promotion—and escape from night/day shift work—with a depreciation of the profession.

"Speaking Mandarin": remnants of economic protectionism

In what is expressed as a forlorn attempt to teach rookies the importance of duties and taxes, some officers were dismayed at the lack of interest dis-played by their junior colleagues in trade regulation. For William, having new officers show concern for "the economic aspect of our jobs" and "protecting the interests of Canadians" in trade is akin to having them "speak Mandarin." William's protectionism stems from a concern for local jobs and businesses in a border region with a struggling economy. As did others, William told tales of a disappearing time when the ports of entry were helping locals with their customs papers and when officers were glad to enforce national taxation in order to shelter local businesses from US competition. Such surviving remnants of economic protectionism could be found in every port I visited.

Given a strong policy orientation towards trade facilitation, I had expected to find officers adopting a conception of their role that reflects their legislated mandate. But for many mid-career and experienced officers, their understanding of their work's purpose is at variance with this official language. They lament the loss of a time when land ports of entry were seen to be essential to local economic life. This nostalgia, and its impact on daily decision-making, is to be taken seriously: more than 20 years after free trade, these experienced officers still saw economic protectionism as a significant aspect of their work and associated the protection of Canadians' livelihood with a more virtuous take on border control than law enforcement. Their views diverge from the official economic partnership language adopted by Canadian border and foreign trade authorities reviewed in Chapter 2, whose policy acquiesces to increased security measures at the border in exchange for a continuation of free trade with its southern neighbour and mobility for their elite citizens.

It matters little whether officers' nostalgia about a lost Canadian economy supported by strong economic protectionism at the border reflects past reality accurately. Nostalgia is not about facts; it evokes glorious bygone times in speaking of a less acceptable present (Davis 1979). Such nostalgic reminiscence does indicate, however, that some officers have come to see themselves as non-contemporaneous to border control as it is practised today. As do reiterations of discretion in a context where effective decision-making is increasingly moved away from ports of entry (a point made in Chapter 4), generational narratives about protectionist borderwork continue to provide officers with an honourable sense of self as they witness their loss of influence in matters relative to national economic well-being. As did their insistence on their high discretion, these narratives also express the "vulnerability" and sense of "social dislocation" (Slutskaya et al. 2016) felt by these officers.

Therefore, it comes as no surprise that nostalgic generational evocations often informed a more or less veiled critique of the political economy of contemporary border control. You may remember Ronald, the officer commenting in Chapter 2 on what he saw as the immanent disappearance of the Canada–US land border for trade regulation. Customs is a second career for Ronald. This is not exceptional. Four interviewees became customs officers after being laid off because of downsizing or after working for one or two decades in struggling economic sectors with worsening pay and working conditions. This experience shaped Ronald's outlook. He analysed with subtlety the impact of global economic changes on regional economic conditions and on his work. He discussed at length the interrelations between the 2008 economic downturn and the current decline of the manufacturing sector, and he reflected on a binational relationship that he considers to be unequal and asymmetric: "Because I see protectionism every day from the US. I think we just take things lax in Canada. Where I think we should become just like them, as protectionists as them."

Having grown up in the vicinity of their workplace and having spent most of their careers involved in borderwork, experienced officers have had time to gauge the effects of a global market economy on local well-being in the Canada–US borderland: labour casualization, deindustrialization, downsizing and the loss of well-paying and unionized jobs. Charles, an experienced officer, asked me whether I shopped at Walmart as a test of my solidarity with small businesses and unionized workers and, encouraged by my negative answer, spoke at length about what he considered to be the damaging impact of NAFTA on the Southern Ontario manufacturing sector and the automotive industry. Similarly, Raymond commented on the serial manufacturing closures in his region, their delocalization in non-unionized Mexican and US rural areas and how his neighbours were now making ends meet through low-paid service-based and menial jobs. The contrast between a free-trade rhetoric and the uncertainty of socioeconomic life on their neighbours and families provided these experienced officers with critical resources. Meanwhile, their younger colleagues become impatient with these views that seem to come straight out of another era. For them, border control now calls for enforcing an ordered circulation of people and things.

Borderwork's logic of ageing and rejuvenation

As a result of current transformations in bordering, those officers associated with the past of border control have been sidelined. In this section, I consider what we learn more broadly about generational borderwork by looking at the marginalization of what are seen as "old ways" as well as the dynamics of promoting those associated with "new ways" in ports of entry. Emerging from the storytelling world of border control, where transmission, discussion and debate shape how to do bordering (Shearing and Ericson 1991), vernacular generational classifications such as old hush puppies and Dobermans who bite reveal the effects of the passage of time for border officers. These classifications participate in the making of a regime of distinction where the new is rewarded and the old dismissed as redundant. Officers associated with the past of customs go through social demotion as their work experience, gained after years of "working the line," gradually becomes at odds with the changing techno-material culture of their port of entry. In this context, stories of past "cold hits" (where one found large quantities of drugs concealed in a truck without prior intelligence) and of 1990s kilometre-long truck line-ups at the border seem to come out of another era.

As officers stress generational variance in skill and adaptability in colleagues, they create "cultures of difference in the workplace" (McMullin et al. 2007: 312). These cultures influence how ageing and younger officers are viewed by their peers but also support the downgrading of those associated with an obsolete generation. Yet if these classifications stigmatize, they also single out. What Down and Reveley (2004: 235) refer to as a "sense of generational distinctiveness" provides peer recognition and may grant access to official credentials and appointments. By setting aside long-standing abilities as outmoded while praising the adaptability of the young, that which is seen to be generational becomes essentialized in officers' categorization of what constitutes a good border officer. These generational classifications can ultimately sustain what Eyerman and Turner (1998) term the *strategic closure* of resources and affect the distribution of labour, where younger cohorts with the right educational credentials who are seen to be more in tune with innovation in bordering are privileged over older colleagues. Generational classifications thus give insight into the logic of ageing in borderwork, where one's past feats become snubbed in favour of novel kinds of achievements that appear more in tune with the present and future of borderwork. This is significant, because making alternative approaches to borderwork appear out of date has been central to effecting the shift to enforcement and security in border control.

Of course, the "old ways" of hush puppies and "new ways" of Dobermans do not come neatly packaged in single individuals but indicate conflicting views on procedures and practices associated with young officers and old officers. For instance, I met an officer who gave equal importance to basic border enforcement skills (new) and public service (old). Another officer was technologically savvy and open to carrying a firearm (new) yet still cared for the implementation of French labelling on products entering the country (old) despite what he saw as the lack of official interest for enforcing this type of national regulation in a free-trade era. But tensions over classifications of work methods and representations of border control produce informal rankings called upon in disputes over status in bordering. Asserting yourself in a collective ("older" and "younger" generations) strengthens your claim to be taken seriously; it helps substantiate the assertion that you are being demoted by new officers or that your own group thinks many older officers are not up to the task of securing borders anymore.

Interviewing or computers? Arthur wants "to look you in the eye"

A major point of generational contention between border officers concerns bordering technologies, particularly the importance that they are given in contrast to other border control methods. Interestingly, officers I spoke with associated questions about their work routines with the respective effectiveness of computers, enforcement data, interviewing skills and interpreting behavioural, oral and visual "risk indicators." Officers' assessments of these differences were based on competing portrayals of the reliability and relevance of these methods for daily decision-making at the border and the reliability and relevance of the steps and techniques involved in making a release/refer decision, evaluating a truck driver and a shipment or investigating them further at secondary inspection docks. While the capacity to interview and interpret signs of nervousness were valued by all, they were understood by older officers to be the result of their training and experience—an experience that younger officers would never acquire, because of their dependence on computers. Meanwhile, younger officers looked with pity on those—generally older officers—who lacked technological proficiency and displayed an inability to assimilate new tools. These views were almost always expressed in generational terms and pointed to a regime of distinction where divergent understandings of valuable border-policing skills compete in designating who does border control best.

When it comes to the respective effectiveness of data and interviewing in border policing, my conversation with Arthur is revealing. An experienced officer, Arthur calls himself "an old fart." Throughout our discussion, he kept insisting on his proficiency with visual and behavioural assessments, thus privileging face-to-face interactions with drivers. He boasted of his interviewing abilities, which he had developed over the years. Even his manner of speaking was a reminder of the embodied nature of these skills: he spoke in staccato sentences, his speech shaped by years of asking short questions and getting short answers. Arthur uttered a sentence then waited for a reply; he sometimes answered a few questions with a question of his own, testing my knowledge. In this way, years of interviewing travellers and truck drivers have shaped Arthur's manner of conversing. When he is interviewed, he recreates the quick back-and-forth dynamic of the booth where he spent hundreds of hours honing his interviewing skills.

Displaying limited technological literacy, Arthur admits typing slowly and having difficulties using the databases at his disposal. When queried about customs regulations and enforcement databases, Arthur proved to be surprisingly uninformed. Arthur distrusts intelligence: for him, "nothing has changed" in border control since he started as an officer two decades earlier. When one is skilled at interviewing, no intelligence or automated risk profile is necessary to evaluate a traveller or a shipment: there is only the truck driver, the officer and the relation they establish in a 30-second interaction at the booth:

ARTHUR: That's what I'm here for. To protect. I try to do that every interview. (. . .) How do I know who's high-risk or low-risk without an interview? [*short pause*] Do I know you're high-risk or low-risk? Without knowing you?

KARINE: Maybe you received intelligence, or . . .

A: Well receiving intelligence is different. If I have the intelligence in front of me, I listen to the intelligence, I send them in. But if I don't have intelligence . . . our intelligence system is weak. We have a programme out front where we run everybody's ID but only . . . what's in there is what we input into there. (. . .)

So, the guy from Texas,[2] first time here, we have nothing on him. So now I have to really concentrate on his eyes. And a lot of young officers, because they're not used to it, they're more used to computers. . . . So, when I'm interviewing—as a young officer now, keying, "Where do you live? How long you've been away?" [*Arthur mimics typing and looking at the computer while asking questions*]. The eye contact is missed. (. . .)

And I try to learn . . . like I . . . I can do very well on the computers. I learn. I'm not . . . I'm not afraid of them. I will learn, but I just . . . old ways. [*short pause*]

I want to look you in the eye.

Officers' narratives are replete with evidence that the introduction of enforcement-related technologies is productive of new bodily dispositions that challenge established borderwork practice centred on seeing. As illustrated by this excerpt, Arthur has strong views regarding the greater emphasis put on information technologies by his younger colleagues and the diminished importance given to visual evaluations in border decisions. These views are widely shared; many career officers expressed variations on this theme. They deliberately drew my attention to what they see as the gradual loss of interviewing skills and of the ability to recognize visual indicators of risk— such as signs of nervousness in drivers. In nearly the same terms and gestures, senior officers from different ports of entry mimicked an imaginary rookie concentrated on a computer screen, entering information provided by a border crosser but failing to make eye contact. They also doubted the efficiency of young officers' overreliance on often-dated—and sometimes-unreliable— computer-generated data. As Nathan, another experienced officer, claimed, "We are losing what we used to do: look at people."

Senior officers and being "out of the game"

With the remodelling of their mandate, the arrival of new enforcement and data management technologies and the arming of younger officers, ageing officers such as Arthur feel that they are "out of the game." This experience may be compounded by health problems (work or non-work related) and an increasing difficulty in adapting to the incessant rolling of a night/day shift routine. Chronic illness or injuries sustained by their ageing bodies may prevent them from bending, kneeling and crawling during truck and car inspections. The changing nature of borderwork also brings its own set of physical challenges; some older officers simply could not train to obtain a firearm (even when they would have been interested in doing so), and others dread their recurring control and defence tactics training, where they practice how to contain, takedown and arrest.

During our conversations, these officers worked hard to conceal their symbolic (or effective) demotion in their port of entry. To do so, they relied on different narrative strategies. Two of these officers described their exploits in traffic, where they worked before sustaining injuries that required them to transfer to the commercial section. This was the case for Nathan, whom I mentioned first in the introduction. Having spent more than a decade away from the frontline, Nathan offered dated anecdotes—for instance, he refers to ID cards that have now been replaced. Nathan used to be a successful traffic officer but was injured and had to quit "working the line." He received compensatory work after being incapacitated, but he "would give [his] right arm to be back in traffic":

> Because that's what I like to do. I love playing the mind games with the travelling public. You know, I've done quite well at it. When I was [at the traffic section], four years in a row, I was the number one enforcement officer. Guns and drugs [*he lies back on his seat and expands his chest with pride*]. I got a kidnapper, I got bank robbers, I got plaques on the wall. I got all kinds of awards. But then I [was injured] and never got better, so then I had to argue with them to give me another job that wasn't on the line. So, we finally came up with a job, so . . .

Another experienced officer, Jacob, concealed his troubles with computers by explaining how he learned to use risk-management tools alongside his younger colleagues:

> Well, for sure, some are more. . . . I would say that these databases, I learned them especially with the new officers who were hired . . . who went to [Customs] college and who learned them at college. Then they came to the office and it is more by working with them that I learned. . . . Well, we did not have training on this, it is a process of learning through practice if you wish. (. . .) And . . . no, it is taking the trouble to learn it, and you know, it is a tool we use daily.

The day of his interview, Jacob was drained. His speech was slow. He had been working nights that week and had barely slept four hours that day. Given his exhaustion, I was grateful that he took the time to speak with me. Jacob spoke at length of what he intended to do on his pension, and he offered a sophisticated calculation of hours and days of work that established when he would be able to do so. Jacob was ready for retirement.

These officers may also be pushed to the margins in everyday interactions with colleagues. Paul, who feels at ease with computers and databases and who often trains rookies when they first join his port of entry, is nevertheless confronted with the disapproving comments of trainees who question his methods and insist that "This is not how we learned it in Rigaud." Paul is slowly passing out of a position of authority, which granted him his colleagues' esteem, to that of an aged officer who is smiled at patiently, sometimes mocked and generally not taken seriously. He is now "an old fart" to quote Arthur again who also complained of occasional stigmatization by younger officers: "I know they tease a lot . . . Young people think old people are old, right? And they have no respect to begin with." Commenting on an occasion when supervisors did not notice that an officer had not shown up for a shift, he adds, "They made a mistake. They don't even know that he's not in, three hours later. So that's why they're not very good supervisors. I offered to train them, but they laughed at me because I'm old." Generational classifications are particularly important to the formation of subjectivity (Aboim and Vasconcelos 2014), impacting one's sense of self-worth. Some career officers' view of themselves as qualified border workers is seriously challenged; much of what characterized their work environment and provided them with a distinct sense of self as border officers has changed.

As a result of a perception that they cannot keep up, experienced officers may be singled out for their "old ways." On the one hand, port practice can contribute to marginalizing "out-of-the-game" officers. Years of night shifts in those ports where shift distribution is not based on seniority creates a long-term fatigue that can make older officers less attentive and focused. Further, these officers' expertise, gained after years of working the line, ceases to be sought and recognized by management. They slowly become somewhat forgotten in the institutional memory of their port that welcomes a new influx of officers, supervisors and managers who did not know them during their prime years. In fact, the transformation of border control not only is affected by introducing technologies or guns in borderwork but also happens through the sidelining of experienced officers associated with past times, who are pushed away from the centre of action and into the margins of border control.

Move over grandpa: frictions over promotions

Not only do new officers enter ports of entry with prized enforcement skills; they also have better diplomas. Based on civil service competition, promotions at the CBSA now reward university education. In a system that privileges testing abilities over years of experience, postsecondary education ensures a greater possibility of advancement. This novel redistribution of status, access to perks and better wages produces tensions between newer officers and career officers. In the context of increased competition over promotions in the policing world, where abilities to process information and acquire knowledge have become valued, the "formats and thinking associated with administrative rule" are increasingly seen as a resource to select those who should move up the hierarchy (Ericson and Haggerty 1997: 349, quoted in Sheptycki 2017: 8). "Dobermans" are thus more likely to be promoted than "hush puppies," thereby speeding up the shift to enforcement in those ports and within the whole CBSA.

I have seen this promotional dynamic create awkward situations in which younger officers with less experience become supervisors, overseeing the older, experienced colleagues who trained them. Paul's case illustrates this dynamic well. At times, our conversation seemed copied word for word from Pierre Bourdieu's (1979, 1984) reflections on generational struggles over resources and status: the "young" claim access to advantageous positions and pay because of their diplomas, while the "old" insist on having their experience recognized. A senior officer, Paul has cumulated different functions over the years, working as acting supervisor, targeter, trade compliance analyst and in-port trainer. When a supervisor position opened in his port, he expected to obtain it on the basis of that experience. However, a less experienced officer was offered the position after ranking better on written tests. Since then, Paul continued working as an officer. There is an evident bitterness in Paul's tone of voice when he speaks of this missed opportunity. He considers that he has "regressed" and makes clear his frustration about this turn of events: "He took my place," he said, "I was his boss" (as acting supervisor) before this newer officer was promoted:

> It advantages the young. So, we have young people who manage older ones. (. . .) So, let's say, you have a business that you run for 30 years and you have staff who has been there for years. If you wish to have someone to take your place, you will take an older employee and you will say, "You know the drill." But if you show up with a young one who has been working for you for a year and then you say, "OK, you will manage all my staff." . . . The government does that right now.

Of particular interest is how officers deployed generational narratives to make sense of how wider border control transformations are differently embodied in younger or older colleagues' attitudes and dispositions. For instance, older officers were concerned with what they saw as the lack of commitment displayed by rookies. William commented that, unlike his younger colleagues, he was "tattooed with the organization":

> Well, it's a choice, but dedicated ones who will put on three or four hats. (. . .) When these people will have left, you will have a new kind of organization. A younger organization, but, as I see it, not as dedicated as before. They will do their job, they will follow instructions and they will ask for everything they can get.

Versions of these remarks were repeated at length by many, demonstrating how senior officers "put generation in service of the belief that older and younger people today possess fundamentally different attitudes about how a person should relate to his or her work" and how such belief relates to the perception of a "sense of entitlement" in young people and their "work to live" rather than "live to work" ethic—a contemporary discourse well rendered by Foster's (2013: 200) discussion of generations at work.

For younger officers, their dedication expressed itself differently and was more in tune with expectations of social mobility that comes with higher education. In contrast to their experienced colleagues who spent their careers working on the frontline and are "tattooed with the organization," recently recruited officers saw the border agency as a level playing field offering diverse possibilities for career advancement. I can confirm that most students in my university department working as CBSA officers dream of moving up to intelligence and investigation units. This notion of border services as a land of opportunities is especially strong for rookie and mid-career officers with the necessary credentials. Denis was enthused about the array of possibilities awaiting a border officer. He described how one can become a supervisor, a chief of operations or an analyst and noted that officers could even be deployed overseas in international airports. But, in fact, there are few such positions available. Younger officers were waiting for incoming retirements, projected to create a staff reshuffling in the entire border agency. Vincent, who holds a university degree but had only a few years of work experience at the border when we met, provided a useful metaphor for illustrating young officers' great expectations. He was "waiting for the geyser," seeing himself at the bottom of a gushing spring to naturally ascend the promotional ladder after the retirement of older managers.

There is an increasing gap between the hopes raised by improved educational credentials, a selective enrolment process and a demanding training, on the one hand, and the repetitive, routine-like and monotonous nature of frontline borderwork, on the other. In border agencies, as in all bureaucracies, most frontline personnel are destined to be employed in the lower echelons of a pyramidal rank structure, with most positions to be filled at the bottom of the ladder (in contrast to Vincent's reversed geyser image). Consequently, it remains to be seen what impact these obstacles to promotion will have on officers' attitude towards their frontline work over the years. Perhaps these recruits will bring change with their improved education and their less "tattooed," more complex and more nuanced commitment. In fact, some research on policing suggests the importance of higher educational schemes in designing a novel policing ethos at the street level and in management; it would provide officers with a critical perspective and offer the potential to change policing and security into more "sophisticated institution[s]" (Lee and Punch 2004). But others have shown that job satisfaction and positive attitudes towards management for US police officers decrease with higher educational achievements and promotional ambitions (Paoline et al. 2015). Perhaps William is right to ask the rookies he trains, "Can you swear that in 30 years, you will have the same determination, the same motivation?"

Embodying "new ways": the armed border officer

In his reflections about generational borderwork, William tells me that the gun not only epitomized tensions between border officers but also profoundly altered armed officers' attitude towards the travelling public:

> It changed over the years. That is why we have this difficulty. Because now, we are going to arm officers. There are old officers who say, "I was not hired to be armed." And you have new ones who say, "I can't wait to carry my firearm because I will receive the respect that Americans [US border officers] receive from people [on the basis of their occupational position]." There's also the mentality that comes with arming. When you are armed, you really are a "border guard."

Beyond frictions over technologies, discretion and professional socialization, the fiercest debate between officers regarded the requirement to be armed, and this dispute followed generational lines. For young officers, it meant that border control was now really about policing, making any other approach to bordering anachronistic. In contrast, many senior officers thought that the gun presented a relevant but limited border policy value. It really came down, they told me, to a union tactic to increase officers' salaries, a tactic inspired by those Canadian regions in which border officers were more "Rambo-like," as Mario put it.[3] An experienced officer, Mario had "never even used" his baton. In this concluding section, however, I wish to entertain the idea that the gun changed more than officers' bank accounts: it changed them. To fully understand the shift to enforcement as a generational shift, we need to consider how the gun transformed borderwork by reworking officers' bodies.

The gun under fire: generational borderwork and arming

Generational tensions in ports of entry were often expressed as having recourse to the firearm as a narrative device. Guns were brought up time and time again in arguments about generational borderwork, illustrating how border control had been transitioning towards security and law enforcement. This happened during my exchange with Thomas, the rookie who told us in Chapter 6 of his life-altering experience at Rigaud. Thomas had been talking about how "age is still a big, big point because we are in a pivotal time when there are a lot of people who are retiring." He explained that older officers were more interested in trade compliance, younger officers in "security and drug trafficking." These two generations working together "create frictions sometimes" because, according to Thomas, some older officers refuse to see how "customs had reached another phase." I asked Thomas what he meant. If customs had reached another phase, where was it now? This is the point where Thomas and many of his colleagues moved away from talk about databases, preclearance programmes or biometrics to the topic of guns:

I give you an example: the firearm. You go around seeing who is armed, who has volunteered for it.[4] It will be 60, 80 . . . 90% of the people at the start of their careers. And that is understandable, you know. I mean when you are nearing 50 years old, carrying a firearm is not something that is of interest to you, especially when you started as a tax collector at the border. You know, for sure, the 1970s were more like this. They only had their stamps. Starting in 1990, even maybe 2000, they started having their batons and all. . . . And now, we have reached the firearm.

Thomas ends by reflecting on how the gun toughens his colleagues' attitude:

You know, I am not. . . . The idea to be. . . . You know, you are not allowed to be unpleasant. The model of the cop, the wannabe police officer, has a tendency to happen here. But we do now put emphasis on security more than on anything else.

Pro-arming officers often separated what constitutes "real" borderwork from what amounts to technicalities—often in reference to paperwork, taxation and trade compliance responsibilities. For them, the gun firmly anchors borderwork in an enforcement mentality. It speaks to what many rookies and mid-career officers interpret—to paraphrase Mannheim (1952 [1923]) on generations—as the "non-contemporaneous" character of borderwork methods that do not include guns. The firearm thus points to the subjective experience of change in border control where a sensibility more in tune with law enforcement is often seen as better adjusted to what one of my interviewees said was the "future of border security."

In contrast to rookies' reiterated statements (that sometimes bordered on ageism), the attitudes of experienced officers tended to be more critical of arming. As underscored by Bosworth, Franko and Pickering (2018: 42) in the case of the expansion of powers towards border control for a variety of UK and US traditional criminal justice officials (e.g. prison and police officers), changes to their traditional focus are not necessarily welcomed by these frontline workers, and many resist their new role. Similarly, for experienced Canadian customs officers, the depiction of the firearm as *the* enforcement tool barely disguised the disdain that younger officers seemed to have for the numerous years in which they accomplished their work without it. These officers disliked firearms. They did not see the necessity of a uniform or cross-regional implementation of the arming policy, nor did they see the need for it in commercial sections supposed to be more preoccupied with trade compliance. In an ironic contrast to his union's position regarding the safety brought about by firearms,[5] Raymond expressed new apprehension regarding his safety, now that he is required to work in an armed environment. A month earlier, an officer in another port dry fired without emptying his gun's chamber; no one was hurt, but Raymond was clearly flustered by the incident.

Sarah's awareness: a generational politics
of armed suspicion

Intergenerational debates did not stop at whether guns were indispensable to any officer worth their salt. These disagreements also related to the increased physicality of border officers' instruction. This included firearm certification and the need to renew control and defensive tactics training every three years throughout one's career—a training from which even younger officers come back sore and aching. Woven throughout this continuous somatic drill is the pursuit of a vigorous, strong and physically fit officer. Such a postulate shapes border officers' bodies anew with important consequences for the border encounter—that is, for how officers deploy authority in border interactions as a result of seeing those who cross borders as potential threats to their safety. Higate (2012: 357) suggests that "corporeal conditioning is a political matter" that invests bodies with a "durable somatic memory." In Chapter 5, we looked at how the officer's body has been masculinized as a result of a successful labour politics that promotes the virile figure of the border enforcer standing at the state's limits in a constant state of readiness. We can now add to this analysis that this body is assumed to have the strength and agility that comes with youth.

Building on these remarks, I now take another, more-fine-grained look at the gun. Particularly, I am interested in how firearms carry with them what Springwood (2014: 453) terms a particular *affective embodiment*. What does this mean exactly? Springwood (2007: 2) invites us to consider people's "everyday experience with guns, especially the relationship of people to their guns" and to "appreciate the idiomatic meanings of guns in local spaces." As we can recall, adopting the gun in bordering followed a particular historic conjunction in the technological politics of bordering, which was reviewed in Chapters 2, 3 and 4. A sense of abstractness brought by security technologies and remote border control is now accompanied, at least in the Canadian case, by efforts to intimately anchor officers' powers to their bodies or, as Diphoorn (2015: 337) argues in the case of police officers, by efforts to have policing equipment become "experienced as part of the body." Such equipment thus makes officers more amenable to using violence or, at least, to viewing this use as a reasonable outcome of stressful situations.

Consequently, the generational "body-reflexive practices" (Connell 2005: 65) that are introduced with arming participate in producing a skewed perspective of the border. Once seen as peaceful and uneventful, it is now viewed as a potentially dangerous zone. In this context, attending to officers' connection to their guns helps us grasp the degree to which firearms introduce new behavioural patterns into borderwork that dovetail with this view. It also allows us to attend to how guns mediate anew officers' relations to their colleagues but also, and most importantly, to border crossers. As illustrated by Sarah's case, border control in Canada is now predicated on the design of a new corporeality for border officers, one that leads them to inhabit bordering spaces in a more authoritative (but also more detached) manner.

I mentioned Sarah in the preceding chapter. When we spoke, Sarah was armed, a rare occurrence since firearm training was still being implemented at the time of our conversation. A rookie officer, Sarah conceived of her work as chiefly oriented around enforcement. Doing a good job for Sarah is not to "stamp it and send it away" but "to work hard and really dig and look for things." Getting results means making seizures of drugs and noncompliant goods and receiving good assessments about her enforcement skills. She particularly enjoys when colleagues acknowledge her search abilities and ask for her help in inspecting a vehicle. There is no mention in Sarah's interview of "protecting the economy" or of providing a service to drivers and importers, as was the case with many of her experienced colleagues. For Sarah, a job well done stems from an enforcement-oriented take on border control and accompanying expertise. For her, as well as many of those officers hired after the CBSA was created, borderwork carries a different connotation than that expressed by senior officers: for her, it is intimately connected with gun carrying.

Sarah discussed at length the impact of the firearm on her work. Of particular interest was her anecdote about a serious incident triggered by her discovery of a firearm in a truck cab. She described how her bodily dispositions were adapted to that type of situation, thanks to her gun training:

> So I was out there and, all of us were armed and we had discussed, you know, what do we do if we find a gun, where . . . who's going to do what, where you're going to position yourself, and then we found a loaded gun under a guy's pillow in his cab, and automat . . . it was just so natural, it just felt like the training. You know, two of the guys withdrew their guns and I was at the back of the trailer, so I'm behind cover, and I can see, you know, the client and the other teammates of mine as they were going to. . . . Like, they've got their guns drawn as well and they were going through arresting him and everything and. . . . It just, it works like clockwork when you're all trained in that area.

But then Sarah explains that things become more complicated when working with unarmed colleagues, pointing to how firearm training introduces "new ways" into borderwork:

> However, if you've got people who are not armed. . . . You've got people who are and the people who aren't don't really . . . they don't know our training. And they don't really know what . . . what to expect from us, or what we're going to do, so, you know I've heard of one instance where. . . . One officer was armed, one wasn't and they found a gun in the person's

car and the guy who wasn't armed immediately jumps in and grabs him, grabs the client to arrest him, whereas we're like, "No!" "No!" because you don't know if he's got another gun on [him] or not. And that's putting yourself in a really bad position. So, the officer who was armed couldn't draw his gun to a low-ready—it's just down here [*Sarah gestures pointing a gun at the ground*]. You're not pointing at anybody because there was an officer in the way.

You know, so it creates . . . situations that, yeah, when there's . . . when you don't have the same understanding, it might not work as well. . . . Yes. Because they've got an old way of doing things, where there was no guns or, you know, there's just a stamp and some handcuffs or whatever, well that's what they did. They just jumped in and [*gentle mocking voice, mimics taking hold of someone*] grabbed the guy and arrest him or whatever.

I became intrigued by the potential of firearms to modify a border officer's conduct and her interactions with her surroundings when Sarah spoke of the *alertness* the firearm brought into her work—especially since Richard, another pro-arming but unarmed officer, quoted in Chapter 5, had also characterized the effect of the firearm on work routines in exactly the same terms, suggesting perhaps that gun training and everyday use are discussed among colleagues. Asked whether she saw a difference with or without a firearm—that is, before and after her training—Sarah replied,

I think, *you're just more aware* of, once again [risk] indicators, but these indicators could be things where people might potentially get angry and, you know, if they're hiding their hands or like. . . . *You're more aware* of where their hands are, because you're not sure if they've got some sort of weapon, that they're going to produce, or whether they've got their fist clenched. . . . Like, "oh my gosh, I want to beat this person up," that kind of thing. *You're more aware. You're more aware* of keeping your distance and knowing what's around you in case, let's say somebody does have a firearm. You can position yourself behind cover, in a safer spot. You know. *So, you're always looking around* and seeing what other people are around that could be associates to a person, or places that you can go for safety, and, *you're just more aware.*

(emphasis added)

What do we learn from Sarah's remarks? Beyond a narrative in which guns bring a sense of power, Sarah deploys another discursive register often used by gun owners and underscored by Harcourt (2006): respect for (and a related careful handling of) guns. Accordingly, if there is a generational politics of suspicion that emerges from the differential valuations of effectiveness given by officers to face-to-face examinations, interviewing skills, indicators of nervousness, information technologies, enforcement data and intelligence, this politics is further complicated by the introduction of firearms in ports of entry. With arming, face-to-face interactions do not solely offer the possibility of inquiring into clues to criminal activity or customs fraud. The presence of firearms also modifies the logic of suspicion that is characteristic of borderwork by bringing about a cautionary attitude to the encounter with truck drivers and travellers. In an ironic twist, arming makes officers feel vulnerable and exposed to physical aggression. With the gun comes expectations that such violence will materialize, as if the legitimate means of violence calls for more violence from those who really are the ones looking down the barrel of this gun. Described by Sarah as heightened "awareness" towards her surroundings, this metamorphosis in conduct requires her to be in constant alert and to anticipate any indication of aggressive behaviour, despite the fact that such occurrences are infrequent. As a result, truck drivers, migrants and the travelling public thus become treated as if they present a threat to officers' safety. Ronald, a mid-career officer, told me, "You have to worry that every driver has a gun." This amended view of border crossers produces an important shift in the way officers handle problematic situations. Whereas Arthur, an experienced officer, playfully claimed in his interview, "[if] somebody wants to get into a little scuffle, we'll go!" Sarah, the "aware" armed rookie, was more likely to "keep [her] distance."

As a result, if armed officers must now keep a safe distance from those they question and search, this cautious positioning of the border guard body frames border encounters anew. What used to be characterized by more approachability and a capacity to negotiate one's narrative at the border (Rygiel 2013)—especially for non-racialized travellers—has become a more detached interaction. Arming reworks proximity in borderwork. The embodied dispositions of border officers are modified by arming in a way akin to Springwood's claim (2014: 463) that open carry is a political performance that "extends a gun-toter's body, his senses, and her mind(s)." Their bulletproof vest–covered bodies are larger, more imposing, more threatening, which also impacts how border crossers are invited to cooperate with border officers and consent to the authority of those who resemble less "tax collectors" and more a particularly well-equipped police corps. Because of the awareness of the violent potentiality that arises in both officers and border crossers as a result of arming, firearms make border encounters more formal and distant. Such politics of suspicion extends Huysmans's (2014: 91) apt understanding of security as a *dispositif* that "circulates suspicion through surveillance technologies and risk communication," where it becomes a dominant "mode of relating and stratifying" embedded in border technologies. It redirects our attention to how a politics of distrust is also reshaping border control, starting with the immediate interactions that are still happening every day in ports of entry. Gun carrying introduces a new corporeality that filters through the anxieties produced by insecurity politics into everyday border encounters, ultimately reaffirming in each and every one of these encounters the dominant role played by border guards at the land border.

Conclusion

Introducing a generation of officers with a new type of police-oriented training and dispositions into ports of entry has been one of the most important interventions that rendered possible the shift to enforcement in Canadian border control. Yet this great generational replacement wished for by the CBSA and by many of the newer officers I met did not happen overnight; consequently, major conflicts have emerged between generations who work side by side. I have been privileged to meet officers who use "old ways" and "new ways" during this transition, which cued me to think about how major policy changes in bordering and security are fiercely debated on the frontline.

If we follow Sayad (1994), telling generational stories about each other's abilities and deficiencies allow officers to make sense of, and locate themselves within, patterns of continuity and change that emerge from contemporary upheavals in border control regimes. But these stories also signalled a more profound shift. As bordering became centred on enforcement, officers altered the way they feel their way through their day and what objects and people they consider harmful or beneficial—in short, how they sense their world. By moulding anew the habits, attitudes, demeanour and bodies of border guards, by promoting those equipped with "the new" and by pushing aside those associated with the past of borderwork, the new border regime has profoundly modified frontline officers' experience of the frontline and the experience of those they encounter at the border. As policing reforms, as new technologies and intelligence schemes are introduced into various security settings on an increasingly rapid and recurring basis, we can expect that similar generational dynamics will emerge elsewhere and that they are likely to repeat themselves.

Acknowledgements

Parts of this chapter are excerpts from the following article:

Côté-Boucher, K (2018). Of "old" and "new" ways: Generations, border control and the temporality of security, *Theoretical Criminology*, 22 (2): 149–168. First Published February 10, 2017 © 2017 by SAGE. Reprinted by permission of SAGE Publications, Ltd.

With many thanks to SAGE Permissions, Ltd.

Notes

1 This word is commonly used in ports of entry to designate what officers portray as the distant, disengaged and indifferent headquarters located in the capital. See Chapter 4.

2 Truck drivers from US states with widespread gun ownership may receive more scrutiny at the border since they are known to carry firearms in their trucks. This being said, it is important to mention that US truck drivers who show up at the border with firearms do not necessarily mean harm. US long-haul drivers sometimes carry firearms intended for self-protection—leaving aside for now the issue of whether firearms actually protect or further endanger their owners. Because these firearms are not registered in Canada, they cannot enter the country. Some border officers mentioned being tipped off to search for guns in trucks registered in US states known for gun ownership, especially when, in some cases, gun promotion paraphernalia (e.g. National Rifle Association stickers) is found in a truck cab. Foreign gun owners wishing to enter Canada are required to leave their firearm in consignment with the CBSA, which they can recover upon exiting the country. This procedure assumes truck drivers will cross back at the same port of entry, which is in fact entirely dependent on the routing provided by their next client. This may consequently present challenges for these drivers who may then "forget" to declare their firearm.

3 It was difficult to pinpoint where these regions where. Québécois officers mentioned Ontario as an illustration of this overly coercive take on bordering, and Ontario officers mentioned their British Columbia–based colleagues. I do not have enough data to investigate the role of these regional Canadian politics in the shift to enforcement, but based on these comments, they seem to have played a role.

4 At the beginning of the implementation of arming, training was done on a voluntary basis but became compulsory later on for both existing and prospective officers.

5 The argument of increased safety for its members has played a central role in the border officers' union campaign to obtain the firearm. See Chapter 5.

References

Aas, K. F., and H. Gundhus. 2015. Policing humanitarian borderlands: Frontex, human rights and the precariousness of life. *British Journal of Criminology* 55 (1):1–18.

Aboim, S., and P. Vasconcelos. 2014. From political to social generations: A critical reappraisal of Mannheim's classical approach. *European Journal of Social Theory* 17 (2):165–183.

Barker, V. 2013. Democracy and deportation: Why membership matters most. In *The Borders of Punishment: Criminal Justice, Citizenship and Social Exclusion*, edited by K. Franko Aas and M. Bosworth. Oxford: Oxford University Press, 237–254.

Bigo, D. 2014. The (in)securitization practices of the three universes of EU border control: Military/navy-border guards/police-database analysts. *Security Dialogue* 45 (3):209–225.

Bosworth, M., K. Franko, and S. Pickering. 2018. Punishment, globalization and migration control: "Get them the hell out of here". *Punishment & Society* 20 (1):34–53.

Bourdieu, P. 1979. *La distinction. Critique sociale du jugement*. Paris: Les éditions de minuit.

———. 1984. *Questions de sociologie*. Paris: Les Éditions de minuit.

Brodeur, J. P. 2007. An encounter with Egon Bittner. *Crime, Law and Social Change* 48 (3–5): 105–132.

Connell, R. W. 2005. *Masculinities (Second edition)*. Cambridge: Polity Press.

Côté-Boucher, K. 2018. Of "old" and "new" ways: Generations, border control and the temporality of security. *Theoretical Criminology* 22 (2):149–168.

Davis, F. 1979. *Yearning for Yesterday: A Sociology of Nostalgia*. New York: Free Press.

Diphoorn, T. 2015. "It's all about the body": The bodily capital of armed response officers in South Africa. *Medical Anthropology* 34 (4):336–352.

Down, S., and J. Reveley. 2004. Generational encounters and the social formation of entrepreneurial identity: "Young guns" and "old farts." *Organization* 11 (2):233–250.

Ericson, R. V., and K. D. Haggerty. 1997. *Policing the Risk Society*. Toronto: University of Toronto Press.

Eyerman, R., and B. S. Turner. 1998. Outline of a theory of generations. *European Journal of Social Theory* 1 (1):91–106.

Foster, K. 2013. Generation and discourse in working life stories. *British Journal of Sociology* 64 (2):195–215.

Harcourt, B. 2006. *The Language of the Gun: Youth, Crime and Public Policy*. Chicago: University of Chicago Press.

Higate, P. 2012. The private militarized and security contractor as geocorporeal actor. *International Political Sociology* 6 (4):355–372.

Huysmans, J. 2014. *Security Unbound: Enacting Democratic Limits*. London: Routledge.

Lee, M., and M. Punch. 2004. Policing by degrees: Police officers' experience of university education. *Policing and Society* 14 (3):233–249.

Mannheim, K. 1952 [1923]. *Essays on the Sociology of Knowledge*. London: Routledge, K. Paul.

McMullin, J. A., T. Duerden Comeau, and E. Jovic. 2007. Generational affinities and discourses of difference: A case study of highly skilled information technology workers. *The British Journal of Sociology* 58:297–316.

Mezzadra, S., and B. Neilson. 2013. *Border as Method, or the Multiplication of Labour*. Durham, London: Duke University Press.

Pallister-Wilkins, P. 2015. The humanitarian politics of European border policing: Frontex and border police in Evros. *International Political Sociology* 9 (1):53–69.

Paoline, E. A. III, W. Terrill, and M. T. Rossler. 2015. Higher education, college degree major, and police occupational attitudes. *Journal of Criminal Justice Education* 26 (1):49–73.

Parmar, A. 2017. Policing belonging: Race and nation in the UK. In *Race, Criminal Justice and Migration Control: Enforcing the Boundaries of Belonging*, edited by M. Bosworth, A. Parmar and Y. Vásquez. Oxford: Oxford University Press.

Pickering, S., and J. Ham. 2014. Hot pants at the border: Sorting sex work from trafficking. *The British Journal of Criminology* 54 (1):2–19.

Pratt, A., and S. Thompson. 2008. Chivalry, "race" and discretion at the Canadian border. *The British Journal of Criminology* 48 (5):620–640.

Proteau, L., and G. Pruvost. 2008. Se distinguer dans les métiers d'ordre (armée, police, prison, sécurité privé). *Sociétés contemporaines* 72 (déc.):7–14.

Rygiel, K. 2013. Mobile citizens, risky subjects: Security knowledge at the border. In *Mobilities, Knowledge, and Social Justice*, edited by S. Ilcan. Montreal, Kingston: McGill-Queen's University Press.

Sayad, A. 1994. Le mode de génération des générations immigrées. *L'Homme et la Société* 111/112:155–174.

Shearing, C. D., and R. V. Ericson. 1991. Culture as figurative action. *The British Journal of Sociology* 42 (4):481–506.

Sheptycki, J. 2017. Liquid modernity and the police métier: Thinking about information flows in police organisation. *Global Crime* 18 (3):286–302.

Slutskaya, N., R. Simpson, J. Hughes, A. Simpson, and S. Uygur. 2016. Masculinity and class in the context of dirty work. *Gender, Work & Organization* 23 (2):165–182.

Springwood, C. F. 2007. The social life of guns: An introduction. In *Open Fire: Understanding Global Gun Culture*, edited by C. F. Springwood. Oxford, NY: Berg.

———. 2014. Gun concealment, display, and other magical habits of the body. *Critique of Anthropology* 34 (4):450–471.

Tanner, S., and M. Meyer. 2015. Police work and new "security devices": A tale from the beat. *Security Dialogue* 46 (4):384–400.

van der Woude, M., and J. van der Leun. 2017. Crimmigration checks in the internal border areas of the EU: Finding the discretion that matters. *European Journal of Criminology* 14 (1):27–45.

Vega, I. 2019. Toward a cultural sociology of immigration control: A call for research. *American Behavioural Scientist* 63 (9):1172–1184.

Conclusion

Why should we care about the Canadian border?

Convincing someone that Canada offers important insights into border control is, each time, a small achievement. I once found myself reminding a European colleague that when she wrote of "North American" mobilities, she might wish to include in her analysis the border shared by the US with its neighbour up north. This neglect is perhaps understandable. At first glance, the Canadian border appears less problematic than other, more-researched borders. In scholarly fields such as criminology, geography and anthropology, the US and European cases have sharpened the critical conceptual tools used in border studies. For better or for worse, our perspective on bordering is circumscribed by the empirical knowledge gathered in these settings. But as a result of our concern with the human consequences of European and US efforts to stem irregular migration, we have missed what makes border control politically contentious from within.

Against a backdrop of harsh border policing and migrant suffering at these sites, the Canadian border appears seemingly uncontroversial. Canadian bordering (and all things Canadian for that matter) benefits from the country's liberal-democratic reputation and its immigration policy, which is cited as a model everywhere. In reality, Canada is more indebted to its geography than to its putative humanitarian soul in matters relative to bordering. Canada washes its hands of "migration crises." It is surrounded by ice in the north and two oceans east and west and shares at the south a long land border with a country that generally affords a comparable standard of living to its citizens, who are thus less likely to cross the border in search of work or protection. Canada also counts on its reputation to foster a convenient ignorance of its colonial history of immigration and settlement over Indigenous lands, a legacy that underpins its border politics to this day (LaDow 2002; Simpson 2014). Finally, it has been slowly securitizing its borders since the beginning of 1990s through a mix of external, land-based and internal border controls that have prevented tens of thousands of refugees and many vulnerable and poor migrants from reaching its shores (Arbel and Brenner 2013; Gilbert 2018; Whitaker 1998).

Taking into account Canada's history, geography and current restrictive border policies over irregular migration allows us to be more level-headed with regard to the apparent lack of tensions that are said to characterize border control in this country. In fact, these particularities make it possible to account for other underestimated trends in bordering that may be less visible but are just as important to the regulation of people and goods across borders. Taking the North American political and economic context into account, this book has provided a textured analysis that has charted and sought to explain the factors that have driven the evolution of Canadian border control towards more enforcement over the past three decades and has considered what this case tells us more broadly about the changing nature of borderwork and how contentious it has become. If someone were to have asked before reading this book, "Is there anything new that can be said about borders?" I hope to have convinced them by its end that there are still plenty of border frictions left to unpack.

The contentious Canadian border: what more do we learn about border control?

What do we learn about the politics of border control when tracing the trajectory of the shift to border enforcement in Canada? First, border scholarship across disciplines would be well served to investigate the integration of policing models, such as more coercive law enforcement methods, into bordering, particularly in view of arguments considering the role of the military in this domain. Compelling studies, again frequently located at the southern European and US borders, highlight the growing militarization of border control (Jones and Johnson 2016; Topak and Vives 2018; Wilson 2014)—that is, the recourse in bordering to military-grade weapons and surveillance technologies (such as drones) as well as to command structures and tactics, intelligence schemes and zonal models of spatial control inspired by the world of defence.

In contrast, the Canadian case provides evidence that the multivalent social control templates formatted in the area of policing also prompt reforms in bordering regulations, policies and practices. These templates may range from intelligence-led to nodal security (Shearing 2016)—the former being proactive, data-led forms of policing and the latter involving cooperation between public and private actors in securing flows—to a more oppressive model influenced by law enforcement. But whatever the models chosen, they affect the modalities of risk assessment, whether and how information from the private sector (carriers, transporters, importers) is collected and analysed, how border guards are trained and with which tools and weapons they are equipped to do their work. These multiple policing models now often coexist in border control agencies and are sometimes at variance with one another.

The weight of these policing templates in bordering has been increasing in maritime, air, land and internal border controls. Our knowledge of the role played by policing models and agencies in bordering remains fragmentary despite a few recent contributions. These include a study on the networked security of maritime ports (Brewer 2014), others concerned with the coercive surveillance role played by municipal and border police forces in countries such as the US, the Netherlands and Australia (Provine et al. 2016; Brouwer, van der Woude and van der Leun 2018; Weber 2011) and works that identify racialized immigration policing practices in the UK (Bowling and Westenra 2018; Parmar 2018).

Intrigued by its growing significance, I have focused on the rise of one of these models in Canadian bordering, that of law enforcement. Beyond algorithms and remote-control risk assessments, law enforcement is one of the major ways that the securitization of bordering has been unfolding in this country. Under this model, border flows are not only interpreted as a security problem that requires risk and contingencies to be anticipated but also apprehended as a law and order concern where the land border and ports of entry stand as a last resort for the interception of criminals and other "bad guys." The results of this shift have been consequential. They have affected not only customs but also immigration and borderwork as a whole, giving more prominence to coercive policing tools and methods in Canadian border control.

The shift to enforcement widens the accountability gap in border control

Such importance taken by policing models in bordering raises urgent accountability issues. Because the police is granted with significant means of coercion, it is generally submitted, at least in countries where the rule of law is respected, to institutionalized mechanisms such as independent review and complaint boards that ensure that these agencies are publicly answerable.[1] However, as argued by the Standing Senate Committee on National Security and Defence in one of the latest official reports on the matter, accountability in Canadian border control is most deficient.[2] This is not really surprising. After all, the late criminologist Jean-Paul Brodeur has made it clear throughout his career that the country has long had a historical problem with state secrecy and has lacked independent and truly effective public oversight mechanisms that would watch over its intelligence and security community. This accountability gap is now widening, especially in border control. We saw in Chapter 2 that the policing powers granted to the CBSA have become greater over the past two decades, giving its employees wide-ranging authority to arrest, search and detain and greater legal discretion than that already afforded to police officers. These powers are also associated with widespread capabilities in matters related to national security, data-led risk management and intelligence production. Despite these prerogatives, there is to date no independent mechanism in Canada to ensure the oversight and review of the actions of the CBSA or those of its 13,000 employees (including 7200 ground officers).[3]

When combined with the increased potential of state violence embedded in the spreading of the law enforcement model, the lack of proper mechanisms to hold the CBSA accountable cannot be underestimated. Indications of increased use of force as well as restrictive and coercive bordering have started piling up in Canada. Published two years after border officers started being trained in firearm carrying and less than a decade after officers started training in control and defence tactics, a 2009 report signalled a rise in the use of physical containment tools, such as pepper spray and batons, by border officers. In a report from the Faculty of Law at the University of Toronto (Gros and Van Groll 2015: 49) regarding the deteriorating detention conditions for migrants with mental health issues, a former director of immigration enforcement at the CBSA is cited as arguing that arming has negatively impacted the handling of immigration control cases in Canada—making intervention with refugees and irregular migrants for these authorities a matter of security rather than one that requires counselling skills.[4] Meanwhile, media reports of misconduct and intrusive behaviour at ports of entry[5] suggest that law enforcement dispositions described in this book are even starting to affect elite travellers, either by subjecting them to lengthy questioning or by requiring some to hand in their phones for data extraction.[6]

Labour politics can shape the border control agenda

How did we get there? Legal analyses of these issues that insist on better oversight, respect of refugee and human rights and clearer privacy and data protection laws are essential.[7] But with this book, I have taken another route and teased out the political and sociological factors that propelled this shift towards law enforcement in Canadian bordering. One factor is the role played by unions in steering the security and border control agenda. Labour politics add another valuable dimension to our study of border politics—one that has been essentially ignored up until now. We frequently assume that technocrats and politicians "think" policy, while street-level border and security workers "implement" it. I have seen this view expressed in both academic work and border high management. Those familiar with how Lipsky's (2010) work on discretion takes this division of labour to task oppose this reasoning, arguing that frontline workers are in fact policymakers in their own right because they effectively "create" policy through their everyday decisions.

However, these debates overlook the fact that criminal justice, security and border workers' unions have a vested interest in keeping their concerns alive in the public eye. Using the case of the Canadian border officer's union fight for arming and shedding light on those perspectives held at the bottom of the bureaucratic hierarchy, I have shown how security workers can effectively dispute official rhetoric on various areas of policing, including border control. Such challenges influence how bordering is framed in public policy, organized by security agencies, supplied in resources by governments and enacted through overhauled bordering practices. As a result, when collectively organized, street-level workers do actively "think" and propose policy. In this sense, they also inspire and propel the security orientations that they believe are the most relevant to the daily realities of their work and that may most benefit them.

Examining how unions influence border policy also helps us see how political frictions rework security and border organizations' priorities from within. At this point, you may ask, why should we bother dissecting these conflicts in such detail? To this, I answer that when we do, we scratch the seemingly slick and monolithic surface of border agencies. For instance, when viewed under this light, the decision to provide border officers with firearms appears less to emerge out of a concern for effective border control than to be the result of internal tensions between the different occupational sectors that make up border agencies. When we approach the CBSA—but also the US-CBP or the Australian Border Force—as diversified in their bordering practice priorities and when we attune to how they are prone to factions, jealousies and power struggles, they appear less as all-powerful entities that should be left alone to decide on our collective security and more as publicly funded and fallible bureaucracies acting within democratic states that are thus required to account for their actions.

Hardened borders: getting serious about the masculinization of bordering

It is puzzling that critical border scholarship pays so little attention to gendered bordering. In a rare and compelling article on the masculinized logics that make up bordering, Agius and Edenborg (2019: 56) claim that border practices "are rendered intelligible and justifiable because they tap into and reproduce specific gendered discourses of space and state identity." In the Canadian context, I have examined the political weight taken by such deeply masculinized language under the guise of the *enforcement narrative*. But what I called the *masculinization of bordering* is more than a matter of discourse. Consider the follow: whether we think of security technologies, border agencies are frontline officers or whether we are interested in the private security agencies involved in bordering, border control is overwhelmingly designed, organized and made possible everywhere by men. It is also striking that bordering is placed under the authority of state organizations that are tasked with responsibilities conceived as men's prerogative in most societies by virtue of their long involvement in defence, protection and security. Comparably to the CBSA, these organizations may also carefully select their frontline workers through masculinist behavioural and attitudinal requirements. Officers' professional socialization even entails what I have referred to in Chapter 6 as an "apprenticeship in dominance" where young officers and female officers test different strategies to assert state authority, learning to abide by the gendered expectations of command that come with their work.

A closer look at these gendering processes can galvanize current critiques of border control. For instance, let's pause on the metaphor of "hardened borders." Entire books have been written that use this trope without even a gesture towards the profoundly gendered undertones of that statement. Yet, as I have shown in this book, in a period in which border spaces are being extended through programmes of dataveillance and mobility tracking, calls for militarized borders, border walls and increased frontline border policing carry with them a particular, masculinized political agenda—the effects of which are to remap bordering activities back onto the state's geopolitical limits through aggressive and potentially lethal forms of control.

Hardened borders are spaces where rigid masculinist fantasies of rule and order are projected onto the control of people's mobilities. Wendy Brown (2010) has made that point in relation to border walls, but the adoption of firearms by Canadian frontline border officers also illustrates this aspect well. The fact that firearms have been primarily granted to *land* border officers in Canada is to be taken seriously. Associating firearms with the protection of the outer limits of the body politic has wider implications for how borders and borderwork are conceived. Theweleit (1987 [1977], 1989 [1978]) underlined in his classic historical work on the Freikorps and the rise of fascism in post–World War I Germany the symbolic importance of firearms in promoting the violent deployment of a masculinity, which Theweleit characterizes by its repulsion towards a femininity conceived as fluidity. This fluidity is what threatens to unravel and melt the body politic. We might not follow Theweleit to the end of his psychoanalytical route but still take seriously his insights into a gendered security imagery that associates flows with the feminine and perceives those that circulate irregularly with a threat that must be stopped, repelled and even injured or killed (even if only in potentiality) by the hard, armed security body of the nation's border corps. Therefore, bordering is part of the sociopolitical factors and logics that make up what Brown (1995: 167) designates as the "masculinism of the state." By conceiving the border as a threatened space in need of (male) protection, gendered imaginaries of border control shape how people and things are treated in border spaces. As Herbert (2001) suggests in the case of US urban policing, gendered dynamics in border control must be taken into account if we are to illuminate how and why efforts to make bordering more humane and democratic and in accordance with human rights fail to take hold.

The changing experiential and organizational life of borderwork

Making a detour by way of labour politics and gendered bordering helped sustain my thesis that Canadian border authorities have adopted a law enforcement policing model for frontline border control. Given that the CBSA and many other bordering agencies around the world emphasize a proactive data-oriented model for remote bordering in the form of targeting, automated decision-making and preclearance, the concern for law enforcement in officers' remarks was at first perplexing. Without a closer look at the inner life of borderwork, it would have been difficult to appreciate the intimate connections between bordering at a distance and a more immediate, embodied and coercive model of border control. I would have missed how, having acutely altered customs and air traveller control to fulfil trade promotion and risk-management objectives, computer-mediated bordering has also ushered in a sensory disorientation in borderwork. Border technologies have rendered decision-making increasingly intangible, inviting officers to spend a good part of their days reviewing data on their screens and processing decisions made remotely about the people and cargo that pass through their port of entry. Coinciding with this experience of intangibility, I have argued, is a significant sense of social demotion. Officers' extended legal prerogatives do not protect them any longer against a feeling that they are losing their hold over border decisions. It should not surprise us that the vision of bordering that emerged out of this experience of intangibility and gradual marginalization from decision-making was one that emphasized a more concrete, armed, coercive and reactive border policing.

Examining the details of daily life in ports of entry sheds light on bordering practices and puts the experiential features of borderwork front and centre. This approach has helped me highlight some of the less-explored dynamics of border agencies' organizational life. First, I have examined how the fraught circulation of data redefines bordering into a contested set of technologized activities. Running against studies that assume an unimpeded circulation of data in border control, I have teased out some of the complex interactions between data management and officers' experience of data-led bordering. The social and interpretive aspects of bordering—whether in the form of officers' relative distrust in data validity, their interpretations of what constitutes a risk or their disappointment in being considered mere data collectors rather than trusted actors that can contextualize and make sense of data—feed back into data systems with consequences that remain to be fully investigated. I hope to have demonstrated that the divisions of labour emerging in data-led bordering present us with a new set of research questions worth exploring. These questions concern the strategic access to data, who has the capacity to intervene on what information is collected and how data is analysed and the types of decisions made on the basis of such analysis. These questions are integral to understanding the organizational life of border, policing and security organizations.

Second, I have described how the transition to enforcement was actually received, experienced and even contested by border officers through intergenerational conflict and suggested that similar conflicts are here to stay. Given the constant changes brought into border agencies by data-led security, border technologies, political struggles over who is in charge of bordering and the various policing models that make up border control, officers' dispositions acquired during their professional socialization are bound to age quickly and appear old in the eyes of recruits who are better acquainted with the new. Given this argument, it might be possible to restructure border control away from enforcement by ushering in a new generation of officers in bordering who would be differently socialized. This would require sweeping reforms in a range of areas that would alter divisions of border labour and access to technologies, the preferred tools of bordering and the mandate given to border actors. These reforms would also be reflected in hiring and training schemes. This would no doubt be a daunting task but not an impossible one, given that it has been undertaken by Canadian border authorities in the past decades with the results described in this book.

Is bordering really about global exclusion?

Given the variegated frictions that make up bordering, painting a monolithic picture of border control would be limiting. Nevertheless, this is the argument often made by critics of bordering who are concerned with restrictions to migration. When looked at through the prism of migration control, deterrence-oriented border policies appear to be expanding everywhere, which come with severe consequences for migrants—whether we are looking at the route to Europe from West Africa (Andersson 2014), transit countries such as Mexico (Brigden 2018) or death while crossing borders (Pickering and Cochrane 2013). Given this fact, border scholars in various disciplines have argued some version of what refugee scholar Anthony Richmond (1994) and geographer Reece Jones (2016) claim in their respective books: we have been witnessing since the 1990s the emergence of a global, single border regime of unparalleled structural violence, the primary function of which is to limit access to the richest countries' territories for the poorest and most vulnerable people of the world. Some anthropological analyses of the strategy of border externalization echo this claim, speaking in unequivocal terms about borders as a "militarized global apartheid" apparatus (Besteman 2019). Similarly, border studies scholars such as van Houtum (2010: 917) have associated the EU treatment of migrants with "human blacklisting," which interprets migrant lives as "waste that can be dumped." In a parallel development over the past decade, the criminology of mobility (Franko Aas and Bosworth 2013) has proposed robust conceptual tools to better comprehend how internalized bordering mechanisms such as detention and deportation are also involved in this mass social dumping. These scholars expose how the aims of criminal justice in many countries are being repurposed to fulfil migrant banishment objectives.

This body of work is incredibly useful. It has prompted us to focus our attention on the securitization and criminalization of migration—in other words, onto the processes through which irregular migration, once considered by many a humanitarian and social justice issue, has been made into security and criminal justice concerns. Borders have now become great open sky laboratories of social control that stretch along migrant routes, compelling those on the move to search for even-more-dangerous paths; migrants testify to being victims and witnesses to sexual assault, criminality and the corruption of officials (Campos-Delgado 2018). Fear of arrest and deportation is a feature of daily life for migrants who live irregularly (Bibler Coutin 2010), making them more vulnerable to labour exploitation (Harrison and Lloyd 2012). No one can deny the severe global injustices generated by border controls, and these scholars give us the empirical knowledge and theoretical resources to better understand, teach about and challenge this state of affairs.

Nevertheless, as I hope to have convinced you throughout this book, the oft-repeated argument that borders constitute primarily exclusionary mechanisms makes for a one-sided reading of the inchoate tensions that now shape borders. Insisting on the role they play in global exclusion leaves us with the skewed impression that borders fulfil only one function. Yet borders are not "hardening" for everyone; in fact, the cross-border mobility of people and cargo is in full swing around the planet. A harsher attitude towards vulnerable migrants parallels costly investment schemes in border infrastructures that facilitate trillions of dollars in global trade and ensure that billions of tourists and business people can land in airports around the globe every year.[8] The policing of this global circulation does not happen through closure, nor is it left to the invisible hand of the market. To keep merchandise and the privileged populations of the world on the move, sophisticated technological forms of surveillance and risk management are used to track and preclear, and these are combined, as far as merchandise is concerned, with complex trade regulations. Because of these diverse objectives and instruments, border policy and border practice are dynamic and changeable.

The border regimes governing the movements of people and goods are related analytically and empirically and therefore need to be investigated together. If the politics of bordering is too narrowly conceived as migration control, leaving trade and customs issues unexamined, then we miss how both interact with one another in particular border regimes. For instance, instead of assuming that an extended legal discretion and powers of arrest at the border will inevitably be acted on, I have shown that these prerogatives may be severely constrained by preclearance and the automation of risk management, especially in the area of customs because of its concern with the promotion of rapid crossings for shipments. Further, we cannot ignore that border management also responds to a neoliberal market agenda. National and international politics, particularly in the form of trade agreements and spats over trade policy, carry tangible and structural effects on bordering. I described in Chapter 2 how this is reflected by the role of NAFTA in North American border policy, a trend that will likely continue with its replacement agreement, the 2018 CUSMA. Because of its dependence on exports to its southern neighbour, Canadian governments have agreed since 2001 to implement more border security in exchange for the protection of Canadian industries' access to the US market. Another clear illustration of how international border politics frequently articulate trade with migration control can be found in US threats levelled at Mexico in 2019 to impose customs tariffs on its exports if the country did not beef up its migrant apprehensions and deportations.[9] In all such cases, free trade, limited customs controls and economic development are wielded as carrots to push for increased border policing against the circulation of undesired migrant bodies (Vives 2017).

Whether trade, traveller and migrant policing comes under the purview of a single border agency (as in the Canadian case) or is the responsibility of several agencies, border control is made up of multiple mobility governance trends, jurisdictions and private and public actors with contrasting agendas that can hardly be subsumed, or synthesized, under an overarching imperative. This is why I have analysed the shift to enforcement not as the single force reshaping the Canadian border but as a local reaction to how diverse political, economic and accompanying policing trends are transforming border control here and elsewhere. If anything, border decisions respond to different logics that sometimes work together but are often at variance with one another. Border decisions that process the privileged movement of people may not be made in parallel to those concerned with the movements of irregular migrants or with those promoting cargo mobilities. In fact, the opposite is often the case. To underscore the profound injustices embedded in border policing requires us to make transparent how some die trying to cross borders while others (and the goods they consume) circulate even more rapidly and comfortably than before. I believe that this is one of the most important questions of global social justice in the 21st century and that it should be couched in those terms.

Notes

1 Whether or not these mechanism function effectively and prevent police deviance is another matter that I cannot discuss here. But let it be said that these institutional mechanisms generally exist for the police, whereas they are inexistent for border control in Canada.

2 Standing Senate Committee on National Security and Defence (2015), *Vigilance, Accountability and Security at Canada's Borders*, https://sencanada.ca/content/sen/Committee/412/secd/rep/rep16jun15a-e.pdf (last consulted 14 Oct. 2019).

3 As explained by Atak et al. (2019), the newly National Security and Intelligence Review Agency is an independent review body which purview covers the CBSA. However, it has a national security focus and does not include a review of day-to-day operations.

4 See T. Wright (2019), Critics question why Canada's border officers need bulletproof vests to work with migrants, *The Canadian Press*, www.cbc.ca/news/politics/critics-question-why-canada-s-border-officers-need-bulletproof-vests-to-work-with-migrants-1.5211439 (last modified 14 July 2019; last consulted 14 Oct. 2019).

5 D. Swain, A. Wesley and S. Davis (2019), Harassment, sexual assault among alleged misconduct by border agents investigated by CBSA, *CBC*, www.cbc.ca/news/canada/cbsa-files-abuse-atip-1.4999473 (last modified 4 Feb. 2019; last consulted 14 Oct. 2019).

6 In an 2019 op-ed, the well-known University of Toronto urban scholar Richard Florida (who incidentally has coined the notion of the high-flying, mobile creative class) expressed his outrage at the repeated invasive treatment that he and his wife are submitted to when they comes back to Canada from the US—interestingly, without acknowledging that such treatment might be a daily occurrence for less-influential and more-vulnerable border crossers less likely to obtain the ear of the media. In another case, a business lawyer saw his laptop and cell phone confiscated after he refused to submit his passwords to a CBSA officer over concern for attorney–client privilege. He has since alerted the media and complained to the CBSA to contest this treatment and says he is considering legal action. These two cases suggest that perhaps, in the case of data collection at the border, the shift to law enforcement involves a sort of twisted "equalization" of treatment for advantaged border crossers whose expectations of priority treatment are not always met. See R. Florida, R. Florida (2019), The border problem at Pearson airport, *Toronto Star*, www.thestar.com/opinion/contributors/2019/07/11/the-border-problem-at-pearson-airport.html (last modified 11 July 2019; last consulted 14 Oct. 2019); S. Harris (2019), Canada border services seizes lawyer's phone, laptop for not sharing passwords, *CBC*, www.cbc.ca/news/business/cbsa-boarder-security-search-phone-travellers-openmedia-1.5119017 (last modified 5 May 2019; last consulted 14 Oct. 2019).

7 In the area of migrant rights, this has been done convincingly for the past two decades by Canadian legal scholars Sharryn Aiken, Idil Atak, François Crépeau, Catherine Dauvergne, Audrey Macklin and Delphine Nakache.

8 For instance, the total number of air passengers (including on national routes) reached 4 billion in 2017, while the global cargo shipping industry, responsible for about 90% of global trade, loaded 10.7 tons of goods onto ships in 2017. See ICAO (2017), *The World of Air Transport in 2017*, www.icao.int/annual-report-2017/Pages/the-world-of-air-transport-in-2017.aspx (last consulted 14 Oct. 2019); UNCTAD (2018), *2018 e-Handbook of Statistics*, https://stats.unctad.org/handbook/ (last modified 5 Dec. 2018; last consulted 14 Oct. 2019).

9 N. Miroff, K. Sieff and J. Wagner (2019), How Mexico talked Trump out of tariff threat with immigration crackdown pact, *The Washington Post*, www.washingtonpost.com/immigration/trump-mexico-immigration-deal-has-additional-measures-not-yet-made-public/2019/06/10/967e4e56-8b8e-11e9-b08e-cfd89bd36d4e_story.html (last modified 10 June 2019; last consulted 14 Oct. 2019).

References

Agius, C., and E. Edenborg. 2019. Gendered bordering practices in Swedish and Russian foreign and security policy. *Political Geography* 71:56–66.

Andersson, R. 2014. *Illegality, Inc. Clandestine Migration and the Business of Bordering Europe.* Oakland: University of California Press.

Arbel, E., and A. Brenner. 2013. *Bordering on Failure: Canada-U.S. Border Policy and the Politics of Refugee Exclusion.* Harvard Immigration and Refugee Law Clinical Program. Cambridge: Harvard Law School.

Besteman, C. 2019. Militarized global apartheid. *Current Anthropology* 60 (S19):S26–S38.

Bibler Coutin, S. 2010. Confined within: National territories as zones of confinement. *Political Geography* 29 (4):200–208.

Bowling, B., and S. Westenra. 2018. Racism, immigration and policing. In *Race, Criminal Justice, and Migration Control: Enforcing the Boundaries of Belonging*, edited by M. Bosworth, A. Parmar and Y. Vásquez. Oxford: Oxford University Press, 61–77.

Brewer, R. 2014. *Policing the Waterfront: Networks, Partnerships and the Governance of Security.* Oxford: Oxford University Press.

Brigden, N. K. 2018. Gender mobility: Survival plays and performing Central American migration in passage. *Mobilities* 13 (1):111–125.

Brouwer, J., M. van der Woude, and J. van der Leun. 2018. (Cr)immigrant framing in border areas: Decision-making processes of Dutch border police officers. *Policing and Society* 28 (4):448–463.

Brown, W. 1995. *States of Injury: Power and Freedom in Late Modernity*. Princeton: Princeton University Press.

———. 2010. *Walled States, Waning Sovereignty*. Cambridge, MA: MIT Press.

Campos-Delgado, A. 2018. Counter-mapping migration: Irregular migrants' stories through cognitive mapping. *Mobilities* 13 (4):488–504.

Franko Aas, K., and M. Bosworth, eds. 2013. *The Borders of Punishment: Migration, Citizenship, and Social Exclusion*. Oxford: Oxford University Press.

Gilbert, E. 2019. Elasticity at the Canada-US border: Jurisdiction, rights, accountability. *Environment and Planning C: Politics and Space*, 37 (3): 424–441.

Gros, H., and P. van Groll. 2015. *"We Have No Rights": Arbitrary Imprisonment and Cruel Treatment of Migrants with Mental Health Issues in Canada*. Toronto: Faculty of Law, University of Toronto.

Harrison, J. L., and S. Lloyd. 2012. Illegality at work: Deportability and the productive new era of immigration enforcement. *Antipode* 44 (2):365–385.

Herbert, S. 2001. "Hard charger" or "station queen"? Policing and the masculinist state. *Gender, Place & Culture* 8 (1):55–71.

Jones, R. 2016. *Violent Borders: Refugees and the Right to Move*. London: Verso.

Jones, R., and C. Johnson. 2016. Border militarisation and the re-articulation of sovereignty. *Transactions of the Institute of British Geographers* 41 (2):187–200.

LaDow, B. 2002. *The Medicine Line: Life and Death on a North American Borderland*. New York and London: Routledge.

Lipsky, M. 2010 [1980]. *Street-Level Bureaucracy: Dilemmas of the Individual in Public Services (30th anniversary expanded edition)*. New York: Russell Sage Foundation.

Parmar, A. 2018. Policing belonging: Race and nation in the UK. In *Race, Criminal Justice, and Migration Control: Enforcing the Boundaries of Belonging*, edited by M. Bosworth, A. Parmar and Y. Vásquez. Oxford: Oxford University Press, 108–124.

Pickering, S., and B. Cochrane. 2013. Irregular border-crossing deaths and gender: Where, how and why women die crossing borders. *Theoretical Criminology* 17 (1):27–48.

Provine, D. M., M. W. Varsanyi, P. G. Lewis, and S. H. Decker. 2016. *Policing Immigrants: Local Law Enforcement on the Front Lines*. Chicago: University of Chicago Press.

Richmond, A. 1994. *Global Apartheid: Refugees, Racism, and the New World Order*. Oxford: Oxford University Press.

Shearing, C. 2016. Reflections on the nature of policing and its development. *Police Practice and Research* 17 (1):84–91.

Simpson, A. 2014. *Mohawk Interruptus: Political Life across the Borders of Settler States*. Durham: Duke University Press.

Theweleit, K. 1987 [1977]. *Male Fantasies Vol. 1 Women Floods Bodies History*. Minneapolis: University of Minnesota Press.

———. 1989 [1978]. *Male Fantasies Vol. 2 Male Bodies: Psychoanalyzing the White Terror*. Minneapolis: University of Minnesota Press.

Topak, Ö. E., and L. Vives. 2018. A comparative analysis of migration control strategies along the Western and Eastern Mediterranean routes: Sovereign interventions through militarization and deportation. *Migration Studies* mny029, DOI: 10.1093/migration/mny029:1–24.

van Houtum, H. 2010. Human blacklisting: The global apartheid of the EU's external border regime. *Environment and Planning D: Society and Space* 28 (6):957–976.

Vives, L. 2017. The European Union-West African sea border: Anti-immigration strategies and territoriality. *European Urban and Regional Studies* 24 (2):209–224.

Weber, L. 2011. "It sounds like they shouldn't be here": Immigration checks on the streets of Sydney. *Policing and Society* 21 (4):456–467.

Whitaker, R. 1998. Refugees: The security dimension. *Citizenship Studies* 2 (3):365–376.

Wilson, D. 2014. Border militarization, technology and crime control. In *The Routledge Handbook on Crime and International Migration*, edited by S. Pickering and J. Ham. London: Routledge, 141–151.

Index